# Horizons

# Mathematics 5

## Book 1

Authors:
*Cindi Mitchell & Lori Fowler*

Editor:
*Alan Christopherson*

Graphic Design:

*Chris Burkholder*
*Mark Aguilar*
*Brian Ring*

*JoAnn Cumming*
*Keith Piccolo*
*Marybeth Graville*

*Annette Walker*
*Lisa Kelly*

**Alpha Omega Publications, Inc.**
Rock Rapids, IA

Horizons Mathematics 5, Student Workbook 1
804 N. 2nd Ave. E., Rock Rapids, IA 51246-1759
© MCMXCVIII by Alpha Omega Publications, Inc.® All rights reserved.

*All rights reserved.* No part of this publication may be reproduced, stored in an electronic retrieval system, or transmitted, in any form or by any means, electronic, mechanical, photocopying, recording, or otherwise, without the prior written permission of the publisher. Brief quotations may be used in literary review.

*Printed in the United States of America*
ISBN 978-1-58095-997-1

# Properties of Addition

**Lesson 1**

Addition is used when we want to find the total of two or more amounts put together.

Addition can be shown in two ways:

```
    4      addend           4    +    7    =    11
  + 7      addend         (addend) (addend)   (sum)
   11      sum                 Horizontal Form
  Vertical Form
```

**Addition properties help us find sums.**

**ORDER PROPERTY OF ADDITION**
When the order of the addends is changed, the sum is the same.

4 + 6 = 10, so 6 + 4 = 10

**ZERO PROPERTY OF ADDITION**
When one addend is zero, the sum is the other number.

8 + 0 = 8

**GROUPING PROPERTY OF ADDITION**
When the grouping of the numbers is changed, the answer is the same.

(5 + 2) + 1 = 8        5 + (2 + 1) = 8        Work inside the ( ) first.
  7    + 1 = 8         5 +    3    = 8

**1** Find each sum. Label the first problem with the following terms: addend, addend, or sum.

```
  4  _____      6          8          3          2
+ 9  _____    + 3        + 7        + 2        + 9
     _____

  5               7          9          0          1          7
+ 9             + 6        + 8        + 8        + 9        + 4


  2               7          3          9          4          5
+ 7             + 3        + 8        + 9        + 4        + 6
```

6 + 6 = _____        3 + 5 = _____        4 + 2 = _____

**2** Match.

1. 7 + (1 + 4) = (7 + 1) + 4      a. Order Property of Addition
2. 3 + 5 = 8 so 5 + 3 = 8      b. Grouping Property of Addition
3. 3 + 0 = 3      c. Zero Property of Addition

**3** Add. Be sure and write the fractions in lowest terms. Connect the answers in order of the problems to uncover the hidden picture.

1. $\frac{1}{7} + \frac{2}{7} =$ _____
2. $\frac{1}{10} + \frac{3}{10} =$ _____
3. $\frac{2}{8} + \frac{4}{8} =$ _____
4. $\frac{2}{9} + \frac{3}{9} =$ _____
5. $\frac{4}{9} + \frac{3}{9} =$ _____
6. $\frac{4}{5} + \frac{1}{5} =$ _____
7. $\frac{2}{17} + \frac{7}{17} =$ _____
8. $\frac{1}{3} + \frac{1}{3} =$ _____
9. $\frac{3}{15} + \frac{2}{15} =$ _____
10. $\frac{3}{7} + \frac{1}{7} =$ _____
11. $\frac{6}{9} + \frac{2}{9} =$ _____

•$\frac{8}{9}$   •$\frac{3}{7}$

•$\frac{1}{3}$    •$\frac{4}{7}$    •$\frac{2}{5}$    •$\frac{3}{4}$

•$\frac{2}{3}$    •1    •$\frac{5}{9}$

•$\frac{9}{17}$      •$\frac{7}{9}$

*Those who are wise will shine like the brightness of the heavens, and those who lead many to righteousness, like the stars for ever and ever. Daniel 12:3*

**4** Define using the following words: parallel, intersecting, perpendicular.

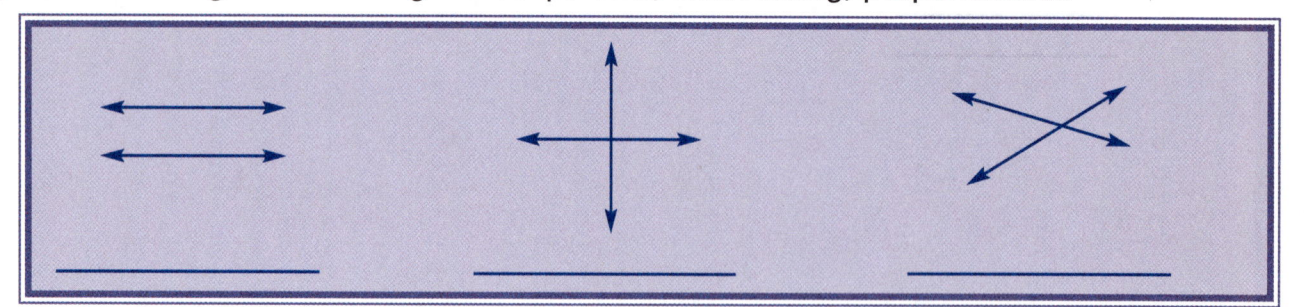

_____      _____      _____

**5** Arrange the numbers in the spaces below to make the largest number possible.

1, 7, 3, 0, 5, 7      3, 3, 5, 8, 1, 0, 2      7, 9, 7, 9, 2, 1

_ _ _ _ . _ _      _ _ _ _ _ . _ _      _ _ _ _ _ . _ _

**Lesson 2**

# Properties of Subtraction

Subtraction is used when we want to take away, or compare amounts. Subtraction can be shown in two ways:

```
  9    minuend           9  −  1  =  8
− 1    subtrahend    (minuend) (subtrahend) (difference)
  8    difference          Horizontal Form
Vertical Form
```

**Subtraction properties help us find differences.**

**ZERO PROPERTY OF SUBTRACTION**
The difference between any number and zero is that number.
   $6 - 0 = 6$
The difference between any number and itself is zero.
   $8 - 8 = 0$

**THE OPPOSITES PROPERTY**
Subtraction "undoes" addition, and addition "undoes" subtraction.
   $8 + 9 = 17$, so $17 - 9 = 8$
   and
   $11 + 5 = 16$, so $16 - 5 = 11$

**1** Find each difference. Label the first problem with the following terms: minuend, subtrahend, or difference.

| 14 | _____ | 16 | 8 | 13 | 12 |
|----|--------|----|----|----|----|
| −7 | _____ | −7 | −2 | −9 | −9 |
| 7  | _____ |    |    |    |    |

| 15 | 17 | 9  | 8  | 10 | 7  |
|----|----|----|----|----|----|
| −9 | −6 | −8 | −8 | −9 | −4 |

| 12 | 7  | 9  | 19 | 4  | 7  |
|----|----|----|----|----|----|
| −7 | −3 | −8 | −8 | −2 | −6 |

16 − 6 = _____        13 − 5 = _____        4 − 2 = _____

**2** Use the zero property to complete.

9 – 9 = \_\_\_\_    1 0 – 0 = \_\_\_\_    1 2 – 0 = \_\_\_\_    2 7 – 2 7 = \_\_\_\_

Use the opposites property to complete.

8 + 7 = 15, so 15 – 7 = \_\_\_\_
9 + 8 = 17, so 17 – 8 = \_\_\_\_
7 – 1 = 6, so 6 + 1 = \_\_\_\_
9 – 2 = 7, so 7 + 2 = \_\_\_\_

**3** Arrange the numbers in the spaces below to make the smallest number possible.

1, 8, 4, 0, 5, 7            4, 4, 5, 7, 1, 0, 2            6, 4, 7, 8, 3, 1

\_ \_ \_ \_ . \_ \_        \_ \_ \_ \_ \_ . \_ \_        \_ \_ \_ \_ \_ . \_

**4** Match.

one-fifth            $\frac{1}{4}$

five-eighths         $\frac{1}{5}$

two-thirds           $\frac{2}{9}$

eleven-twelfths      $\frac{2}{3}$

two-ninths           $\frac{11}{12}$

one-fourth           $\frac{5}{8}$

**5**

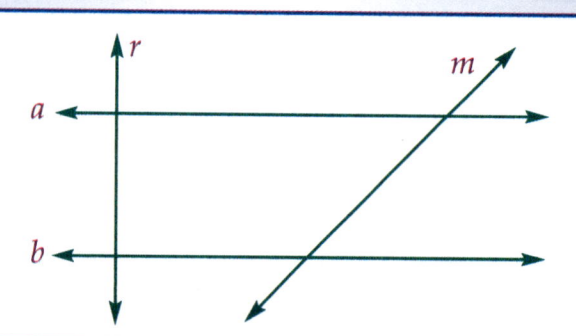

Name a pair of parallel lines. _____

Name a pair of perpendicular lines. _____

Name two pair of intersecting lines. _____

**6** Add each fraction and write it in lowest terms. Find the letter in the roof that matches the sum, and write it in the box in the window. The message will complete the statement; **A house** ............

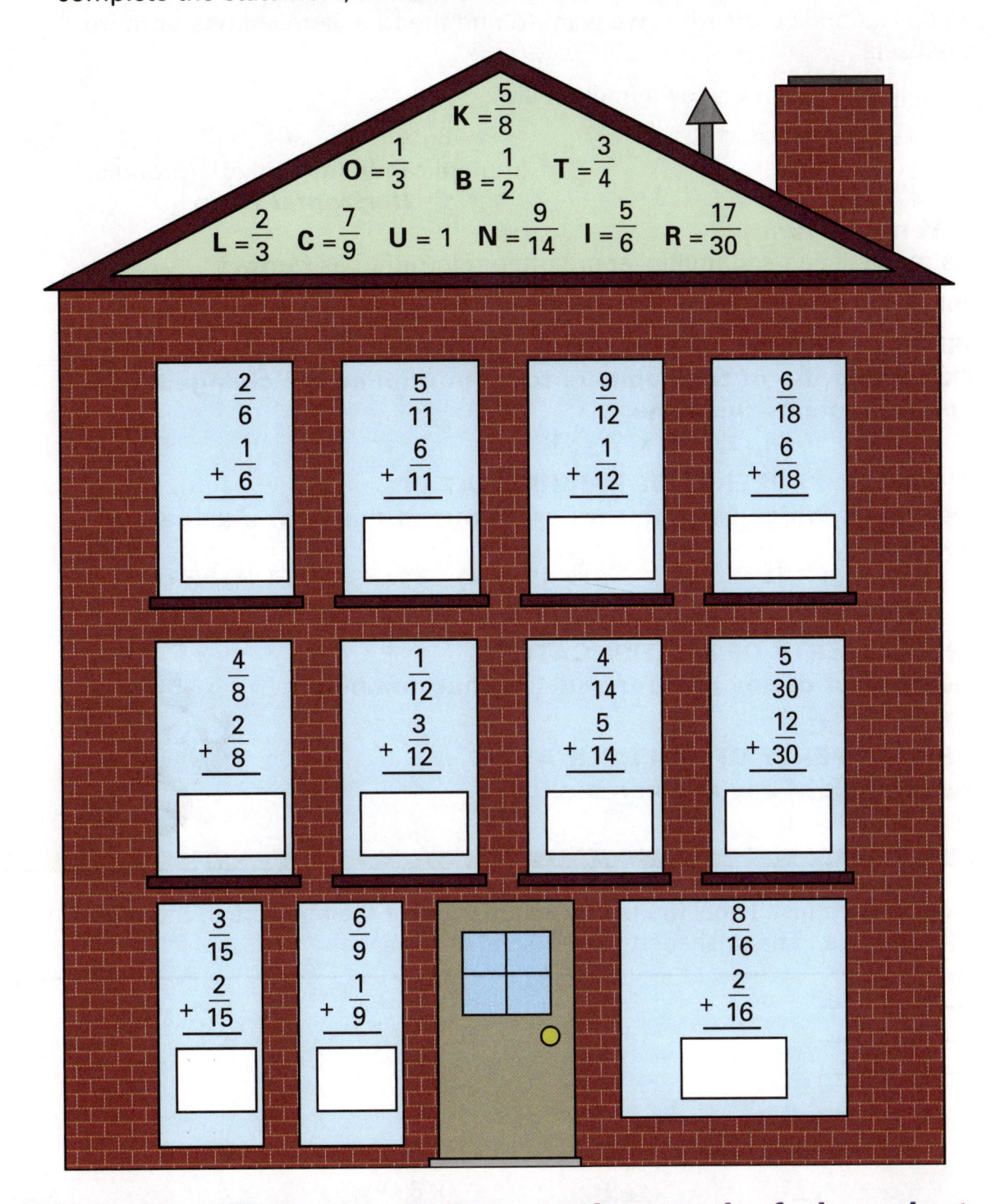

Roof key:
- K = $\frac{5}{8}$
- O = $\frac{1}{3}$, B = $\frac{1}{2}$, T = $\frac{3}{4}$
- L = $\frac{2}{3}$, C = $\frac{7}{9}$, U = 1, N = $\frac{9}{14}$, I = $\frac{5}{6}$, R = $\frac{17}{30}$

Windows:

1. $\frac{2}{6} + \frac{1}{6} = \frac{1}{2}$ → **B**
2. $\frac{5}{11} + \frac{6}{11} = 1$ → **U**
3. $\frac{9}{12} + \frac{1}{12} = \frac{5}{6}$ → **I**
4. $\frac{6}{18} + \frac{6}{18} = \frac{2}{3}$ → **L**
5. $\frac{4}{8} + \frac{2}{8} = \frac{3}{4}$ → **T**
6. $\frac{1}{12} + \frac{3}{12} = \frac{1}{3}$ → **O**
7. $\frac{4}{14} + \frac{5}{14} = \frac{9}{14}$ → **N**
8. $\frac{5}{30} + \frac{12}{30} = \frac{17}{30}$ → **R**
9. $\frac{3}{15} + \frac{2}{15} = \frac{1}{3}$ → **O**
10. $\frac{6}{9} + \frac{1}{9} = \frac{7}{9}$ → **C**
11. $\frac{8}{16} + \frac{2}{16} = \frac{5}{8}$ → **K**

**Matthew 7:24-25:** Everyone who listens to these words of mine and acts on them will be like a wise man who _ _ _ _ _ his house _ _  _ _ _ _ . The rain fell, the floods came, and the winds flew and buffeted the house. But it did not collapse; it had been set solidly on rock.

# Properties of Multiplication

**Lesson 3**

Multiplication is used when we want to find the total items in one or more equal sets.

Multiplication can be shown in two ways:

```
  6    multiplicand          6    x    4    =    24
x 4    multiplier        (multiplicand) (multiplier) (product)
 24    product                    Horizontal Form
Vertical Form
```

The multiplicand and multiplier are often referred to as **factors**.

Multiplication of properties helps us find products.

### ORDER PROPERTY OF MULTIPLICATION
When the order of the numbers to be multiplied are changed, the product remains the same.

3 x 6 = 18,  so  6 x 3 = 18

### GROUPING PROPERTY OF MULTIPLICATION
The way in which the numbers are grouped does not change the product.

(3 x 2) x 4 = 24     3 x (2 x 4) = 24     Work inside the ( ) first.
  6   x 4 = 24       3 x   8   = 24

### ONE PROPERTY OF MULTIPLICATION
The product of any number and 1 is that number.

4 x 1 = 4

### ZERO PROPERTY OF MULTIPLICATION
The product of any number and 0 is 0.

6 x 0 = 0

**1** Find each product. Label the first problem. Shade the answers in the table on the next page. The unshaded spaces spell a message.

|   8 _____ |   3  |   3  |   7  |   3  |   7  |
|  x 9 _____ |  x 2 |  x 9 |  x 4 |  x 6 |  x 1 |
|  72 _____ |      |      |      |      |      |

|   7  |   3  |   7  |   3  |   7  |   3  |
|  x 7 |  x 7 |  x 9 |  x 8 |  x 6 |  x 3 |

|   2  |   5  |   3  |   5  |   7  |   7  |
|  x 7 |  x 7 |  x 4 |  x 3 |  x 8 |  x 0 |

8  Horizons Math 5, Student Workbook 1

Shade the answers from the previous problems in the table below.

| 81 | 0 | 35 | 6 | 45 | 49 | 18 | 70 | 21 | 72 | 7 | 24 |
|---|---|---|---|---|---|---|---|---|---|---|---|
| G | P | O | U | R | F | D | E | B | X | Q | C |

| 15 | 63 | 9 | 46 | 14 | 65 | 42 | 12 | 56 | 27 | 28 | 19 |
|---|---|---|---|---|---|---|---|---|---|---|---|
| N | W | S | A | I | T | M | V | L | H | K | ! |

What is the hidden word? _____

**2** Solve the problems by applying the multiplication properties.

3 × (2 × 4) = ____, so (3 × 2) × 4 = ____        3 × (5 × 2) = ____, so (3 × 5) × 2 = ____

8 × 0 = ____    0 × 1 = ____    5 × 1 = ____    1 × 23 = ____    0 × 17 = ____    1 × 231 = ____

**3** Draw and label.

| ray AB | right angle ∠XYZ | acute angle ∠LMN | obtuse angle ∠QRS |
|---|---|---|---|
|  |  |  |  |

**4** Find the sum or difference.

| 6<br>+ 3 | 4<br>+ 7 | 8<br>+ 8 | 9<br>+ 6 | 6<br>+ 2 |
|---|---|---|---|---|

| 9<br>− 6 | 11<br>− 5 | 6<br>− 6 | 18<br>− 9 | 13<br>− 6 |
|---|---|---|---|---|

**5** Use the table to answer the questions.

| 1 cup | 1 pint | 1 quart | 1 gallon |
|---|---|---|---|
| 8 fluid ounces | 2 cups | 2 pints | 4 quarts |
| | 16 fluid ounces | 4 cups | 8 pints |
| | | 32 fluid ounces | 16 cups |
| | | | 128 fluid ounces |

4 cups = _____ pints     8 quarts = _____ gallons     1 quart = _____ cups

16 cups = _____ gallon     1 gallon = _____ pints     8 pints = _____ gallon

64 ounces = _____ quarts     32 cups = _____ gallons     8 cups = _____ quarts

**6** Add and subtract. Circle the footballs with the correct answers to solve the riddle:

**What grades would a football player always get?** _____

5 + 3 → 8 A
4 + 6 → 8 A
8 + 7 → 12 B
9 + 6 → 15 L
3 + 7 → 10 W

9 − 3 → 6 A
14 − 6 → 8 Y
6 − 2 → 4 S
18 − 9 → 8 D
13 − 4 → 9 P

5 + 5 → 10 A
13 − 7 → 7 K
9 + 1 → 10 S
19 − 7 → 11 O
9 + 7 → 16 S

**7** Shade the even numbers and read the number formed by the shading.

| 2 | 3 | 4 | 54 | 7 | 6 | 548 | 116 |
|---|---|---|---|---|---|---|---|
| 90 | 11 | 5 | 86 | 409 | 8 | 3 | 422 |
| 368 | 17 | 1 | 902 | 707 | 508 | 10 | 806 |

10  Horizons Math 5, Student Workbook 1

# Properties of Division

**Lesson 4**

We use division to solve problems that involve finding how many equal sets or how many items are in each set.
Division can be shown in two ways:

divisor 4)$\overline{36}$ dividend (quotient 9) — **Vertical Form**

36 ÷ 4 = 9
dividend   divisor   quotient — **Horizontal Form**

**Division properties help us find quotients.**

**DIVISION BY ONE**
Any number divided by one is that number.
8 ÷ 1 = 8

**DIVISION OF A NUMBER BY ITSELF**
Any number divided by itself is one.
7 ÷ 7 = 1

**MULTIPLICATION AND DIVISION ARE RELATED**
Dividing "undoes" multiplying and multiplying "undoes" division.
20 ÷ 5 = 4 and, 4 x 5 = 20

**DIVISION BY ZERO**
We CANNOT divide by zero.
5 ÷ 0 = ? Check ? x 0 = 5 Nothing will check!
We can divide 0 by a number.
0 ÷ 5 = 0 Check 0 x 5 = 0

**1** Find the quotient. Then follow your answers to find your way through the path.

1. 5)$\overline{40}$   2. 6)$\overline{36}$   3. 4)$\overline{16}$   4. 4)$\overline{20}$   5. 6)$\overline{12}$   6. 7)$\overline{7}$

7. 4)$\overline{36}$   8. 4)$\overline{12}$   9. 6)$\overline{60}$   10. 3)$\overline{15}$   11. 3)$\overline{33}$

12. 6)$\overline{18}$   13. 5)$\overline{45}$   14. 7)$\overline{14}$   15. 9)$\overline{63}$

16. 7)$\overline{63}$

**2** Solve the problems by applying the division properties.

49 ÷ 7 = _____ so, _____ x 7 = 49         40 ÷ 8 = _____ so, _____ x 8 = 40

5 ÷ 5 = _____     5 ÷ 1 = _____     10 ÷ 10 = _____     10 ÷ 1 = _____     0 ÷ 9 = _____

What division problem is impossible? _____

**3** Joshua's Hardware Store sells nails, nuts, bolts, and screws individually or by the pound. Andy needs to refill the buckets below so that each one has exactly one pound. How much will he put in each bucket?

**Hint:**

$$1 \text{ lb.} = \frac{9}{9}$$
$$- \frac{1}{9}$$
$$\frac{8}{9}$$

Buckets: $\frac{1}{3}$, $\frac{1}{6}$, $\frac{3}{7}$, $\frac{3}{8}$, $\frac{3}{4}$ (bucket shown with $\frac{1}{9}$)

**4** Define using the following terms: acute angle, obtuse angle, or right angle.

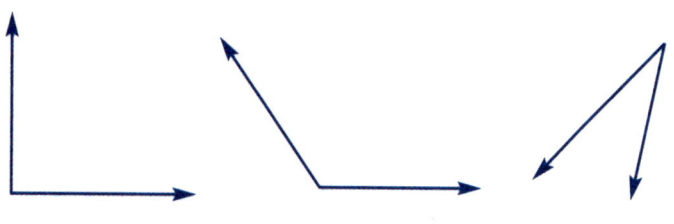

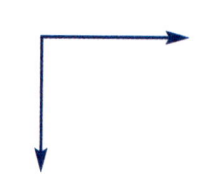

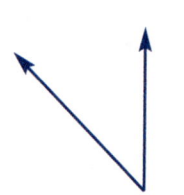

_____    _____    _____    _____    _____

**5** Shade the odd numbers and read the message.

| 9 | 62 | 11 | | 78 | 33 | 22 | | 55 | 65 | 85 | | 17 | 74 | 801 |
|---|----|----|---|----|----|----|---|----|----|----|---|----|----|-----|
| 171 | 5 | 25 | | 679 | 92 | 515 | | 22 | 43 | 4 | | 19 | 80 | 43 |
| 13 | 6 | 133 | | 143 | 9 | 645 | | 64 | 57 | 54 | | 3 | 3 | 75 |
| 21 | 42 | 43 | | 67 | 10 | 7 | | 80 | 89 | 76 | | 1 | 40 | 87 |
| 7 | 2 | 77 | | 9 | 14 | 3 | | 90 | 93 | 88 | | 77 | 30 | 97 |

The message: ___ ___ ___ ___ is AWESOME!

**Lesson 5**

## Missing Addends

The youth group at church is having a bake sale. Jeannine is responsible for getting 18 pies for the sale. Help her determine how many pies she still needs.

| Sign here if you can bring pies. | Please tell what kind and how many. |
|---|---|
| Amy | 2 blueberry pies |
| Stephen | 3 apple pies |
| Karen | 1 cherry pie |
| Trisha | 2 pumpkin pies |

Jeannine turned her problem into a math sentence.
2 + 3 + 1 + 2 + _?_ = 18
       8       + _?_ = 18
       8 + _10_ = 18

**1** Find the missing number.

Sample:
6 + 8 + 9 + _2_ = 25

4 + 17 + 3 + ____ = 37

12 + 6 + ____ + 5 + 1 = 32

13 + 3 + ____ + 8 + 11 = 48

9 + ____ + 8 + 3 + 6 = 33

**2** Find the sum or difference.

```
  5        13         4        17         3
+ 7      − 11       + 1      −  7       + 7
```

**3** Label the first problem and find the products.

|  9    |  9    |  7    |  4    |  2    |  4    |  9    |
| x 9   | x 7   | x 8   | x 5   | x 6   | x 8   | x 6   |
|  81   |       |       |       |       |       |       |

|  3    |  4    |  6    |  2    |  4    |  7    |  9    |  5    |
| x 4   | x 7   | x 2   | x 2   | x 5   | x 9   | x 2   | x 6   |

**4** Find the value of the money and write it on the line provided.

_____

_____

_____

_____

**5** Divide and check.

7)49     4)16     6)30     8)72     7)42

9)45     7)35     3)12     5)20     7)21

## 6  Find each sum.

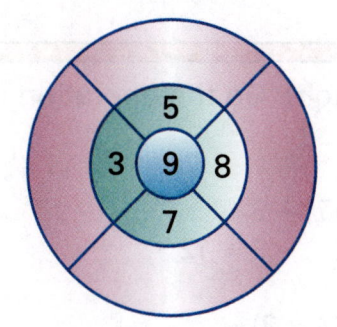

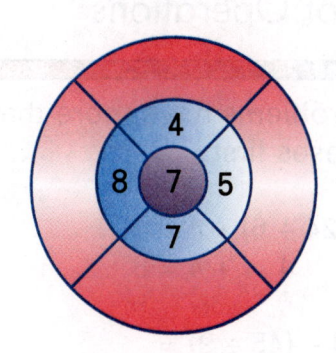

## 7  Identify the missing numerator or denominator.

$\dfrac{3}{9} = \dfrac{n}{18}$     $\dfrac{4}{5} = \dfrac{n}{45}$     $\dfrac{7}{8} = \dfrac{21}{n}$

$\dfrac{1}{7} = \dfrac{n}{49}$     $\dfrac{9}{10} = \dfrac{n}{20}$     $\dfrac{5}{8} = \dfrac{45}{n}$

## 8  Label each figure with one of the following names: triangle, square, pentagon, hexagon, or decagon.

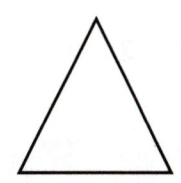

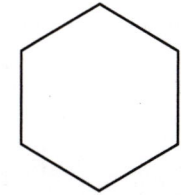

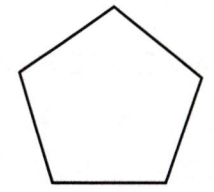

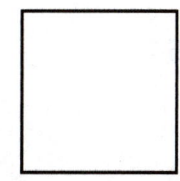

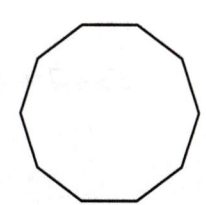

**Lesson 6**

## Order of Operations

Some problems have more than one operation. Do the operation in the parentheses first.

(24 ÷ 6) + 4 =          (3 x 7) – 9 =
    4   + 4 = 8              21  – 9 = 12

14 – (45 ÷ 9) =         8 + (4 x 3) =
14 –     5   = 9        8 +   12  = 20

**1** Solve.

17 – (3 x 4) = _____   14 + (81 ÷ 9) = _____   (32 ÷ 8) – 4 = _____

(9 x 8) + 12 = _____   (13 + 6) – 8 = _____    21 ÷ (7 – 4) = _____

8 x (4 + 3) = _____    (16 – 7) + 3 = _____    (11 + 7) – 4 = _____

**2** Rewrite each problem. Place the parentheses in the proper place to make each statement true.

35 ÷ 7 + 49 = 54        4 x 8 + 12 = 80         15 – 7 x 2 = 16

29 + 3 ÷ 4 = 8          17 + 18 – 5 = 30        16 – 6 + 4 = 14

**3** Find the missing addends.

5 + 6 + _____ + 9 = 28          4 + 7 + 9 + _____ = 35          _____ + 3 + 7 + 12 = 36

**4** Find each quotient. Label the first problem.

_____ 4)12   _____ 7)21   9)81   9)36   2)18

7)49   7)56   6)24   9)72   3)15

**5** Find each product. Label the first problem.

```
  9  _____      9        9        9        9
x 4  _____    x 7      x 2      x 9      x 8
 36  _____
```

```
  9        9        9        9       10
x 1      x 6      x 0      x 5      x 9
```

**6** Find the missing numerator or denominator.

$\frac{4}{5} = \frac{8}{n}$   $\frac{3}{5} = \frac{27}{n}$   $\frac{5}{11} = \frac{n}{22}$   $\frac{6}{7} = \frac{n}{49}$   $\frac{7}{8} = \frac{14}{n}$

n =   n =   n =   n =   n =

**7** Label each shape.

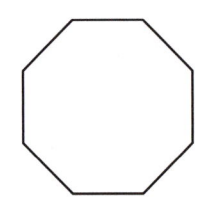

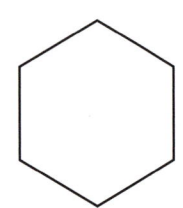

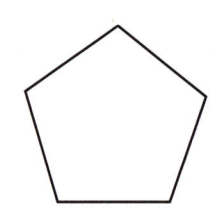

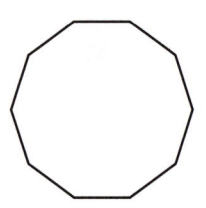

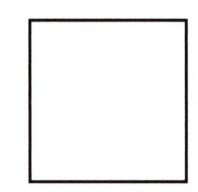

**8** Match the geometric symbol with the corresponding picture.

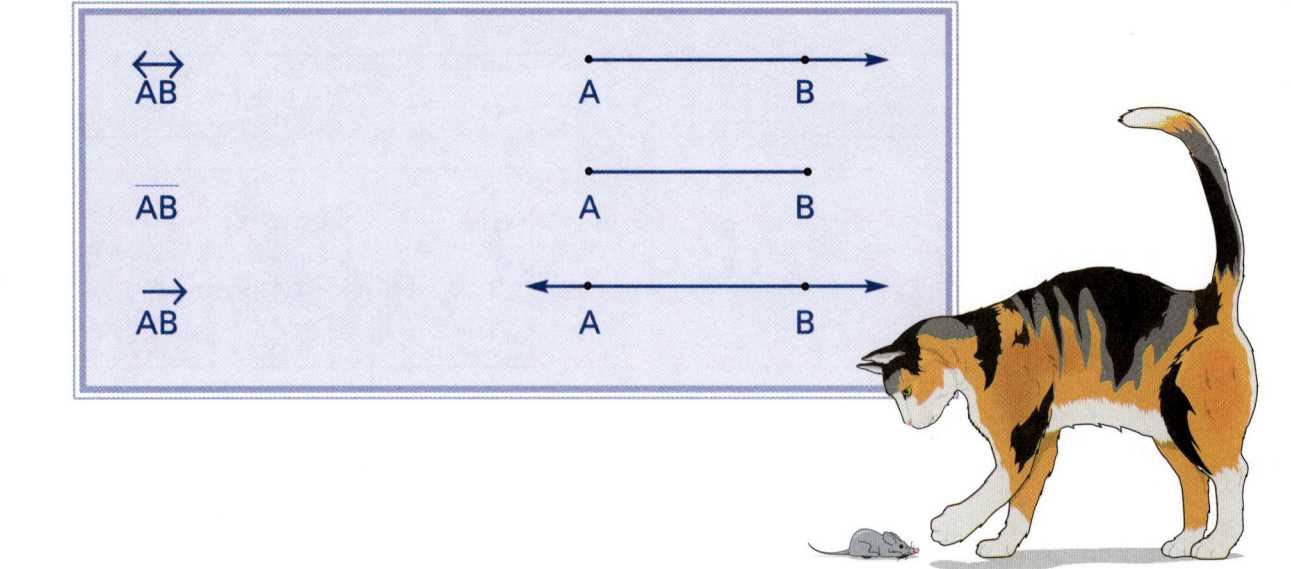

**Lesson 7**

# Equations

A number sentence which contains an equals sign is called an **equation**. A **variable** is a letter that stands for a number.

Paul and Steve need to sell 60 raffle tickets to help pay their camp tuition. Paul sold 45 raffle tickets. How many does Steve need to sell? This problem can be expressed as an equation. ($n$) will be the variable, or the letter that stands for how many raffle tickets Steve needs to sell.

$$\begin{aligned} n + 45 &= 60 \\ -45 &\phantom{=} -45 \\ n &= 15 \end{aligned}$$

1. To solve an equation the variable ($n$) must be alone on one side. 45 is added to ($n$), so we must subtract 45 from ($n$) to eliminate it from that side.
2. Whatever is done to one side of the equation, must be done to the other. Subtract 45 from the right side, also.
3. $n = 15$, Steve needs to sell 15 raffle tickets.

**Check**

$n + 45 = 60$
$15 + 45 = 60$

1. Plug the answer back into the original problem to check.

**1** Solve the equations and check.

$n + 39 = 49$
$-\phantom{00}\phantom{0}-$

Check

$n + 41 = 174$
$-\phantom{00}\phantom{0}-$

Check

$n + 73 = 97$
$-\phantom{00}\phantom{0}-$

Check

$n + 15 = 91$
$-\phantom{00}\phantom{0}-$

Check

$n + 96 = 179$
$-\phantom{00}\phantom{0}-$

Check

$n + 38 = 49$
$-\phantom{00}\phantom{0}-$

Check

**2** Solve. Find the answer in the solution box. Place the letter next to each answer on the lines beside each problem. Read the solution to the riddle:
**What always keeps its hands on its face?**

| 9 K | 3 A | 91 O | 4 L | 40 C |

11 – (2 x 4) = _____ _____          34 + (54 ÷ 9) = _____ _____

(35 ÷ 7) – 1 = _____ _____          (9 x 9) + 10 = _____ _____

(33 + 16) – 9 = _____ _____          45 ÷ (7 – 2) = _____ _____

**3** Find the missing addends.

4 + 5 + 11 + \_\_\_\_\_ = 47          3 + \_\_\_\_\_ + 8 + 5 + 1 = 23          \_\_\_\_\_ + 4 + 8 + 2 = 28

**4** Find the quotients.

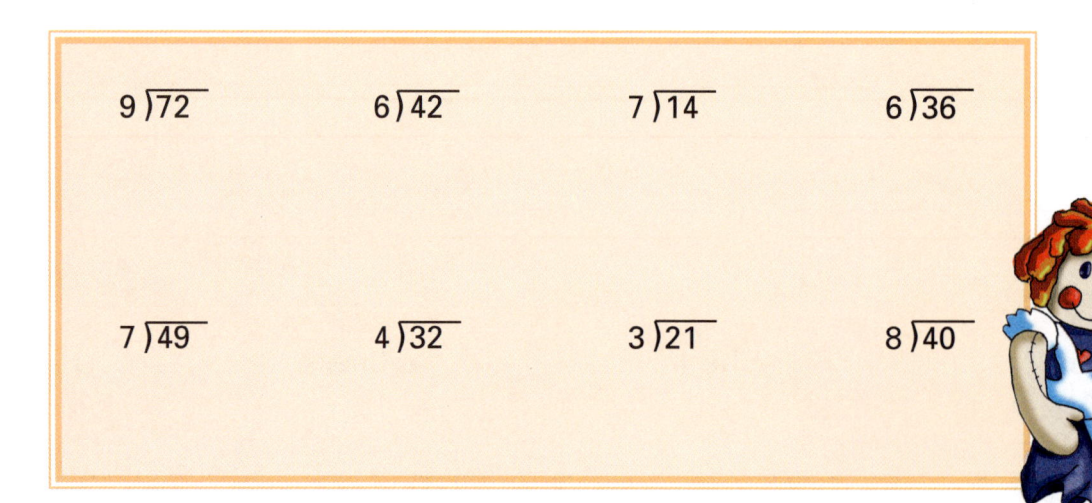

9)72          6)42          7)14          6)36

7)49          4)32          3)21          8)40

**5** Rename each fraction in lowest terms.

$\frac{15}{30} =$ _____   $\frac{16}{32} =$ _____   $\frac{14}{49} =$ _____   $\frac{9}{27} =$ _____

$\frac{10}{20} =$ _____   $\frac{50}{100} =$ _____   $\frac{30}{54} =$ _____   $\frac{35}{45} =$ _____

**6** Compare similar and congruent.

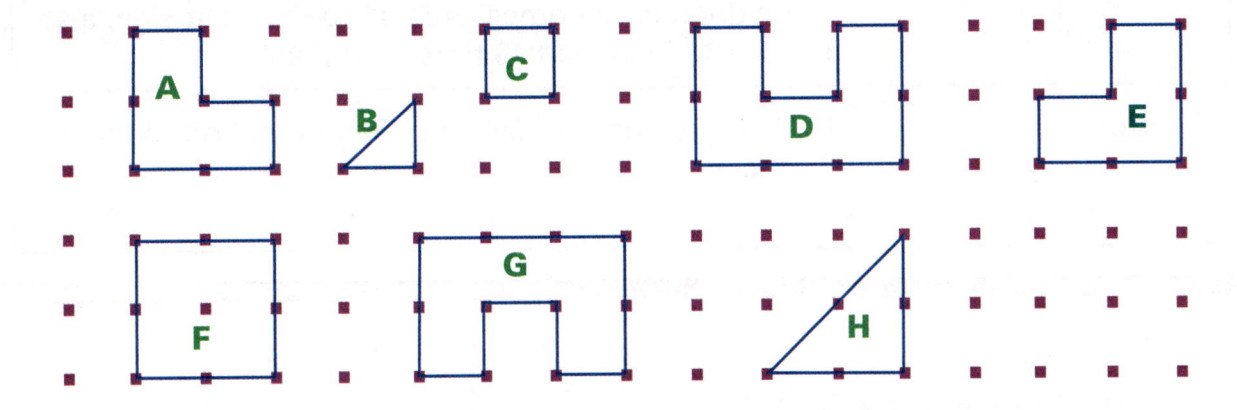

What shapes are similar? _____

What shapes are congruent? _____

**7** Use the table to give the missing numbers.

| 1 gallon = 4 quarts | 1 quart = 2 pints |
|---|---|
| 1 pint = 2 cups | 1 cup = 8 fluid ounces |

8 quarts = _____ gallons   10 cups = _____ pints   5 quarts = _____ pints

1 gallon = _____ pints   16 cups = _____ gallon   3 gallons = _____ quarts

## Lesson 8

## Equations

A number sentence which contains an equals sign is called an **equation**.
A **variable** is a letter that stands for a number.
We can add and subtract in equations.

Timothy and Jason had 28 raffle tickets left after they sold fifteen. How many did they have originally?

$$\begin{array}{rl} n - 15 &= 28 \\ +\ 15 & +15 \\ \hline n &= 43 \end{array}$$

1. To solve an equation the variable ($n$) must be alone on one side. 15 is subtracted from ($n$), so we must add 15 to ($n$) to eliminate it from that side.
2. Whatever is done to one side of the equation, must be done to the other. Add 15 to the right side, also.
3. $n = 43$, They had 43 tickets originally.

**Check:**
$n - 15 = 28$
$43 - 15 = 28$

1. Plug the answer back into the original problem to check.

**1** Solve the equations and check.

$n - 11 = 78$
$\phantom{n}+\phantom{11}\ \ +$

Check

$n - 31 = 181$
$\phantom{n}+\phantom{31}\ \ +$

Check

$n - 3 = 187$
$\phantom{n}+\phantom{3}\ \ +$

Check

$n - 75 = 31$
$\phantom{n}+\phantom{75}\ \ +$

Check

$n - 126 = 19$
$\phantom{n}+\phantom{126}\ \ +$

Check

$n - 238 = 99$
$\phantom{n}+\phantom{238}\ \ +$

Check

**2** Solve each addition equation.

$n + 13 = 78$  $\qquad$ $n + 38 = 903$ $\qquad$ $n + 76 = 77$ $\qquad$ $n + 302 = 608$

**3** Rewrite each problem. Place the parentheses in the proper place to make each statement true.

$45 \div 9 + 4 = 9$  $\qquad$ $2 \times 8 + 16 = 48$ $\qquad$ $34 - 2 \times 2 = 64$

$9 + 3 \div 4 = 3$ $\qquad$ $7 + 20 - 5 = 22$ $\qquad$ $46 - 24 + 6 = 28$

**4** Find the missing addend.

$1 + 8 + 9 + \underline{\phantom{xx}} = 71$

$34 + 21 + \underline{\phantom{xx}} + 12 = 100$

$16 + 13 + \underline{\phantom{xx}} + 12 = 68$

**5** Rename each fraction in lowest terms. Find the fraction in the number bank. Write the letter next to it on the line and read the solution to the riddle: **What is a baby's favorite reptile?** The first one has been done for you.

| $\frac{1}{2}$ = A | $\frac{1}{3}$ = T | $\frac{3}{8}$ = K | $\frac{2}{3}$ = R |
| $\frac{1}{5}$ = L | $\frac{1}{7}$ = N | $\frac{1}{4}$ = E | $\frac{1}{10}$ = S |

$\frac{8}{12}$   $\frac{5}{10}$   $\frac{5}{15}$   $\frac{6}{18}$   $\frac{3}{15}$   $\frac{4}{16}$   $\frac{8}{80}$   $\frac{4}{28}$   $\frac{3}{6}$   $\frac{6}{16}$   $\frac{5}{20}$

$\frac{2}{3}$   ___   ___   ___   ___   ___   ___   ___   ___   ___   ___

R   ___   ___   ___   ___   ___   ___   ___   ___   ___   ___

**6** Draw a similar and a congruent figure.

**7** Use the table to give the missing numbers.

1 foot = 12 inches
1 yard = 3 feet = 36 inches
1 mile = 1,760 yards = 5,280 feet

24 inches = _____ feet       5,280 yards = _____ miles       144 inches = _____ yards

6 feet = _____ inches        2 miles = _____ yards           2 yards = _____ inches

## Calculating

**Lesson 9**

This lesson requires the use of a calculator. Calculators are useful tools in helping to solve problems quickly. Students should learn basic facts, and calculators should never be a substitute for gaining that knowledge. When you use a calculator, follow these steps:

1. Write the stated problem.
2. Estimate the answer.
3. Put data into the calculator.
4. Compare the answer on the calculator with the estimated answer.

Adrienne and Kayli are on the decorating committee for their Sunday School Valentines Day party. They want to string red crepe paper all the way around the room. The measurement of one side of the room is 360 inches. If all four sides of the room are equal in length, how many inches is the perimeter? If they add 12 inches more to each side, so the crepe paper will drape down, how much crepe paper will they need?

Multiply:   360   x   4   =   1,440 inches
Multiply:   12    x   4   =   48 inches
Add:        1,440 +   48  =   1,488 inches

The perimeter of the room in 1,440 inches.
They will need 1,488 inches of crepe paper.

**1** Solve each problem.

Stan Cottrell is an ultramarathon runner. He founded Friendship Sports. It promotes friendship among nations through sports to bring people to a personal relationship with God. Use your calculator to answer the questions about Stan's many runs across states, countries, and continents.

1. Stan Cottrell runs about 140 miles a week when he is in training. How many miles does he run a day if he runs seven days a week?

2. Stan ran across Europe from Edinburgh, Scotland to the Rock of Gibraltar in 80 days. He averaged 44 miles a day. How far was his total run?

3. When Stan was planning his run across the United States, he figured that running 62 miles a day for fifty days would easily get him from New York City to San Francisco. How many miles would he run?

4. No one had ever run for twenty-four hours in a row. Stan decided to set the world's record. He ran about seven miles an hour for twenty-four hours. How long was the run?

**2** Solve each addition equation.

$n + 67 = 165$     $n + 43 = 93$     $n + 156 = 177$     $n + 102 = 675$

**3** Solve each subtraction equation.

$n - 53 = 98$     $n - 63 = 345$     $n - 70 = 157$     $n - 76 = 406$

**4** Complete each pattern.

2, 4, 6, 8, ____, ____, ____

10, 5, 9, 4, 8, ____, ____, ____

1, 2, 4, 8, ____, ____, ____

**5** Order the fractions from least to greatest.

$\frac{1}{16}$  $\frac{4}{16}$  $\frac{2}{16}$  $\frac{9}{16}$  $\frac{16}{16}$  $\frac{12}{16}$  $\frac{3}{16}$

____  ____  ____  ____  ____  ____  ____

**6** Draw a symmetrical shape for each figure.

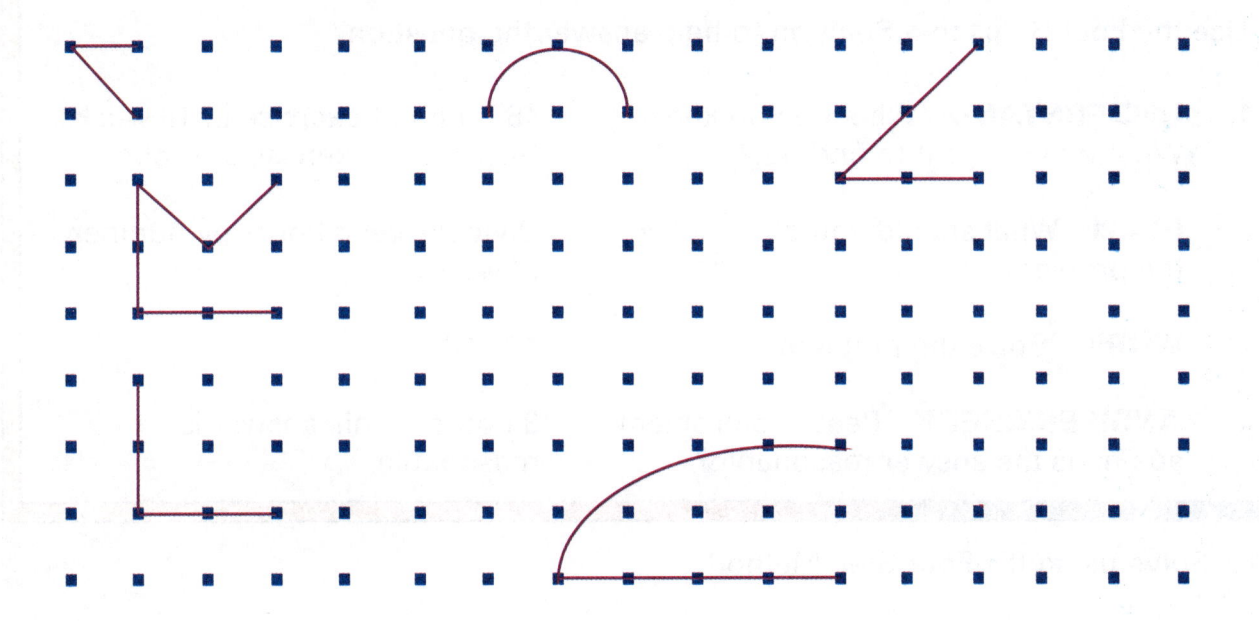

# Investigating Problems

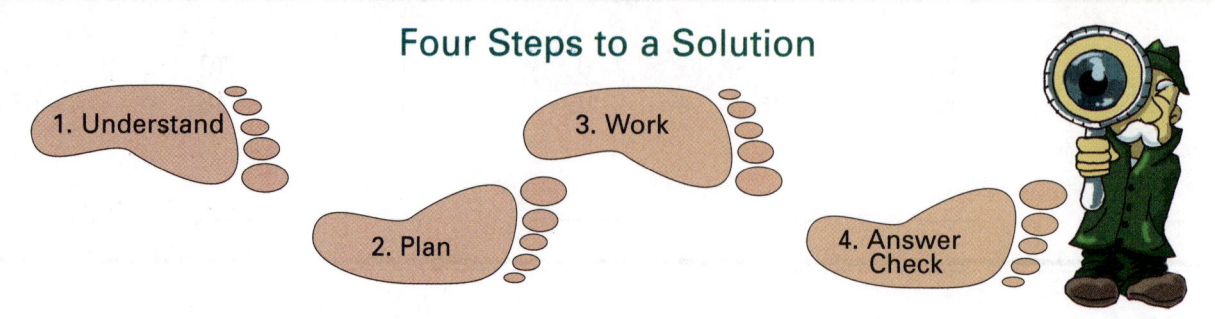

Lesson 10

## Four Steps to a Solution

1. Understand
2. Plan
3. Work
4. Answer Check

Amelia is working for a Presidential Sports Award. She needs to do 48 hours of exercise in a four month period (16 weeks). How much does she need to exercise every week?

Use the Four Steps to a Solution to help answer the question.

1. **UNDERSTAND** - What do you know? What do you want to find out?

   48 hours of exercise in 16 weeks. How much exercise a week?

2. **PLAN** - What should you do to solve the problem?

   Divide: total # hours by number of weeks

3. **WORK** - Solve the problem.

   48 ÷ 16 =

4. **ANSWER/CHECK** - Read the problem again. Is the answer reasonable?

   3 hours. This answer is reasonable.

**1** Solve using the Four Step Method.

1. Amelia needs to exercise for 3 hours a week to get her sports award. If she wants to exercise 30 minutes each day, how many days will she need to exercise per week?

2. Amelia takes 10 minutes to warm up, 10 minutes to cool down, and 30 minutes to exercise. How much time does she spend in all?

3. Amelia runs a 10 minute mile. How many miles will she run by the end of her 30 minute workout?

4. The Red Mountain Fun Run is a five mile run around Amelia's neighborhood. If she runs her usual 10 minute a mile pace, how long will it take her to complete the race?

**2** Solve the addition or subtraction equations.

$n - 35 = 56$    $n + 42 = 67$    $n - 14 = 89$    $n + 89 = 138$

$n - 45 = 52$    $n + 40 = 87$    $n - 102 = 645$    $n + 34 = 549$

**3** Use a calculator to solve the problems.

| Trail Name | Elevation | Length |
|---|---|---|
| Amethyst Trail | 5800 ft to 6880 ft | 3 miles one way |
| Sixshooter Canyon | 3800 ft to 7560 ft | 4.7 miles one way |
| Strayhorse Canyon | 5000 ft to 8200 ft | 12.7 miles one way |
| Highline Trail | 7000 ft to 7600 ft | 14.6 miles one way |
| Palo Verde Trail | 1820 ft to 1840 ft | 4 miles one way |
| Horton Creek Trail | 5500 ft to 6420 ft | 3.8 miles one way |
| Dan's Trail | 6720 ft to 7120 ft | 4.8 miles round trip |

1. Andrew wants to go on a hike in central Arizona. He does not like to climb uphill. Look at the elevations on the table, and choose the best hike for Andrew.

2. Susan wants to hike about 8 miles round trip. Which hikes could she choose?

3. Jamie and Andrew want to hike a trail that has an elevation change of less than 1,000 feet. Which four trails on the chart above fit that description?

4. The Red Mountain Hiking Club wants to hike the trail with the steepest elevation. Which hike should they take?

4. Draw lines of symmetry on the numbers. Place an X on the numbers that have no lines of symmetry.

1   2   3   4   5

6   7   8   9   0

5. Find the pattern, and write the next three numbers.

2, 4, 3, 9, 4, 16, 5, 25, ____, ____, ____

1, 1, 2, 3, 5, 8, ____, ____, ____

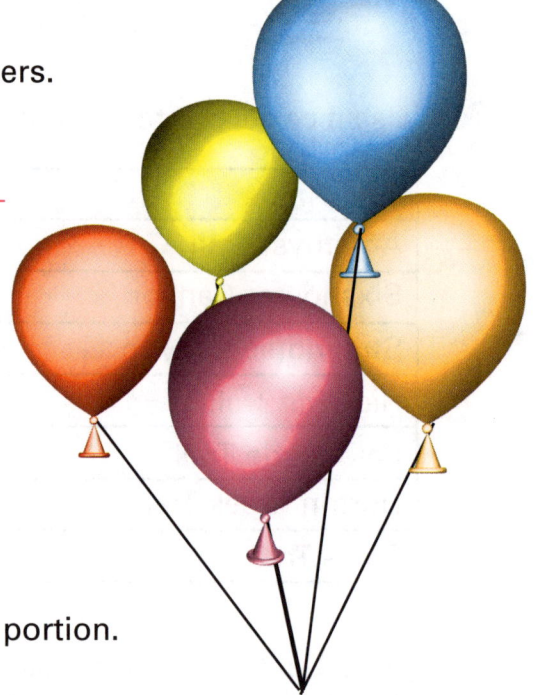

6. Write the fraction that represents each colored portion.

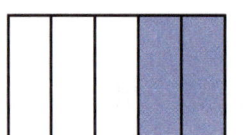

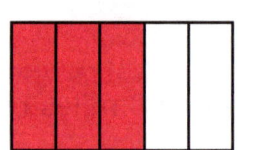

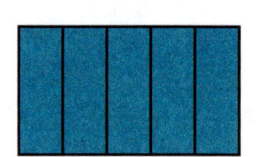

_____      _____      _____      _____

Order the fractions from least to greatest.

_____      _____      _____      _____

**Test 1**

**1** Label each addition property with one of the following terms: grouping property of addition, order property of addition, or zero property of addition. Then apply each property to solve the equations below. 11 pts.

25 + 10 = 35     _____
10 + 25 = 35

89 + 0 = 89     _____

(13 + 3) + 5 = 21     _____
13 + (3 + 5) = 21

90 + 15 =          10 + 56 =          54 + 19 =          12 + 9 =

2 + (14 + 5) =     (10 + 5) + 3 =     45 + (3 + 3) =     (89 + 0) + 1 =

**2** Use the Properties of Subtraction to help you solve the following problems. Label each part of the first problem. 16 pts. total for this exercise.

```
  14    _____        10         8        13        12
-  7    _____       - 3       - 2       - 0       - 5
---
   7
```

```
  25      19         9         6        10         7
-  5     - 6       - 8       - 6       - 9       - 2
```

18 − 6 = _____          13 − 3 = _____          4 − 4 = _____

Horizons Math 5, Student Workbook 1   31

**3** Use your knowledge of the Multiplication Properties to find the incorrect answers below. Circle all the incorrect answers and correct them. 8 pts. total for this exercise.

(15 x 2) x 1 = 30          25 x 4 = 50          5 x (4 x 0) = 20          (8 x 1) x 9 = 72

6 x 8 = 46          1 x 7 = 7          (9 x 9) x 1 = 81          9 x (9 x 1) = 81

**4** Use your knowledge of Division Properties to solve the following problems. 7 pts.

5 ÷ 1 =          25 ÷ 25 =          15 ÷ 0 =          100 ÷ 4 =

0 ÷ 7 =          (7 x 4) ÷ 28 =

What process "undoes" division? _____

**5** Find the missing addends. 4 pts. total for this exercise.

4 + 19 + 3 + _____ = 39          10 + 6 + _____ 5 + 1 = 32

13 + 3 + _____ 8 + 12 = 48          9 + _____ + 5 + 3 + 6 = 33

46 pts. Total

# Lesson 11

## Place Value

Remember that every number has a specific value on the place value chart. When reading written numbers, these place value names are used to specify the value of each number. Look at the examples below.

|  | thousands | hundreds | tens | ones |
|---|---|---|---|---|
| Standard Form: | 5 | 4 | 6 | 2 |
| Word Equivalents: | five thousand | four hundred | sixty | two |
| Standard Form: | 1 | 9 | 0 | 0 |
| Word Equivalents: | one thousand | nine hundred | | |

Written Form: Five thousand, four hundred sixty-two

Written Form: One thousand, nine hundred

**1** Write each number in written form.

6,003 = _____

2,149 = _____

4,976 = _____

3,041 = _____

**2** Solve.

$$\begin{array}{r}10\\-\ n\\\hline 4\end{array} \qquad \begin{array}{r}25\\-\ n\\\hline 15\end{array} \qquad \begin{array}{r}37\\-\ n\\\hline 24\end{array} \qquad \begin{array}{r}100\\-\ n\\\hline 25\end{array}$$

**3** Write as an improper fraction.

$3\frac{4}{5}$ $\qquad$ $2\frac{6}{8}$ $\qquad$ $1\frac{1}{3}$ $\qquad$ $8\frac{1}{4}$

1. Understand
2. Plan
3. Work
4. Answer & Check

**4** Use the four step problem solving method listed above to solve the following problems.

Paul traveled approximately 360 miles to Tarsus while fleeing from Grecian Jews. If he traveled 20 miles per day, how long would it take him to complete this journey?

The trip Paul and Barnabas took to Jerusalem from Antioch took approximately 18 days. If they traveled 15 miles per day, how long was the trip (in miles)?

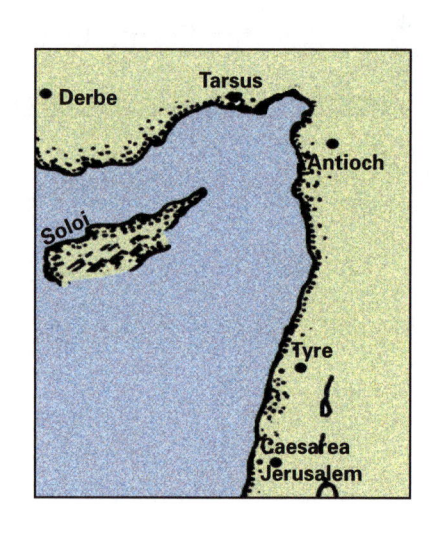

**5** Use a calculator to solve these problems.

Mr. Smith's Convenience Store was selling several items in multiple packages. Look at the chart below.

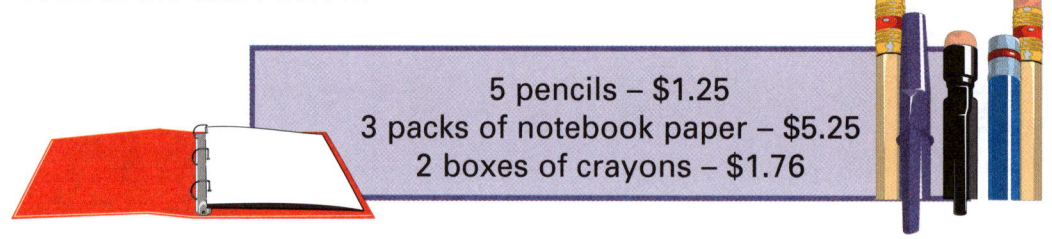

5 pencils – $1.25
3 packs of notebook paper – $5.25
2 boxes of crayons – $1.76

How much would each individual item cost?

Mrs. Calloway's store is selling several items in multiple packs. Look at the chart below.

3 pencils – $0.90
2 packs of notebook paper – $3.00
3 boxes of crayons – $2.40

How much would each individual item cost? Which store has the better individual cost on each item, Mr. Smith's or Mrs. Calloway's?

Pencils – _____

Notebook paper – _____

Crayons – _____

**6** Label each part.

Label the blue line CD.
Label the green line AB.

$\overline{CD}$ is the _____ of the circle.

$\overline{AB}$ is the _____ of the circle.

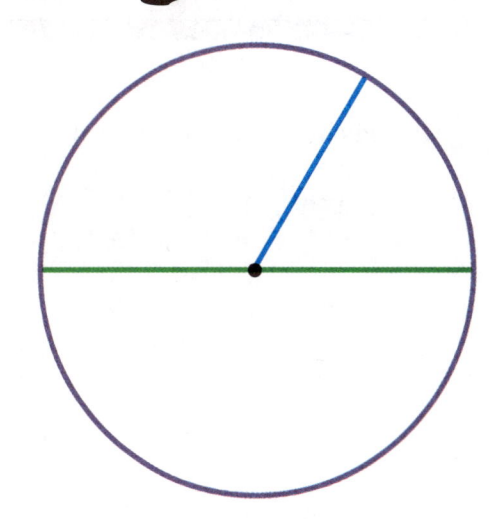

**7** Add.

| 32.4 + 68.7 = | 21.5 + 33 + 76.3 = | 70 + 63.1 + 17.6 = |

**Lesson 12**

## Place Value

It can get confusing when reading larger numbers if you do not know each number's place value. The chart below will help you to read these numbers correctly.

Melon's Amusement Park had 4,321,496 people visit the park in 1995. In 1996 they counted 6,014,722 visitors to the park. Which year had more visitors; 1995 or 1996?

|  | millions | hundred thousand | ten thousands | thousands | hundreds | tens | ones |
|---|---|---|---|---|---|---|---|
| 1995 | 4 | 3 | 2 | 1 | 4 | 9 | 6 |
| 1996 | 6 | 0 | 1 | 4 | 7 | 2 | 2 |

Four million, three hundred twenty-one thousand, four hundred, ninety-six

Six million, fourteen thousand, seven hundred, twenty-two

Melon's Amusement Park had more visitors in 1996 than in 1995.

**1** Write each number in written form.

6,459,021

_____

5,830,412

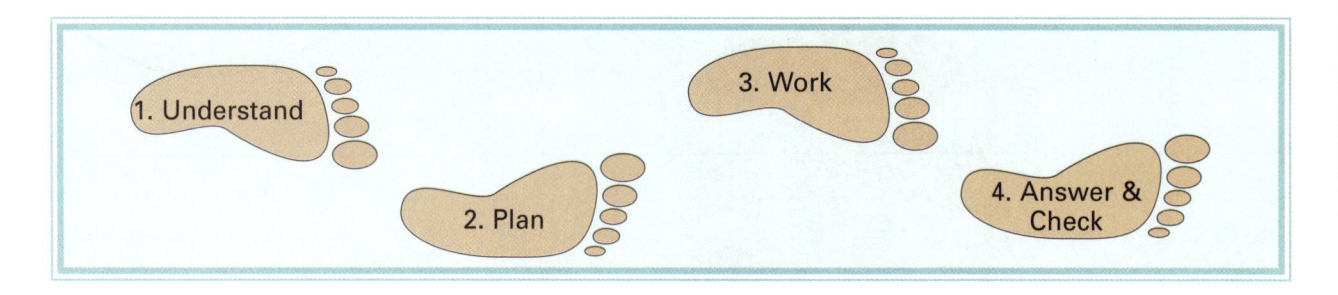

_____

1. Understand
2. Plan
3. Work
4. Answer & Check

**2** Solve.
The printer made exactly 42 posters from a roll of paper. If each poster was 15 inches long, how long was the roll of paper?

Callie needs to cover a bulletin board in her classroom. If the bulletin board is 180 inches wide, and each strip of paper is 15 inches wide, how many sheets will be needed to cover the board?

**3** Solve using a calculator

Kimberly needs to purchase several items at the store. She needs 2 bottles of shampoo, 1 box of soap, 4 pounds of ground beef, and 2 pounds of cheese. How much is her total bill?

| | |
|---|---|
| Shampoo | $1.33 each (bottle) |
| Soap | $2.49 for 3 boxes |
| Ground beef | $1.29 per pound |
| Cheese | $1.45 per pound |

Mount Keel is an active volcano which measures 2,558 meters high. After erupting, 534 meters was blown off the top. How high was the mountain after the eruption?

**4** If the statement is true, color the box red. If the statement is not true, color it blue. Do you see a symbol?

| | | | | |
|---|---|---|---|---|
| $1\frac{2}{7} = \frac{10}{7}$ | $4\frac{2}{5} = \frac{25}{5}$ | $1\frac{2}{5} = \frac{7}{5}$ | $1\frac{2}{3} = \frac{7}{3}$ | $6\frac{1}{8} = 5\frac{6}{8}$ |
| $5\frac{7}{8} = \frac{42}{8}$ | $3\frac{3}{5} = \frac{18}{5}$ | $2\frac{3}{4} = \frac{11}{4}$ | $3\frac{1}{3} = \frac{10}{3}$ | $6 = \frac{37}{6}$ |
| $1\frac{3}{6} = \frac{8}{6}$ | $2\frac{1}{8} = \frac{15}{8}$ | $3\frac{2}{4} = \frac{14}{4}$ | $2\frac{1}{3} = \frac{9}{3}$ | $1\frac{1}{16} = \frac{18}{16}$ |
| $1\frac{4}{10} = \frac{15}{10}$ | $1\frac{2}{5} = \frac{6}{5}$ | $2\frac{3}{4} = \frac{11}{4}$ | $3\frac{6}{7} = 22$ | $7\frac{3}{4} = \frac{30}{4}$ |

**Galatians 2:20**

**5** Which one circle has the following:

A radius labeled AB.

A diameter labeled AD.

A chord labeled CD. _____

Note: A chord is a line that has both end points on the circle.

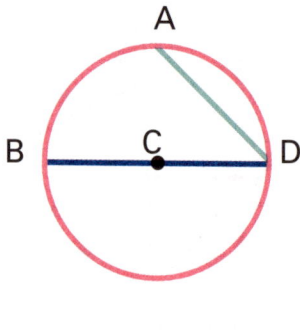

Circle 1 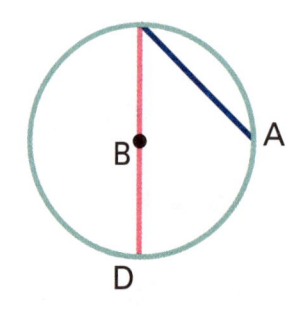   Circle 2 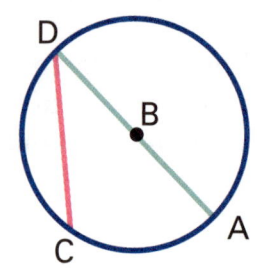   Circle 3

**6** Circle the incorrect answers and correct them.

| 0.6 | 17.6 | 8.59 | 3.80 | 4.68 |
|---|---|---|---|---|
| + 1.8 | + 6.2 | + 2.37 | + 2.35 | + 7.5 |
| 2.4 | 23.8 | 1.96 | 5.16 | 18.33 |

**7** Write the amount shown.

38  Horizons Math 5, Student Workbook 1

**Lesson 13**

# Place Value

The population of Mainland China (in 1993) was 1,178,500,000. At the current rate of growth, Mainland China is estimated to have a population of 1,280,000,000 in the year 2000, and 1,397,800,000 in the year 2010. What is the projected population increase from 1993 to 2000? What is the projected population increase from 2000 to 2010?

These are very large numbers! Use the chart below if you need assistance remembering each digit's place value.

| ten billions | billions | hundred millions | ten millions | millions | hundred thousands | ten thousands | thousands | hundreds | tens | ones |
|---|---|---|---|---|---|---|---|---|---|---|
|  | 1 | 1 | 7 | 8 | 5 | 0 | 0 | 0 | 0 | 0 |
|  | 1 | 2 | 8 | 0 | 0 | 0 | 0 | 0 | 0 | 0 |
|  | 1 | 3 | 9 | 7 | 8 | 0 | 0 | 0 | 0 | 0 |

We read: One billion, one hundred seventy-eight million, five hundred thousand
We read: One billion, two hundred eighty million
We read: One billion three hundred ninety-seven million eight hundred thousand

The difference between the estimated population growth of 1993 and 2000 is 101,500,000.
The difference between the estimated population growth of 2000 and 2010 is 117,800,000.

**1** Write in standard form.

Eight billion, two hundred fifty-four million, two hundred fifteen thousand, seven hundred fifty-four

_____

Nine billion, four hundred thirty-three million, six hundred two thousand, ninety-one

_____

Twenty billion, ninety-six million, fifty-one

_____

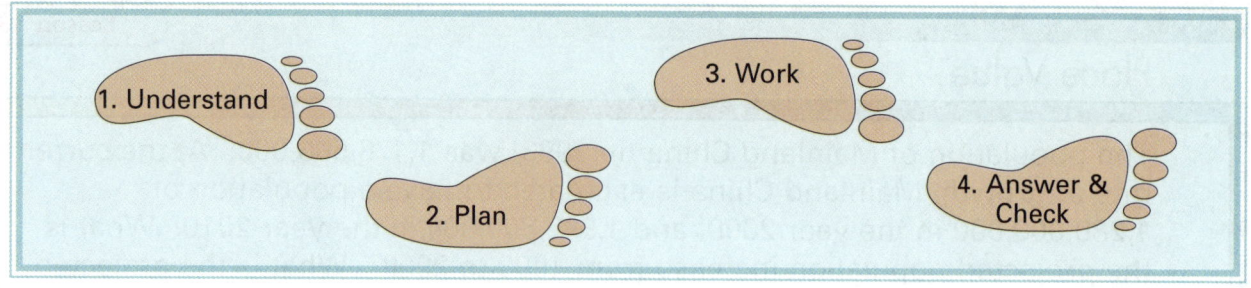

1. Understand
2. Plan
3. Work
4. Answer & Check

**2** Solve.

At 8:00 P.M., 4 of Lisa's friends arrived at her New Years Eve party. At 9:00 P.M., 8 more friends arrived. By 11:30 P.M., 10 more had arrived, but 2 had left. How many friends were at the party at 11:30 P.M.?

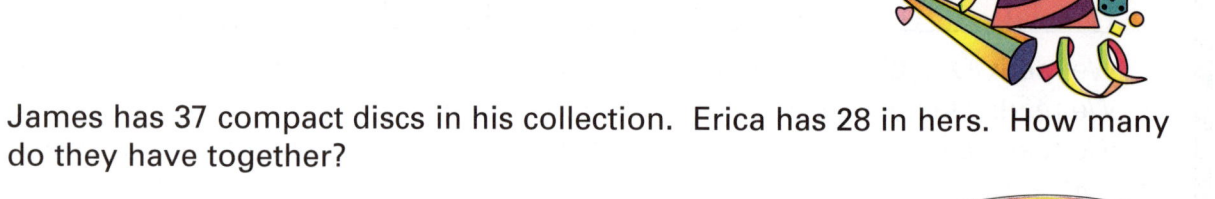

James has 37 compact discs in his collection. Erica has 28 in hers. How many do they have together?

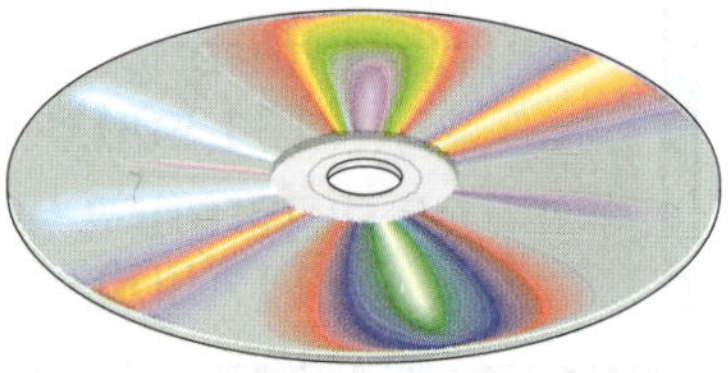

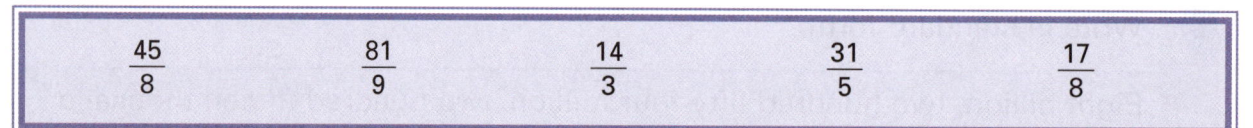

**3** Write as mixed numbers.

| $\frac{45}{8}$ | $\frac{81}{9}$ | $\frac{14}{3}$ | $\frac{31}{5}$ | $\frac{17}{8}$ |

**4** Label.

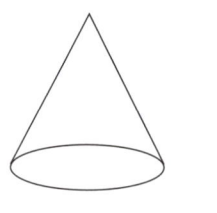

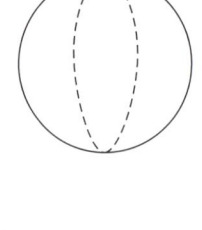

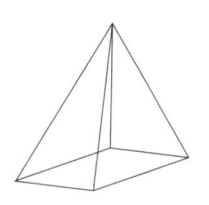

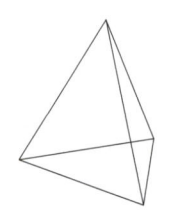

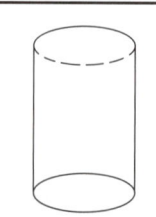

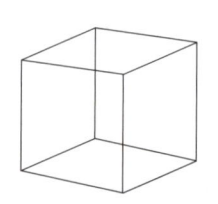

5) Find the difference.

| 5.82 | 6.50 | 0.71 | 0.93 | 30.17 |
|---|---|---|---|---|
| −1.65 | −3.68 | −0.68 | −0.05 | −18.92 |

6) Solve.

Mr. Jones purchased a set of wrenches for $49.99. He also purchased a tool box for $25.50. What was his total bill, excluding tax? _____

How much money is shown below?

7) Color the even numbered boxes yellow and the odd numbered boxes black.

| 33 | 25 | 24 | 55 | 71 |
|---|---|---|---|---|
| 3 | 88 | 2 | 12 | 9 |
| 7 | 13 | 50 | 15 | 1 |
| 79 | 11 | 6 | 69 | 5 |

*Isaiah 5:20a*

**Lesson 14**

# Place Value

Numbers may be written in standard from, written form, or **expanded form**. Look at the examples below.

Standard: 6,978

Written: Six thousand, nine hundred seventy-eight

Expanded: 6,000 + 900 + 70 + 8

OR

(6 × 1,000) + (9 × 100) + (7 × 10) + (8 × 1)

**1** Write in expanded and written form.

56,243

245

1,089

981,341

2. Write in standard form.

Five hundred billion, sixty-four million, two hundred thirty-three thousand, nine hundred two

_____

Ten billion, sixty-five thousand, seven hundred eighty-nine

_____

3. Match.

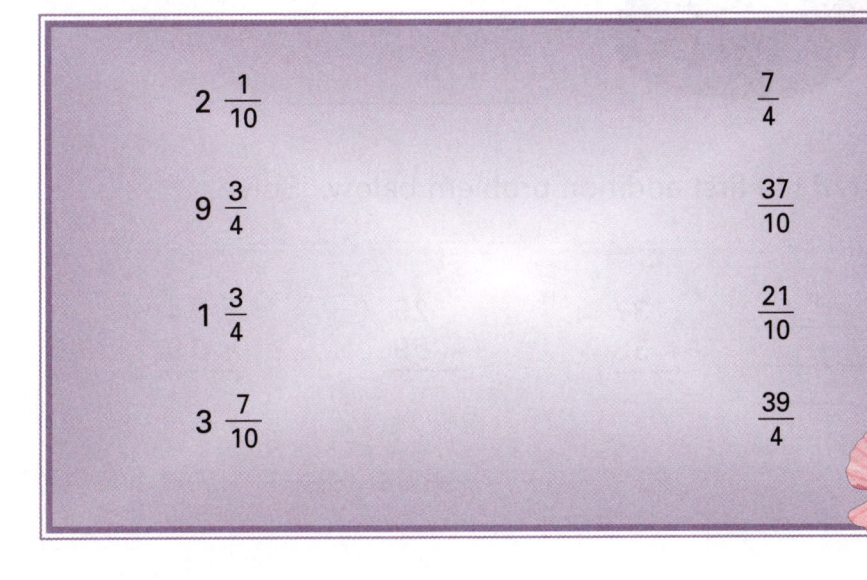

$2\frac{1}{10}$         $\frac{7}{4}$

$9\frac{3}{4}$         $\frac{37}{10}$

$1\frac{3}{4}$         $\frac{21}{10}$

$3\frac{7}{10}$        $\frac{39}{4}$

4. Draw the following space figures.

rectangular pyramid          triangular prism          cone

5. Write the temperature.

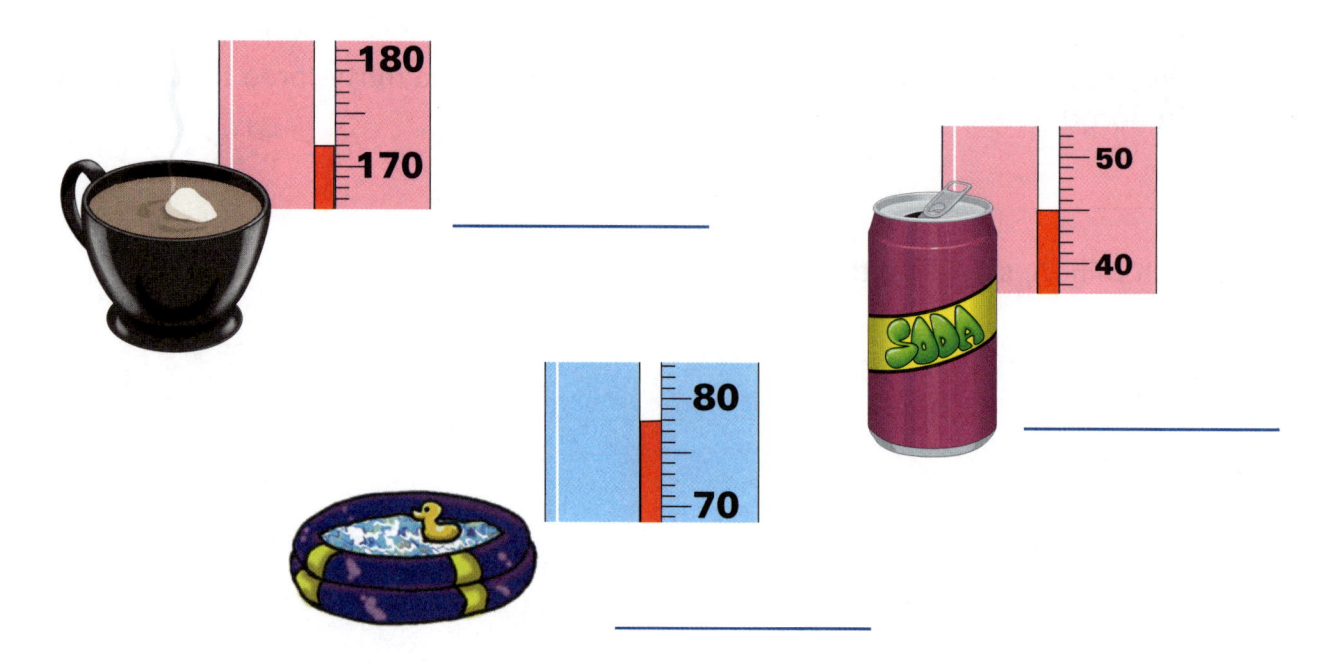

_____

_____

_____

6. Label each part of the first addition problem below. Solve.

```
   59   a. _____        37           29           84           56
 + 47   b. _____      + 58         + 59         + 79         + 87
        c. _____
```

7. Solve as quickly as possible! Try not to make any errors!

```
    9           8           5           4           6           7
  x 3         x 1         x 2         x 5         x 7         x 8


    5           6           9           2           3           7
  x 8         x 6         x 9         x 3         x 0         x 4
```

# Roman Numerals

Lesson 15

People have used Roman numerals for hundreds of years. These numerals are a different way of writing numbers. Today they can be seen on, and in, many things including clocks, books, and even buildings.

Basic Roman numerals:

| I | V | X | L | C | D | M |
|---|---|---|---|---|---|---|
| 1 | 5 | 10 | 50 | 100 | 500 | 1000 |

The letter values are added to attain the desired amount when writing some numerals.

Example:
LXXXIV
50 + 30 + 4 = 84

MMI
1000 + 1000 + 1 = 2001

In other numerals, the first letter value is subtracted for the second letter value to attain the desired number.

Example:
IX
10 − 1 = 9

IV
5 − 1 = 4

XL
50 − 10 = 40

Understanding place value is very important if one is to understand and read Roman numerals. Each Roman numeral holds a value on the place value chart, just like our standard Arabic numbers.

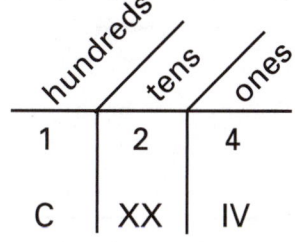

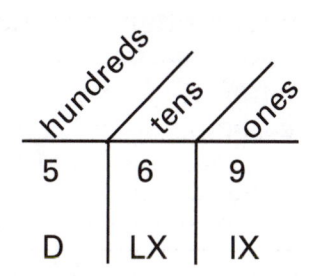

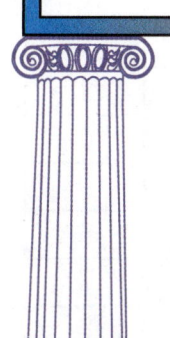

Example:

| hundreds | tens | ones |
|---|---|---|
| 1 | 2 | 4 |
| C | XX | IV |

| hundreds | tens | ones |
|---|---|---|
| 5 | 6 | 9 |
| D | LX | IX |

**1** Write the Roman numeral under each standard number.

Example:

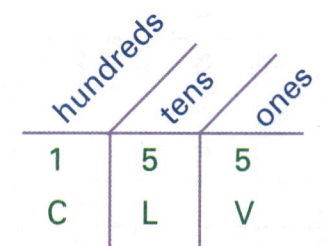

| hundreds | tens | ones |
|---|---|---|
| 1 | 5 | 5 |
| C | L | V |

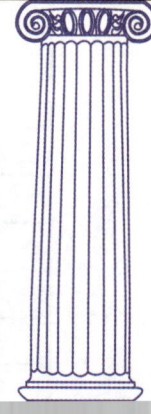

② Match each standard number with the written or expanded form of that number.

| | |
|---|---|
| 296 | Two thousand, nine hundred sixty |
| 2,096 | Two hundred ninety-six |
| 296,000 | 200,000 + 900 + 60 |
| 2,960 | Two thousand, ninety-six |
| 200,960 | 200,000 + 90,000 + 6,000 |

③ Find each number written in standard form in the puzzle below.

Five hundred thousand, forty-five
One billion, six hundred thousand
Eleven million, four hundred seventy-five thousand, nine hundred
Two thousand fourteen

| 1 | 0 | 0 | 0 | 6 | 0 | 0 | 0 | 0 | 0 |
|---|---|---|---|---|---|---|---|---|---|
| 1 | 5 | 3 | 1 | 0 | 5 | 7 | 9 | 2 | 4 |
| 4 | 7 | 6 | 3 | 8 | 4 | 5 | 1 | 3 | 1 |
| 7 | 4 | 0 | 4 | 8 | 9 | 9 | 1 | 4 | 0 |
| 5 | 0 | 0 | 0 | 4 | 5 | 0 | 4 | 7 | 9 |
| 9 | 3 | 5 | 9 | 8 | 2 | 1 | 8 | 2 | 5 |
| 0 | 4 | 0 | 0 | 7 | 2 | 5 | 5 | 3 | 7 |
| 0 | 6 | 5 | 9 | 8 | 0 | 0 | 9 | 6 | 8 |
| 9 | 8 | 8 | 1 | 8 | 3 | 2 | 0 | 1 | 4 |
| 6 | 5 | 2 | 3 | 5 | 6 | 1 | 0 | 4 | 9 |

**4** Add. Reduce to lowest terms.

$3\frac{1}{8} + 5\frac{3}{8} =$  $\qquad$  $2\frac{4}{5} + 5\frac{1}{5} =$

$20\frac{10}{21} + 12\frac{5}{21} =$  $\qquad$  $13\frac{1}{3} + 15\frac{1}{3} =$

**5** Find the perimeter.

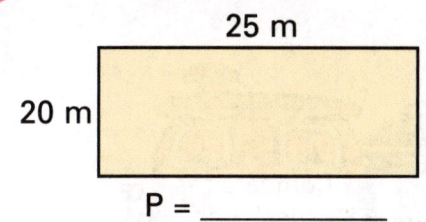

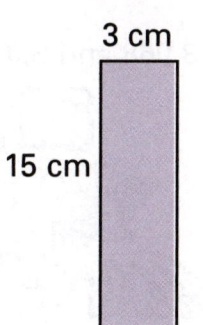

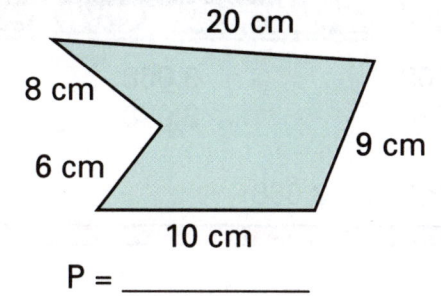

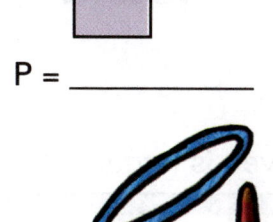

25 m
20 m

P = _____

3 cm
15 cm

P = _____

20 cm
8 cm
6 cm
9 cm
10 cm

P = _____

**6** Add as quickly as possible. Try not to make any errors!

| 8 | 1 | 6 | 2 | 9 | 10 |
|---|---|---|---|---|---|
| + 3 | + 9 | + 4 | + 8 | + 5 | + 4 |

| 5 | 2 | 3 | 1 | 0 | 7 |
|---|---|---|---|---|---|
| + 3 | + 5 | + 6 | + 3 | + 5 | + 4 |

**7** Write <, >, or =.

5.65 ____ 5.56        2.09 ____ 2.90        33.10 ____ 33.1

142.06 ____ 141.06   54.256 ____ 54.257   9.00 ____ 9

Lesson 16

## Order Numbers

The steps below will help you compare and order numbers.

1. Compare each digit starting at the left.

2. When 2 digits are the same, determine which digit is larger. The number with the larger digit is the larger number.

Compare 3,068 and 3,078

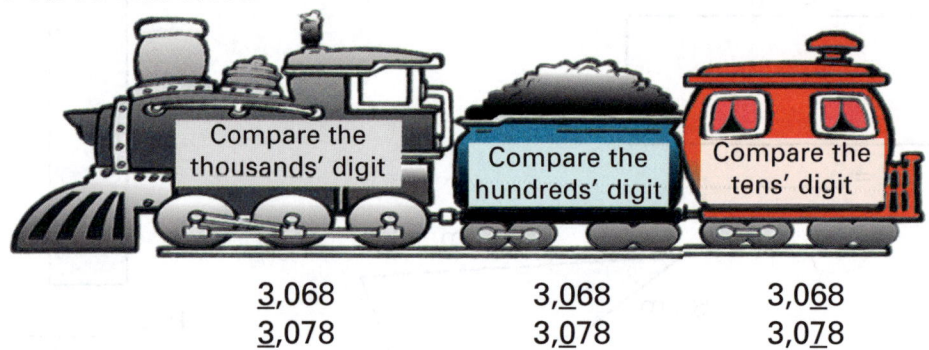

Compare the thousands' digit
Compare the hundreds' digit
Compare the tens' digit

3,068          3,068          3,068
3,078          3,078          3,078

Seven is larger than six so, 3,078 > 3,068

**1** Circle the larger number in each pair.

3,274    3,742

12,655    12,556

7,612    7,216

2,779    2,774

284,643    283,643

19,682    18,682

**2** Write each Roman numeral in standard, written, and expanded form.

Example:
LVII = 57
Fifty-seven
50 + 7

CXV =

XXIV =

MDCXX =

XLII =

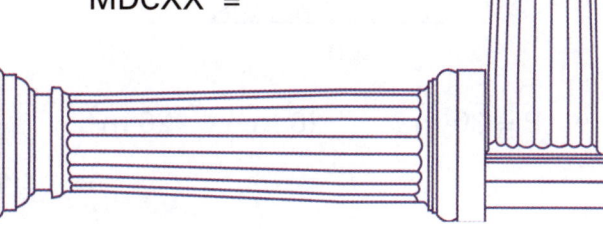

**3** Match with the numbers in the Data Bank.

Forty-four million, seven hundred sixteen thousand, two hundred twenty-five
_____

Six million, seven hundred ten thousand, eight hundred fifty-five
_____

Seven hundred thirty-five billion, three hundred twenty million, three hundred ten thousand, four
_____

**Data Bank**

735,320,310,004        44,716,225        6,710,855

**4** Match.

$4\frac{2}{6} + 5\frac{3}{6} =$         $5\frac{7}{8}$

$6\frac{5}{8} + 9\frac{2}{8} =$         $37\frac{5}{6}$

$3\frac{5}{8} + 2\frac{2}{8} =$         $15\frac{7}{8}$

$22\frac{3}{6} + 15\frac{2}{6} =$         $9\frac{5}{6}$

**5** Circle the correct perimeter.

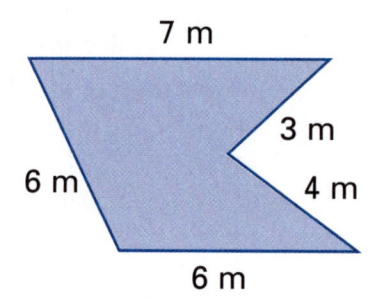

7 m
3 m
6 m
4 m
6 m

P = 30 m    26 m    26 m²

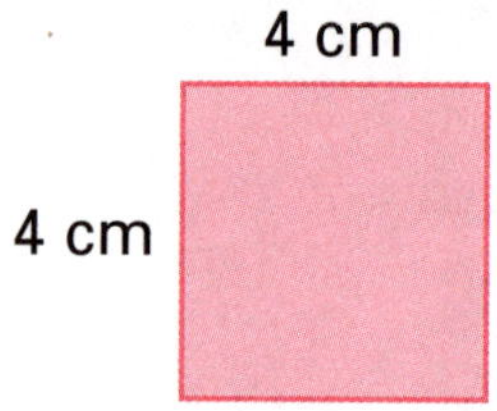

4 cm
4 cm

P = 8 cm    12 cm    16 cm

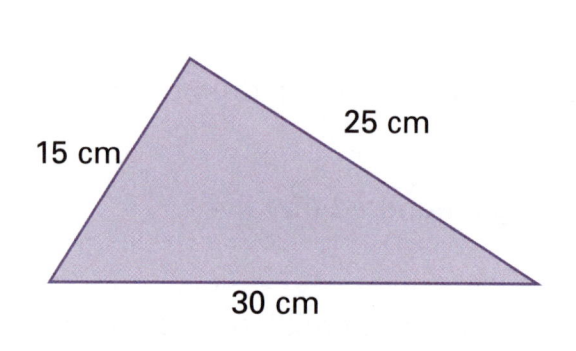

25 cm
15 cm
30 cm

P = 70 cm    65 cm    55 cm

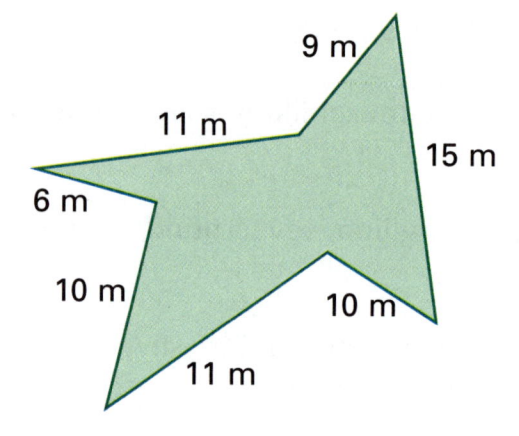

9 m
11 m
15 m
6 m
10 m    10 m
11 m

P = 70 m    73 m    72 m

**6** Find the difference as quickly as possible. Try not to make any errors!

```
  16        4        5        7        8        9
-  5      - 3      - 2      - 6      - 0      - 7



   4        6       15        3        0       12
-  1      - 2      - 10      - 3      - 0      - 2
```

**Lesson 17**

# Round Numbers

Sometimes we don't need an exact answer. We can round and get an estimated answer.

Chad and Bryan were making a poster for a report on Georgia. The actual population of Georgia's major cities are very large numbers. It was easier and acceptable for Chad and Bryan to round each population number rather than give an exact number.

**Georgia's Five Major Cities and Their Populations**

| City | Population | | Rounded |
|------|-----------|---|---------|
| Atlanta | 394,017 | is rounded to | 394,000 |
| Columbus | 179,278 | is rounded to | 179,000 |
| Savannah | 137,560 | is rounded to | 138,000 |
| Macon | 106,612 | is rounded to | 107,000 |
| Albany | 78,122 | is rounded to | 78,000 |

When rounding a number, you are estimating which place value the number is closest to. To round a number to the tens place:

1. Find the digit in the tens place.

    <u>3</u>4

2. Think of a number line.

    30 31 32 33 34 35 36 37 38 39 40

If 35 is exactly half way between 30 and 40, is 34 lower than 35 or higher than 35? It is lower than 35, and therefore closer to 30.

3. The number 34 rounds to 30.

4. If the number is 35 or higher it is rounded to 40.

**1** Work these problems by rounding each number.

80 81 82 83 84 85 86 87 88 89 90

Round the number 87. Is it closer to 80 or 90 on the number line?

```
←——+——+——+——+——+——+——+——+——+——+——→
  350 351 352 353 354 355 356 357 358 359 360
```

Round the number 352 to the tens' place. Is 352 closer to 350 or 360?

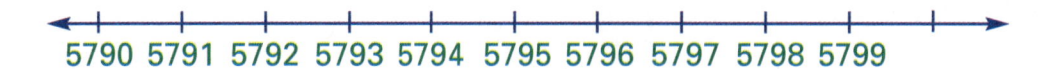

```
←——+——+——+——+——+——+——+——+——+——+——→
  5790 5791 5792 5793 5794 5795 5796 5797 5798 5799
```

Round the number 5,793 to the tens' place. Fill in the missing number on the number line. What does 5,793 round to?

Round the numbers to the tens' place.

61 = _____

82 = _____

38 = _____

56 = _____

**2** Order from the smallest to the largest. Solve the message.

| N | C | R | E | T |
|---|---|---|---|---|
| 5,649 | 6,218 | 4,825 | 4,843 | 5,745 |

| E | A | P | E | N |
|---|---|---|---|---|
| 4,829 | 5,809 | 4,832 | 6,812 | 6,028 |

___  ___  ___  ___  ___  ___  ___  ___  ___  ___

___  ___  ___  ___  ___  ___  ___  ___

*Luke 15:10*

**3** Write the Roman numeral.

| 34 | 56 | 3 | 17 | 125 | 1,000 |
|----|----|----|----|-----|-------|
| ___ | ___ | ___ | ___ | ___ | ___ |

**4** Match each set.

| 1,060 | One thousand, six hundred | 1,000 + 6 |
| 1,006 | One thousand, sixty | 1,000 + 600 |
| 1,600 | One thousand, six | 1,000 + 60 |

**5** Find the difference.

$5\frac{4}{10}$     $10\frac{2}{3}$     $7\frac{21}{25}$     $3\frac{1}{2}$     $34\frac{2}{5}$

$-3\frac{1}{10}$    $-9\frac{1}{3}$    $-5\frac{15}{25}$    $-2\frac{1}{2}$    $-25\frac{1}{5}$

**6** Find the area.

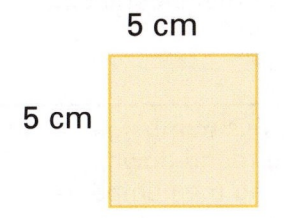

5 cm
5 cm

Area = _____

20 cm
3 cm

Area = _____

**7** Fill in the bars on the graph from the Data Bank.

**Fall Festival Booth Proceeds**

Concessions
Garage Sale
Pony Rides
Train Rides
Moon Walk

$0   $100   $150   $200   $250   $300

**Data Bank**

| Item | Total Sales |
|---|---|
| Moon Walk | $100 |
| Train Rides | $200 |
| Pony Rides | $275 |
| Garage Sale | $225 |
| Concessions | $300 |

**8** Quickly find the difference.

  8      10      15      3      17
−5      − 8     −10     − 3     −12

**Lesson 18**

# Rounding Numbers

Round 5,862 to the nearest 10, 100, and 1,000. Look at the chart below to help you do this.

| **5,862 Rounded to 10** | **Rounded to 100** | **Rounded to 1,000** |
|---|---|---|
| 1. Underline the number in the **tens'** place. 5,8<u>6</u>2 | 1. Underline the number in the **hundreds'** place. 5,<u>8</u>62 | 1. Underline the number in the **thousands'** place. <u>5</u>,862 |
| 2. Look at the number to the right of the underlined number.  5,86<u>2</u> ← | 2. Look at the number to the right of the underlined number.  5,8<u>6</u>2 ↑ | 2. Look at the number to the right of the underlined number.  5,<u>8</u>62 ↑ |
| 3. If this number is less than 5, you round down, meaning the 6 stays the same and the 2 becomes a zero. Remember: When rounding 5,862 to the tens' you are estimating whether 5,862 is closer to 5,860 or 5,870. Think of a number line as in Lesson 17. | 3. If this number is less than 5, you round down, meaning the number is closer to 5,800 than 5,900. This is not true because the number to the right of the underlined place is 6. | 3. If this number is less than 5, you round down, meaning the number is closer to 5,000 than 6,000. This is not true because the number to the right of the underlined place is 8. |
| 4. 2 is less than 5, so the number rounds to 5,860 when rounded to the nearest 10. | 4. 6 is larger than 5, so the number rounds up, meaning that 5,862 is closer to 5,900. | 4. 8 is larger than 5, so the number rounds up, meaning that 5,862 is closer to 6,000. |
| Picture reference:  ←———|———|———|———→  5,860   5,865   5,870  The red line represents where 5,862 would be on the number line. It is closer to 5,860 when rounded to the nearest 10. | Picture reference:  ←———|———|———|———→  5,800   5,850   5,900  The red line represents where 5,682 would be on the number line. It is closer to 5,900 when rounded to the nearest 100. | Picture reference:  ←———|———|———|———→  5,000   5,500   6,000  The red line represents where 5,682 would be on the number line. It is closer to 6,000 when rounded to the nearest 1,000. |

**1** Round to the nearest 10.

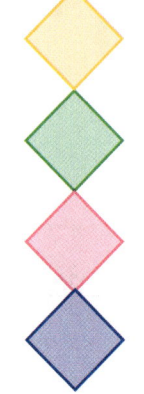

2,5<u>7</u>6 _____     6,8<u>9</u>3 _____     4<u>5</u>9 _____

Round to the nearest 100.

5,<u>9</u>48 _____     1,<u>0</u>81 _____     3,<u>8</u>98 _____

Round to the nearest 1,000.

<u>4</u>,193 _____     <u>3</u>,418 _____     <u>2</u>,991 _____

**2** Compare and order from the smallest to the largest. Solve the message.

| 517 | 24,500 | 762 | 513,902 | 691 |
|---|---|---|---|---|
| T | L | N | O | E |
| 503,002 | 8,090 | 23 | 731 | 698,233 |
| J | A | E | R | Y |

(numbers) _____ _____ _____ _____ _____ _____ _____

(letters) _____ _____ _____ _____ _____ _____ _____

_____ _____ _____

_____ _____ _____   **Luke 15:7**

**3** Write the standard number.

| XXII | LXV | CM | IV | XC |
|---|---|---|---|---|
| _____ | _____ | _____ | _____ | _____ |

**4** Subtract. Reduce to lowest terms.

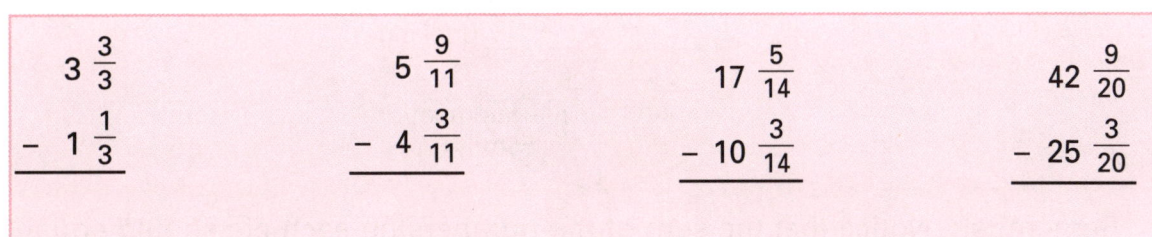

$3 \frac{3}{3}$        $5 \frac{9}{11}$        $17 \frac{5}{14}$        $42 \frac{9}{20}$
$- 1 \frac{1}{3}$      $- 4 \frac{3}{11}$      $- 10 \frac{3}{14}$      $- 25 \frac{3}{20}$

**5** Complete the check.

Kathryn purchased 3 packages of socks at a cost of $3.99 each. How much money did she spend? Fill in the check below for the total purchase amount.

Kathryn Williams
123 South Mabry St.
Smithville, AZ 80289

2001-91

PAY TO THE ORDER OF _____ $ _____

_____ DOLLARS

**6** Find the area.

30 m

25 m

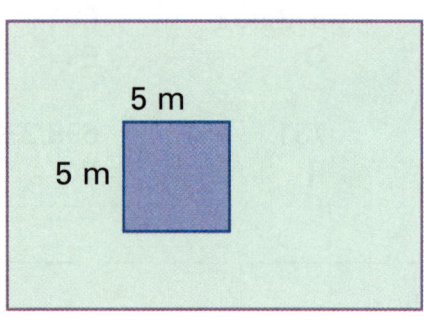

5 m
5 m

Find the area of the larger square NOT INCLUDING the smaller blue square.

Area = _____

15 m

36 m

Find the area of 1/2 of the rectangle.

Area = _____

**7** Use the graphs to answer the questions.
Selita works at a book store. Last week 100 magazines were sold.

### 100 Magazines Sold Last Week

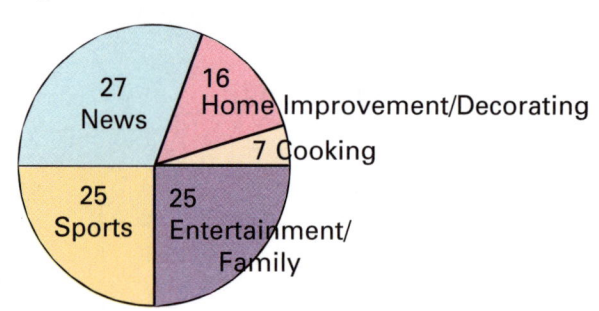

27 News
16 Home Improvement/Decorating
7 Cooking
25 Sports
25 Entertainment/Family

Remember: Notice that the sum of the numbers on each pie should equal 100.
27 + 16 + 7 + 25 + 25 = 100

Which magazine sold the least? _____

Which magazine sold the most? _____

How many of each was sold?   least _____   most _____

How many Home Improvement/Decorating and
Cooking magazines were sold? _____

How many more News magazines were sold than Sports magazines? _____

**8** Multiply.

| 10 | 11 | 6 | 7 | 9 | 5 |
|---|---|---|---|---|---|
| x 4 | x 2 | x 9 | x 6 | x 8 | x 3 |

**Lesson 19**

## Problem Solving

Understand — Plan — Work — Answers & Check

Understanding the question is the first step in problem solving. Read carefully to determine what a word problem is asking you to do.

**1** Decide which of these questions can be answered using the data in the box. Write *yes* if it can be answered and *no* if it can not be answered with the data provided.

**Movie Tickets**
Matinee   $3.00 each
Evening   $6.00 each

_____ How much would 3 matinee tickets cost?

_____ How much change would you get if you bought 2 evening tickets?

_____ What costs more, 3 matinee tickets or 2 evening tickets?

_____ How much would 5 evening tickets cost?

_____ Tom & Sally bought 2 tickets to the matinee, 2 cokes and 2 popcorns. How much money did they spend?

**2** Round to the indicated place.

Round to the nearest 10.
321             8,729           209,325
_____        _____         _____

Round to the nearest 100.
43,835          6,788           7,585
_____        _____         _____

Round to the nearest 1,000.
873,911         2,553           1,234
_____        _____         _____

**3** Write <, >, or =.

3,438 ☐ 3,567         987,321 ☐ 873,911         209 ☐ 290

**4** Color the boxes containing fractions which have been reduced to lowest terms.

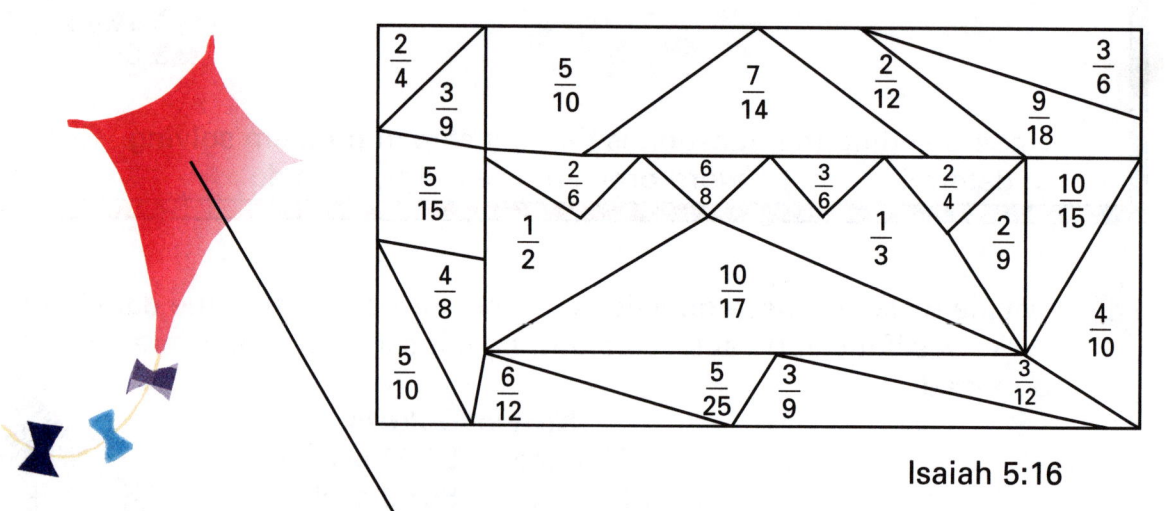

$\frac{2}{4}$  $\frac{3}{9}$  $\frac{5}{10}$  $\frac{7}{14}$  $\frac{2}{12}$  $\frac{9}{18}$  $\frac{3}{6}$

$\frac{5}{15}$  $\frac{2}{6}$  $\frac{6}{8}$  $\frac{3}{6}$  $\frac{2}{4}$  $\frac{10}{15}$

$\frac{1}{2}$  $\frac{1}{3}$  $\frac{2}{9}$

$\frac{4}{8}$  $\frac{10}{17}$  $\frac{4}{10}$

$\frac{5}{10}$  $\frac{6}{12}$  $\frac{5}{25}$  $\frac{3}{9}$  $\frac{3}{12}$

Isaiah 5:16

**5** Write a question for each set of information given and then solve the question.

Bobby wants to buy 3 CDs. Each CD is $13.00.

_____

Karen ran 2 miles on Monday, 3 miles on Wednesday, and 1 mile on Friday.

_____

Sarah earns $7.00 per hour. She works 5 hours on weekdays (Monday - Friday) and 7 hours a day on Saturday.

_____

Tom makes $14.00 commission on every Bible he sells. Last week he sold 15 Bibles.

_____

**6** Complete the line graph by showing Kim's scores for 5 tests:

Kim's scores: 75; 80; 90; 95; 100

**Scores**          **Kim's Social Studies Test Scores**

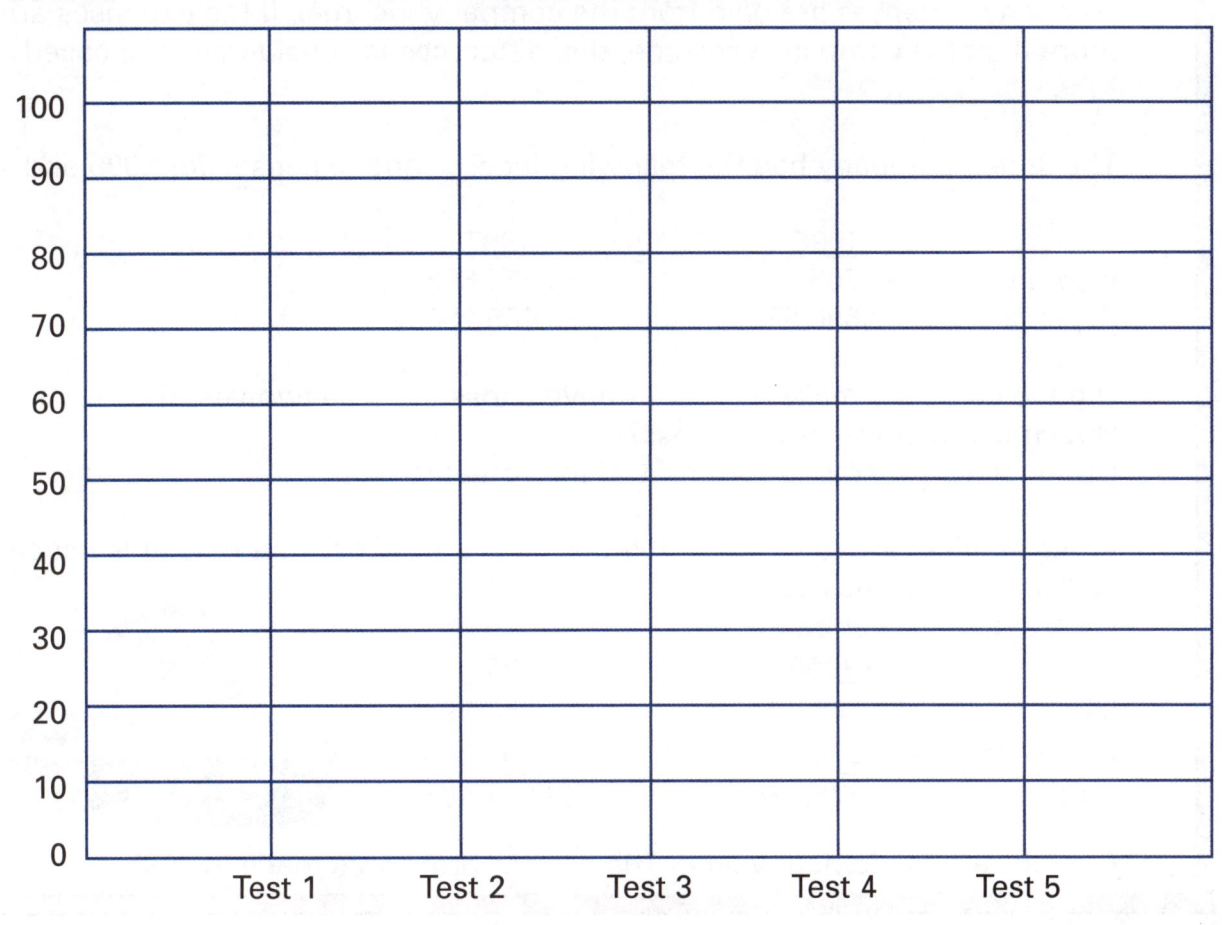

100
90
80
70
60
50
40
30
20
10
0

Test 1    Test 2    Test 3    Test 4    Test 5

**Tests**

**7** Multiply.

| 23 | 45 | 78 | 90 | 23 |
|---|---|---|---|---|
| x 3 | x 10 | x 5 | x 2 | x 12 |

**Lesson 20**

# Calculator

When operating a business, a **profit** is the amount of money left after all company expenses are paid from the company income. If the expenses are more than the company's income, this difference is considered, and called a **loss**.

The Jones Company had the following income and expenses for 1996 and 1997:

|  | 1996 | 1997 |
|---|---|---|
| Income | $3,765,997 | $5,456,892 |
| Expenses | $2,590,573 | $3,165,285 |

Did the company make a profit or have a loss in these two years?
How much was the profit or loss?
During which year was the profit or loss greater?

When solving problems with multiple steps and larger numbers, it is usually easier to use a calculator.
Look at the answer below.

|  | 1996 | 1997 |
|---|---|---|
| Income | $3,765,997 | $5,456,892 |
| Expenses | − $2,590,573 | − $3,165,285 |
| Profit | $1,175,424 | $2,291,607 |

Profits were made both years. The greater profit was made in 1997.

**1** Use a calculator to solve the problem given below.

Mr. Calloway's business posted incomes of $4,893,589; $4,890,874; and $5,012,389 for the years 1995, 1996 and 1997. His expenses were $4,904,733; $3,894,569; and $3,004,358 for the same years. During which years did he make a profit and which years was there a loss?

Hint: When a company sustains losses, the amount of the loss is shown in parentheses ( ) and in red ink.

|  | 1995 | 1996 | 1997 |
|---|---|---|---|
| Income | $4,893,589 | $4,890,874 | $5,012,389 |
| Expenses | $4,904,733 | $3,894,569 | $3,004,358 |

60 Horizons Math 5, Student Workbook 1

**2** Decide which of the questions below can be answered using the data in the problem. Give the answers when possible.

> Problem: At the school bookstore paperback books cost $7.00 each and hardback books cost $10.00 each.
>
> 1. How much more does the hardback book cost than the paperback book?
>
> 2. How much money will it take to purchase 4 paperbacks?
>
> 3. Did Karen spend more on 3 hardback books or 5 paperback books?
>
> 4. How much change will Karen receive from her purchase?

**3** Round each number to the nearest 10, 100 and 1,000.

|  | 451,213 | 2,132 | 8,546 | 5,465 | 123,211 |
|---|---|---|---|---|---|
| Nearest 10 | _____ | _____ | _____ | _____ | _____ |
| Nearest 100 | _____ | _____ | _____ | _____ | _____ |
| Nearest 1,000 | _____ | _____ | _____ | _____ | _____ |

**4** Order from the largest to the smallest.

546,999     943,000     781,908     987,384     564,038

_____    _____    _____    _____    _____

**5** Solve.

$$\begin{array}{r} 5 \\ -\ n \\ \hline 1 \end{array} \qquad \begin{array}{r} n \\ -\ 14 \\ \hline 30 \end{array} \qquad \begin{array}{r} 87 \\ -\ n \\ \hline 50 \end{array} \qquad \begin{array}{r} n \\ -\ 56 \\ \hline 4 \end{array} \qquad \begin{array}{r} 40 \\ -\ n \\ \hline 27 \end{array}$$

6. Complete the pictograph about CD sales. Use the data in the table.

| Monday | Tuesday | Wednesday | Thursday | Friday | Saturday |
|--------|---------|-----------|----------|--------|----------|
| 30 | 25 | 30 | 35 | 60 | 75 |

Monday –

Tuesday –

Wednesday –

Thursday –

Friday –

Saturday –

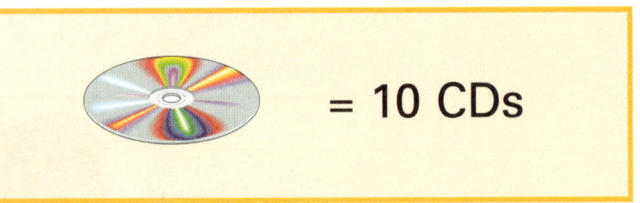

= 10 CDs

7. Solve.

56 ÷ 7        72 ÷ 8        81 ÷ 9        90 ÷ 10        48 ÷ 6

**Test 2**

### 1  Solve. 9 pts. total for this exercise.

17 − (2 × 4) = _____        14 + (81 ÷ 9) = _____        (24 ÷ 8) − 1 = _____

(9 × 8) + 16 = _____        (18 + 6) ÷ 8 = _____        21 ÷ (7 − 4) = _____

8 × (4 + 9) = _____        (16 − 7) + 3 = _____        (11 + 9) − 4 = _____

### 2  Solve. 8 pts. total for this exercise.

6 × $n$ = 36        5 × $n$ = 50        9 × $n$ = 81        $n$ − (4 + 1) = 0

$n$ − 45 = 90        $n$ × 7 = 56        (8 × $n$) + 0 = 24        5 × (1 × $n$) = 5

### 3  Solve each problem. 4 pts.

1. Stan Cottrell runs about 140 miles a week when he is in training. How many miles does he run a day if he runs five days a week?

2. If Calvin runs 35 miles a day for 3 months (31 days in each month), how many total miles will he have run?

3. When Arthur was planning his run across the United States, he figured that running 50 miles a day for sixty-four days would easily get him from New York City to San Francisco. How many miles would he run?

4. If Andy runs 15 miles a day, every day for a whole year (not a leap year), how many miles will he have run that entire year?

### 4  Write each number in written form. 6 pts. total for this exercise.

6,103 = _____

5,149 = _____

4,871 = _____

3,041 = _____

6,059,021 = _____

7,330,412 = _____

**5** Write the number in standard form on the place value chart provided. 3 pts.

| bill. | 100 mill. | 10 mill. | mill. | 100 thou. | 10 thou. | thou. | hundred | tens | ones |
|---|---|---|---|---|---|---|---|---|---|
|  |  |  |  |  |  |  |  |  |  |

1. Six billion, two hundred fifty-four million, two hundred fifteen thousand, seven hundred four.
2. Nine billion, four hundred thirty-three million, two hundred two thousand, ninety-one.
3. One billion, nine hundred seventy-eight thousand.

**6** Write in expanded and written form. 4 pts. total for this exercise.

16,243

545

1,009

981,341

**7** Write the Roman numeral for each number written in standard form. 6 pts.

| Standard Number | Roman Numeral |
|---|---|
| 22 |  |
| 842 |  |
| 14 |  |
| 275 |  |
| 30 |  |
| 41 |  |

40 pts. Total

**Lesson 21**

## Addition with Two & Three Digits

Chad is counting the pennies he collected. There were 38 pennies in his piggy bank. He stacked them in piles of ten for easier counting.

There were 14 pennies in Chad's pocket. He stacked them in piles of ten also. How many pennies does Chad have all together?

Step 1

Add the ones 8 + 4 = 12
Regroup 12 ones so that
there are 1 ten and 2 ones

```
  1
  38
+ 14
   2
```

Step 2

Add the tens 3 + 1 = 4
Add the regrouped ten 4 + 1 = 5
5 tens

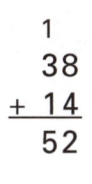

```
  1
  38
+ 14
  52
```

Chad has 52 pennies in all.

What if Chad found one jar with 241 pennies and another jar with 174. How many pennies would this be?

Step 1
Add the ones 1 + 4 = 5
5 ones

```
  241
+ 174
    5
```

Step 2
Add the tens 4 + 7 = 11
Regroup 11 tens so that
there are 1 hundred and 1 ten

```
   1
  241
+ 174
   15
```

Step 3
Add the hundreds 2 + 1 = 3
Add the regrouped hundred
3 + 1 = 4

```
   1
  241
+ 174
  415
```

Chad has 415 pennies when the two jars are added together.

**1** Find the sum.

|   49  |   79  |  651  |  744  |  585  |  176  |
|-------|-------|-------|-------|-------|-------|
| + 15  | + 21  | + 325 | + 455 | + 105 | + 78  |

**2** Find the sum. Reduce to lowest terms, if possible.

$\frac{1}{10} + \frac{4}{10} =$        $\frac{4}{8} + \frac{1}{8} =$        $\frac{5}{12} + \frac{6}{12} =$        $\frac{15}{21} + \frac{3}{21} =$

**3** Match the picture with the correct value.

$5.46

$5.71

$5.98

**4** The Loganville First Baptist men's softball team purchased new jerseys at a total cost of $330.00 and new sliding pants at a total cost of $375.00. If there are 15 players on the team, how much did each player have to pay for his jersey? How much for his pants?

In addition to purchasing uniforms, each player needs to help First Baptist Church pay for the league and umpire fees associated with the season. The total league and umpire fee (for the season) is $500.00. First Baptist Church will pay $200.00 and the balance will be split among the 15 softball players.
How much will each player have to pay for league fees?

**5** Find the volume.

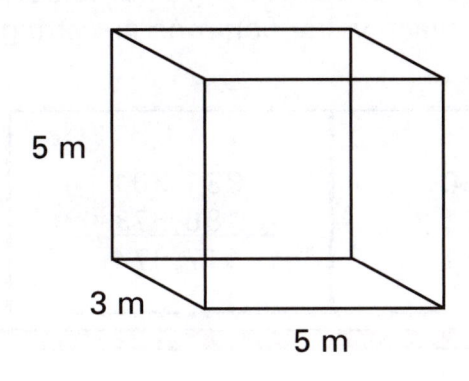

5 m, 3 m, 5 m

15 cm, 4 cm, 5 cm

Volume = _____    Volume = _____

**6** Give the digit that holds the specified place value in the number below.

226, 504, 825, 986

\_\_\_\_ thousands          \_\_\_\_ hundred millions

\_\_\_\_ hundreds           \_\_\_\_ billions

\_\_\_\_ ten thousands      \_\_\_\_ tens

\_\_\_\_ ten millions       \_\_\_\_ hundred billions

**7** Solve.

| 82 | $n$ | 853 | $n$ | 89 |
|---|---|---|---|---|
| $+\ n$ | $+\ 125$ | $+\ n$ | $+\ 13$ | $+\ n$ |
| 99 | 543 | 971 | 78 | 103 |

## Lesson 22

### Addition with Four, Five, and Six Digits

Larger numbers are added in the same way as two- and three-digit numbers. In order to avoid errors, it is important that your place value columns are straight and neat.

```
   1              1 1               1
  3,567          12,480           231,301
+ 1,931        + 10,891         + 186,673
  5,498          23,371           417,974
```

**1** Find the sum.

```
  1,345          3,497          2,124          416          218
+ 1,949        + 1,862         +  571        + 876        + 391
```

**2** Circle the problems with incorrect answers. Correct them.

```
  137          589          279          21          89          56
+  23        + 451        + 106        + 45        + 54        + 33
  161        1,040          365          66         143          99
```

**3** Make the amount of money shown by using the fewest bills and coins possible.

$25.98 = bills: _____
         coins: _____

$53.27 = bills: _____
         coins: _____

$15.33 = bills: _____
         coins: _____

$8.99  = bills: _____
         coins: _____

**4** Solve.

You would like to purchase a new pair of in-line skates. You could sell your old ones through the newspaper, or you could trade them in on the new pair.

Some things to think about before making your decision:

- You can get $35.00 for your old in-line skates if you trade them in on the new ones.

- You can get approximately $50.00 if you sell them through the newspaper advertisement, but it is possible that you would have to come down on the price.

- The newspaper advertisement will cost $5.00 a day.

- The new pair of in-line skates costs $125.00.

- You need the new in-line skates before your church festival (which is in 1 week).

1. If you trade in the old in-line skates, how much will you have to spend for the new ones?

2. If you sell the old skates through the newspaper, and get the asking price, how much money will you make after paying the expenses for a 3 day ad?

3. If the newspaper ad runs for 7 days, and you do not sell the in-line skates, how much money will you spend purchasing the new skates and paying the advertising expenses minus the trade-in amount?

**5** Find the volume.

7 m  5 m  6 m

10 m  5 m  Depth 4 m

_____  _____

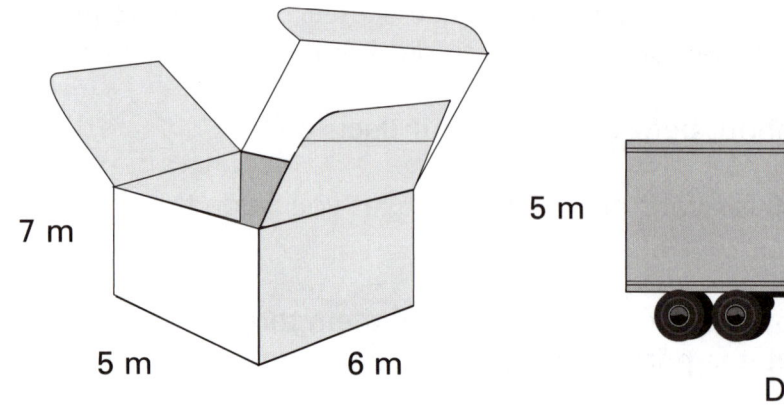

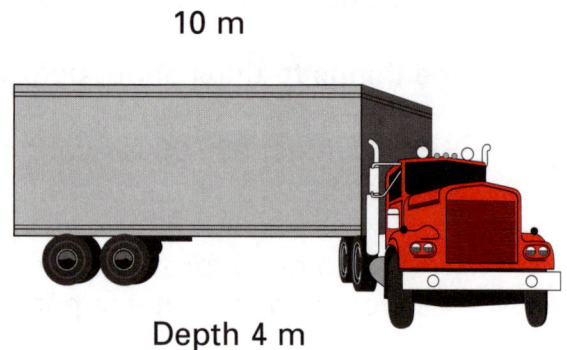

**6** Answer.

Write a number with a 4 in the billions' place: _____

Write a number with a 7 in the millions' place: _____

Write a number with an 8 in the ten millions' place: _____

Write a number with a 0 in the tens' place: _____

**7** Solve.

| 4,82? | 25 | 9? | 1?7 | 56 |
| + 21 | + 1? | + 14 | + 108 | + ?3 |
| 4,844 | 35 | 112 | 235 | 129 |

Lesson 23

## Column Addition

Allison, Kimberly, and Lisa are building an igloo using sugar cubes. Allison brought 40 sugar cubes, Kimberly brought 60, and Lisa brought 55. How many sugar cubes do they have in all?

| Step 1 | Step 2 |
|---|---|
| Add the ones column | Add the tens column |
| 0 + 0 + 5 = 5 | 4 + 6 + 5 = 15 |
| No regrouping is necessary | Regroup 15 tens = |
|  | 1 hundred  5 tens |

Remember to keep your place value columns straight and avoid errors!

```
   40           40
   60           60
 + 55         + 55
    5          155
```

The group has 155 sugar cubes.

**1** Find the sum.

```
   44         13         36         12
   20         16         30          7
 + 15        + 3        + 45       + 10



   27         56         87         89
   12          3         21         81
   11         12         31         45
 +  1        + 2        + 10        + 8
```

**2** Find the sum. Unscramble the message.

| 1,560 **S** | 54,801 **T** | 123 **O** | 549 **L** |
|---|---|---|---|
| + 1,581 | + 34,752 | + 798 | + 340 |

Order the answers from smallest to largest.

_____   _____   _____   _____

*Luke 15:32*

**3** Color the improper fractions which convert to the mixed numbers in the data bank. Find the hidden picture.

Data Bank:   $5\frac{1}{3}$   $6\frac{2}{5}$   $1\frac{3}{10}$   $8\frac{3}{4}$   $3\frac{7}{9}$   $2\frac{11}{12}$

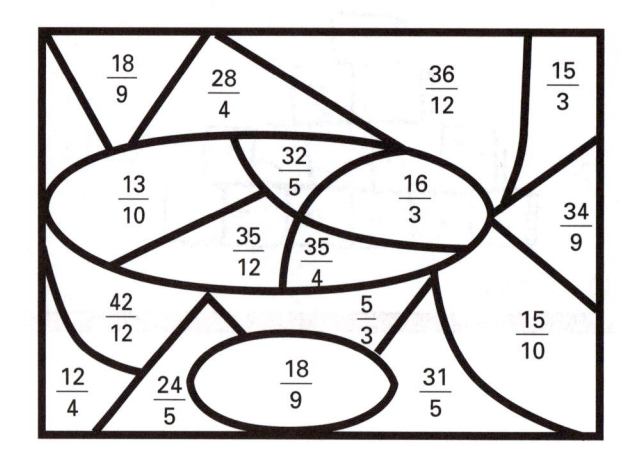

Fractions in the picture:
$\frac{18}{9}$, $\frac{28}{4}$, $\frac{36}{12}$, $\frac{15}{3}$, $\frac{13}{10}$, $\frac{32}{5}$, $\frac{16}{3}$, $\frac{34}{9}$, $\frac{35}{12}$, $\frac{35}{4}$, $\frac{42}{12}$, $\frac{5}{3}$, $\frac{15}{10}$, $\frac{12}{4}$, $\frac{24}{5}$, $\frac{18}{9}$, $\frac{31}{5}$

**4** Solve these multi-step problems.

The Sunday School teacher purchased 12 boxes of crayons, 3 packages of drawing paper, and 10 bottles of glue. If she purchased all of these items at a cost of $1.00 each, how much money did she spend?

Sarah paid $3.00 to get into the softball game. She then paid $5.25 for a slice of pizza and a soft drink. If Sarah only brought a $20.00 bill with her to the game, how much money did she have left after purchasing a ticket and the food?

**5** Order each row from the largest to the smallest.

| 12,144 | 15,928 | 12,441 | 15,298 |
| --- | --- | --- | --- |
| _____ | _____ | _____ | _____ |
| 21,282 | 21,548 | 12,540 | 21,854 |
| _____ | _____ | _____ | _____ |

**6** Label each geometric figure. Use the Data Bank below.

_____    _____    _____

_____    _____

All of these figures are four sided figures, or _____.

**Data Bank:**

square      trapezoid      parallelogram      rectangle

rhombus      quadrilateral      triangle

# Lesson 24

## Estimating Sums

Teresa and Chris are folding programs for the Christmas pageant. Teresa has folded 58 and Chris has folded 89. ABOUT how many programs have they folded together?

The word ABOUT is a key word in the problem above. This word signals that the problem is not looking for an exact answer, but an **estimated** answer. Many times we do not need to know an exact answer to a problem or question. An **estimated** answer will be sufficient. To **estimate** an addition problem, we simply round each addend before adding. Look at the example answer below.

| **Actual Problem** | **Rounded addends** | **Estimated Problem & Answer** |
|---|---|---|
| 58<br>+ 89<br>147 | 60<br>90 | 60<br>+ 90<br>150 |

Teresa and Chris have folded about 150 programs.

**1.** Use rounding (to the nearest ten) to estimate each sum.

```
   58          39          48
   35          19          21
 +  5        + 20         + 9

   68                      27
    8                      12
 + 45                    + 14
```

**2.** Find the sum.

```
   37        7,277       3,941         636          77
 + 16      + 5,341     + 1,597       + 412        + 33


 45,516     71,120      40,006     542,051     102,305
+31,004    +12,189     +67,453    +170,231    +154,280
```

**3** Solve.

Cassie rode 6 laps on her bicycle around the school track. Patrick rode 10 laps on his bicycle. How much farther did Patrick ride than Cassie if each lap was 230 meters?

Kathryn pledged $250.00 to the building program at her church. If she has already given $50.00 and plans to give $10.00 per week until the pledge is given, how many weeks will it take to pay this?

**4** Color the boxes with the 6 largest numbers in the diagram.

| 8,003 | 4,127 | 9,809 | 6,981 | 7,237 |
|---|---|---|---|---|
| 7,053 | 9,000 | 9,005 | 9,543 | 8,865 |
| 8,923 | 5,985 | 9,364 | 3,567 | 4,988 |
| 8,132 | 6,978 | 9,013 | 7,892 | 5,897 |

**Galatians 2:20**

**5** Use your calculator to solve these problems.

3,678 + 543 − (35 x 25) =

3.95 + (4 x 34) − 1.01 =

(79,245 − 53,289) + 234 =

**6** Find the shape and color it the appropriate color.

| PUZZLE CODE ||
|---|---|
| **Shape** | **Color** |
| Trapezoid | Green |
| Rhombus | Red |
| Rectangle | Blue |
| Parallelogram | Yellow |
| Square | Pink |

Use a black marker to outline all the shapes in the diagram that are quadrilaterals.

**Hint:** One shape is drawn twice!

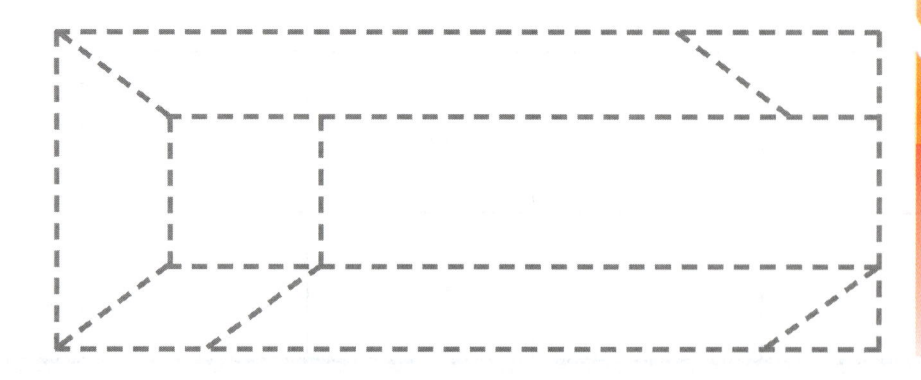

## Lesson 25

## Subtracting Two & Three Digits

There are 27 New Testament books and 39 Old Testament books in the Bible. How many more Old Testament books are there than New Testament books?

    39      1. Subtract the ones' column. Regroup if necessary.
− 27
     2

$9 - 7 = 2$

    39      2. Subtract the tens' column.
− 27
   12      $3 - 2 = 1$

There are 12 more books in the Old Testament than in the New Testament

Adam lived to be 930 years old. His third son, Seth, lived to be 912. How much longer than Seth did Adam live?

1. Subtract the ones' column. Regroup if necessary.

   1
93*0*
91*2*

2 cannot be taken from 0. One group of 10 from the tens' column, must be regrouped to the ones' column. We now subtract $10 - 2 = 8$.

2. Subtract the tens' column. Regroup if necessary.

  2
9*3*0
9*1*2
   8

Because one group of 10 was renamed, we now subtract $2 - 1 = 1$.

3. Subtract the hundreds' column.

*9*30
*9*12
 18

$9 - 9 = 0$

Adam lived 18 years longer than Seth.

**1** Find the difference.

| 36 | 57 | 45 | 60 |
|---|---|---|---|
| − 14 | − 28 | − 21 | − 46 |

| 163 | 193 | 385 | 784 |
|---|---|---|---|
| − 24 | − 25 | − 159 | − 213 |

**2** Estimate by rounding to the nearest 100

$$756 - 657 \qquad 712 - 491 \qquad 415 - 307 \qquad 663 - 121$$

**3** Find the sum. On the numbered lines below, write the letter that matches each answer.

$$1{,}560 + 4{,}680 = C \qquad 2{,}296 + 5{,}399 = D \qquad 131{,}476 + 488{,}081 = G \qquad 3{,}947 + 5{,}546 = I \qquad 546{,}021 + 368{,}429 = M$$

$$461{,}213 + 399{,}300 = S \qquad 899 + 320 = O \qquad 69{,}214 + 24{,}713 = R \qquad 435 + 375 = K \qquad 1{,}572 + 1{,}078 = Y$$

___  ___  ___  ___  ___  ___  ___
619,557  1,219  7,695  9,493  860,513  914,450  2,650

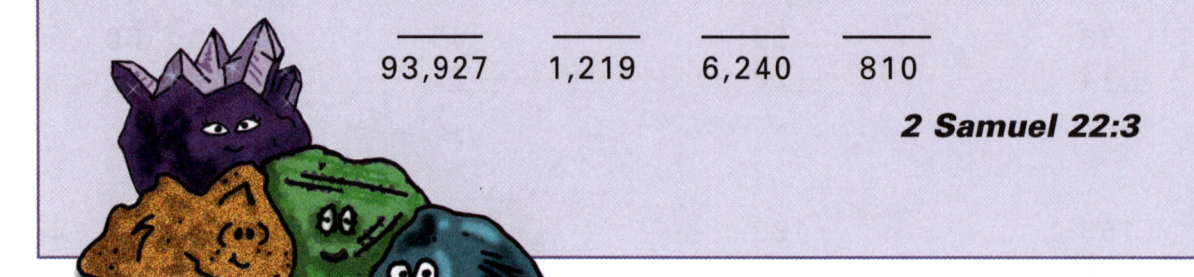

___  ___  ___  ___
93,927  1,219  6,240  810

**2 Samuel 22:3**

## 4. Find the sum.

```
  44        13        36        12
  10         6         7        27
+ 18      + 57      + 45        45
                              +  8


  37        18        17        24
  12        25        25        36
  46        36        48        64
+ 10       + 9      + 57      + 31
```

## 5. Round.

| Nearest 10 | Nearest 100 | Nearest 1,000 |
|---|---|---|
| 23 _____ | 782 _____ | 1,371 _____ |
| 56 _____ | 465 _____ | 2,891 _____ |
| 98 _____ | 213 _____ | 5,231 _____ |

## 6. Solve and check.

$8 + n = 32$        $n + 9 = 55$        $22 + n = 42$        $n + 15 = 35$

_____        _____        _____        _____

Check

**Lesson 26**

## Subtracting Two, Three, Four, Five, & Six Digits

Doug and Karen went mountain climbing. They climbed 1,256 feet on Tuesday. They climbed 947 feet on Wednesday. How much farther did they climb on the first day than the second?

We subtract larger numbers just like we subtract two- and three-digit numbers. It is important, however, that the place value columns are straight. This will help you avoid errors.

```
  1
1,256
-  947
      9
```
1. Subtract the ones. Regrouping is necessary from the tens' to the ones'.

$$16 - 7 = 9$$

```
   4
1,256
-  947
     09
```
2. Subtract the tens'. Due to regrouping we now subtract.

$$4 - 4 = 0$$

```
  1
1,256
-  947
    309
```
3. Subtract the hundreds'. Regrouping is necessary from the thousands' to the hundreds'.

$$12 - 9 = 3$$

```
0
1,256
-  947
    309
```
4. Subtract the thousands'. Due to regrouping, there is nothing left in the thousands' column to subtract.

$$0 - 0 = 0$$

Doug and Karen climbed 309 feet more on Tuesday than Wednesday.

**1** Find the difference.

| 6,470 | 842,078 | 1,743 | 13,572 |
|-------|---------|-------|--------|
| − 2,082 | − 434,132 | − 962 | − 12,835 |

| 7,953 | 15,045 | 67,324 | 647,081 |
|-------|--------|--------|---------|
| − 1,790 | − 8,438 | − 26,275 | − 179,000 |

**2** Find the difference.

```
  600        907        560        805
- 476      - 268      - 287      - 329
```

```
  703        701        906        448
- 233      - 576      - 128      - 285
```

**3** Estimate. Round three-digit numbers to nearest 100. Round four- and five-digit numbers to the nearest 1,000.

```
  647        842       1,743
- 208      - 434      -  862
```

```
 3,572     15,045
-2,873     - 8,152
```

**4** Estimate by rounding to the nearest 10.

```
      13          90          18
      52          67          84
    + 24          78           6
                +  6         + 40
```

**5** Label the first problem.
Find the sum.

```
  12 _____      7         15         18         21
 + 9 _____    + 3        + 10       + 20       + 15
  21 _____
```

**6** Solve.

```
  10         3         8        13        45
 + ?        + ?       + ?       + ?       + ?
  25         9        12        15        50
```

**Lesson 27**

## Estimating Differences

Estimating with subtraction problems is just like estimating with addition problems. To estimate an answer, we round the minuend and subtrahend and then subtract. Look at the examples below.

Round to the nearest 10

```
  76        80
- 38      - 40
          ----
           40    estimated
                 answer
```

Round to the nearest 100

```
 2,107     2,100
-  896    -  900
          ------
           1,200  estimated
                  answer
```

Round to the nearest 1,000

```
 1,975     2,000
- 1,326   - 1,000
          ------
           1,000  estimated answer
```

**1** Estimate by rounding to the indicated place.

**Nearest 10**

```
   63          72         156
 - 27        - 28        - 87
```

**Nearest 100**

```
   726       1,597       1,807
 - 376       - 765       - 598
```

**Nearest 1,000**

```
  7,697     16,203       2,437
 -1,876    - 9,783      -1,129
```

## 2. Find the difference.

$$726 - 511$$    $$1{,}597 - 489$$    $$156 - 23$$

$$24{,}327 - 10{,}561$$    $$451{,}780 - 354{,}087$$

## 3. Estimate.

Round to the 100s'.

$$1{,}375 - 845$$    $$6{,}202 - 3{,}765$$    $$9{,}483 - 7{,}329$$

Round to the 1000s'.

$$7{,}429 - 2{,}059$$    $$8{,}726 - 5{,}394$$    $$2{,}538 - 1{,}460$$

## 4. Solve.

$$5 - n = 2$$    $$10 - n = 5$$    $$20 - n = 15$$    $$100 - n = 30$$

**5** Find the difference.
Label each part of the indicated problem.

|  17       |  21   |  60   |  10  |  8  |
| --------- | ----- | ----- | ---- | --- |
| − 10      | − 11  | − 50  | − 6  | − 3 |

**6** Match.

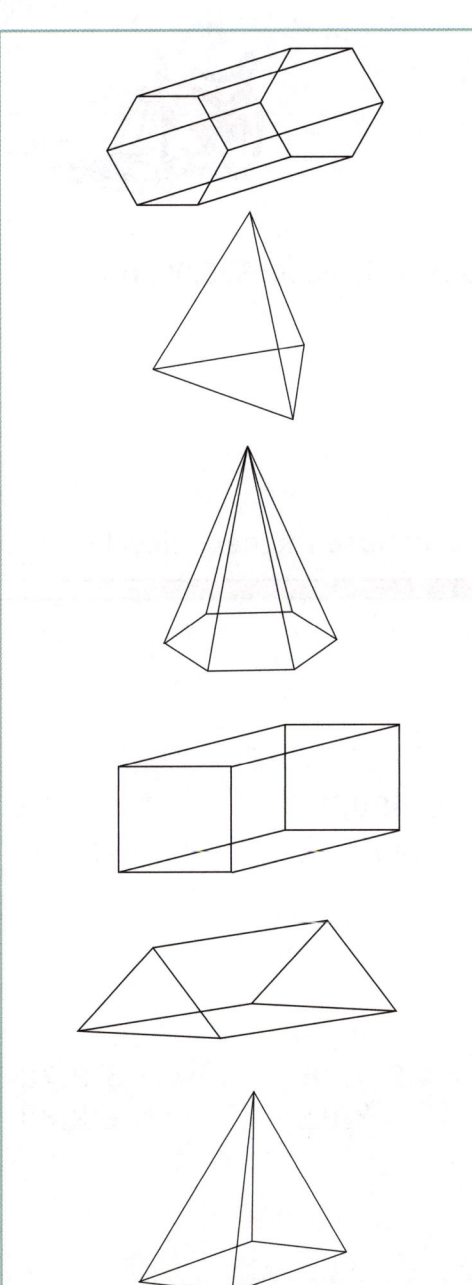

Hexagonal pyramid

Triangular prism

Rectangular pyramid

Rectangular prism

Hexagonal prism

Triangular pyramid

**Lesson 28**

## Addition & Subtraction of Money

Rather than have a gift exchange at their Christmas party, Mrs. Smith's Sunday School class wanted to use the money to purchase a gift for a needy child. Mrs. Smith's class voted to buy a bicycle for a child in a nearby orphanage. Christopher and Maggie collected the money as it came in. Christopher collected $22.97 and Maggie collected $15.89. What was their combined total?

Money is added in the same way as greater numbers. It is important to place the decimal points directly beneath each other and to keep the place value columns in line. This will help you avoid errors.

```
    1 1
  $ 15.89
+ $ 22.97
  $ 38.86
```

The class had $38.86 to buy a bicycle. If the bicycle costs $75.00, how much more money will they need to collect?

```
  $ 75.00
− $ 38.86
  $ 36.14
```

The class still needs $36.14 before they can purchase the new bicycle.

**1** Find the sum or difference.

| $ 235.97 | $ 471.21 | $ 890.71 | $ 432.55 |
|---|---|---|---|
| − 183.32 | − 42.29 | − 599.22 | − 267.09 |

| $ 5.98 | $ 12.54 | $ 4.16 | $ 9.78 |
|---|---|---|---|
| + 3.18 | + 10.25 | + 2.03 | + 2.99 |

**2** Estimate the difference.

Round to the nearest 10.

```
    45              98            123
  - 23            - 54          - 113
```

Round to the nearest 100.

```
   235             546          8,121
 - 106           - 398        - 7,271
```

Round to the nearest 1,000.

```
  2,894          4,810         5,143        12,518
 - 1,244        - 2,346       - 4,841       - 3,451
```

**3** Find the difference.

```
 234,851        687,035       285,381       389,001
- 135,300      - 511,072     - 124,321     - 213,200
```

```
  8,901         25,110         1,111
 -  803       - 10,222        -  823
```

**4** Match the answer with the problem.

Solve the message. The first one is done for you.

$$\begin{array}{cccccc} 69 & 247 & 29 & 570 & 306 & 854 \\ -45 & -136 & -13 & -246 & -200 & -532 \\ \hline 24 & & & & & \end{array}$$

C ___  ___  ___  ___  ___  ___

$$\begin{array}{ccccc} 474 & 45 & 75 & 10 & 25 \\ -224 & -36 & -68 & -7 & -12 \end{array}$$

___  ___  ___  ___  ___

*Isaiah 28:16*

| DATA BANK | | | | |
|---|---|---|---|---|
| 322 = **R** | 9 = **T** | 324 = **N** | 7 = **O** | 111 = **O** |
| 250 = **S** | 3 = **N** | 13 = **E** | 16 = **R** | 106 = **E** |

**5** Label each part. Solve.

$$\begin{array}{cccc} 15 & 21 & 45 & 75 \\ -n & -n & -n & -n \\ \hline 6 & 11 & 36 & 25 \end{array}$$

**6** Label each figure.

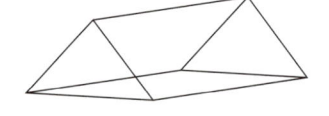

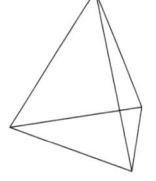

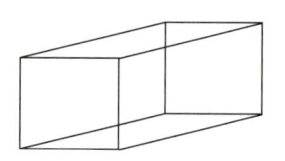

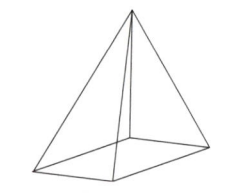

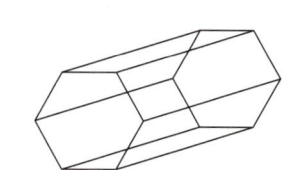

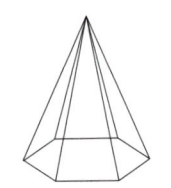

88 Horizons Math 5, Student Workbook 1

**Lesson 29**

## Word Problems

Sum   Difference   **More**   How Many?

Four Steps to a Solution When Working Word Problems:

Cathy makes $4.00 per hour baby-sitting. If she baby-sat for 7 hours on Saturday, how much money did she make?

Use the Four Steps to a Solution to help answer the question.

Less

Quotient   Plan   How Much?   Work   Answer/Check   Product

Understand

1. UNDERSTAND - What do you know? What do you want to find out?
   * Cathy makes $4.00 per hour
   * How much money did she make in 7 hours?

2. PLAN - What should you do to solve the problem?
   * Multiply   $4.00 x 7 hours

3. WORK - Solve the problem.
   * $4.00 x 7 = $28.00

4. ANSWER/CHECK - Read the problem again. Is the answer reasonable? Does it answer the question?
   * Cathy made $28.00 for 7 hours of baby-sitting. Yes the answer is reasonable.

**1** Use the Four Steps to a Solution to solve these problems.

1. Mrs. Jones' class had a bake sale. Suzanne bought a cake for $4.00, a dozen cookies for $2.00, and one brownie for $0.50. How much money did Suzanne spend?

2. Steve purchased 12 cookies and gave away 3. Then he bought 4 more. How many cookies did he have then?

3. Ashley spent $3.50 on cookies and $4.00 on a cake. If she had a $10.00 bill how much money does she still have?

**2** Find the difference or sum.

$5.98          $12.54         $14.16         $41.58
+ 3.18         − 3.92         + 5.37         − 10.09

**3** Estimate. Round to the nearest 100.

4,688                  69,832                 403
− 1,225                − 13,540               − 100


    691                        1,069
  − 312                        − 891

**4** Find the missing number.

15,045         57,802         167,324        9,365
−  8,?68       − 38,9?1       − 12?,875      −  ?,878
   6,577        18,811         40,449         4,487

5. Find the equal ratio by dividing.

$$\frac{8}{36} = \frac{n}{9} \qquad \frac{21}{28} = \frac{3}{n} \qquad \frac{6}{15} = \frac{n}{5} \qquad \frac{12}{24} = \frac{2}{n}$$

6. Match.

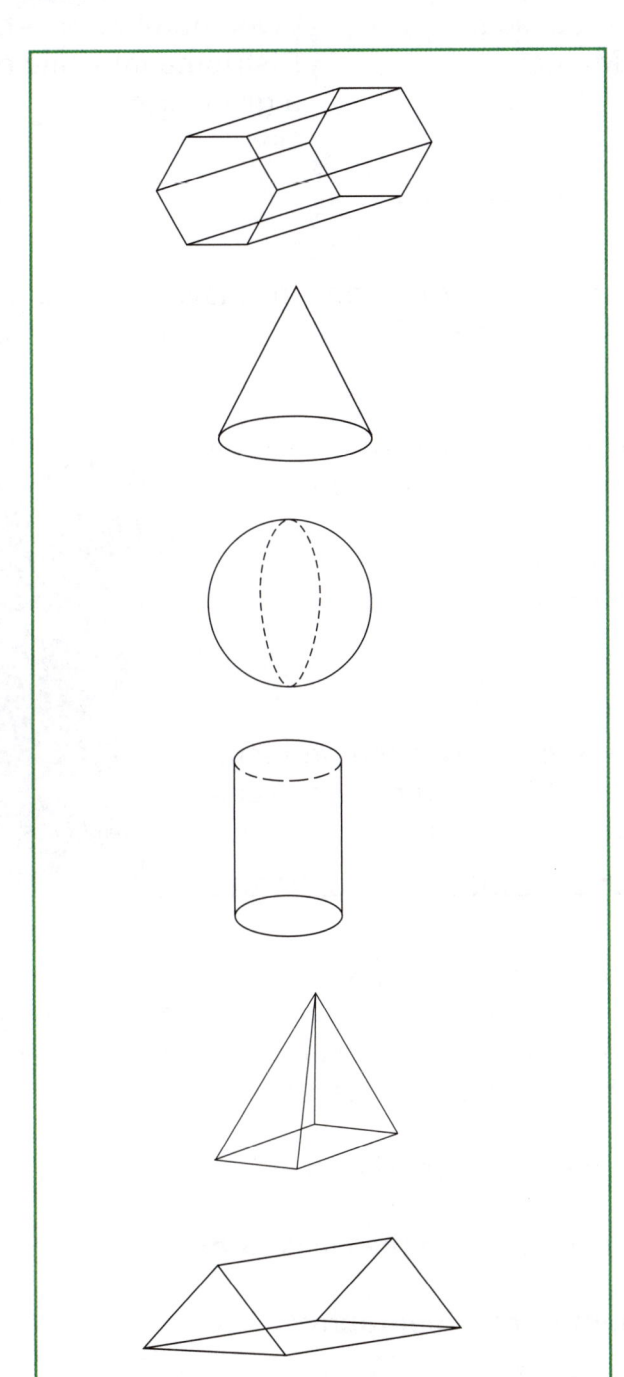

Sphere

Hexagonal prism

Cylinder

Rectangular pyramid

Triangular prism

Cone

Lesson 30

## Problem Solving

It is difficult to decide which operation ( +, –, x, ÷ ) to use in a story problem. The table below shows you key words that signal each operation.

| + | – | x | ÷ |
|---|---|---|---|
| How many in all? Find the total. Add. | How many more? Compare. Take away. Subtract. | Finding the total for equal sets. Multiply. | Distribute evenly into a given number of sets. Distribute into sets of a a given size. Divide. |

Jamie sold 6 boxes of candy on Monday, 4 boxes on Tuesday, 7 boxes on Wednesday, 6 boxes on Thursday, and 2 boxes on Friday. How many boxes of candy did Jamie sell in all?

**UNDERSTAND** You know how many boxes Jamie sold each day. You need to find out the total amount sold.

**PLAN** You want to know the TOTAL amount, so you need to ADD. 6 + 4 + 7 + 6 + 2 =

**WORK** 6 + 4 + 7 + 6 + 2 = **25**

**ANSWER/CHECK** The answer is 25 boxes. Reread the problem and check to see that this answer makes sense. Is 25 a realistic answer to the question? Yes.

**1** Mrs. Price's class conducted a survey to find out what type of books their classmates liked the best. The results were: 12 – Adventure, 11 – Mystery, 6 – Humor, 4 – Biography, and 3 – Other. Using these results, answer the questions. Some key words have been highlighted to help you decide what operation to use.

1. **How many more** people like Adventure than Mystery?

2. If everyone votes, **how many** students are in the class **in all**?

3. **How many more** people like Humor than Biography?

4. What is the **total** number of people who like both Adventure and Mystery?

**2** Find the sum or difference.

| $237.97 | $578.13 | $82.10 | $238.99 |
| − 123.20 | + 169.14 | − 14.99 | + 178.19 |

**3** Estimate each difference. Round to the nearest 10.

| 23 | 56 | 189 | 256 | 450 | 876 |
| − 11 | − 21 | − 154 | − 120 | − 378 | − 764 |

**4** Circle all the even answers. Place the corresponding letter to each answer as you go down the column on the lines below to solve the message.

| 9 x 5 = 45 **H** | 5 x 7 = 35 **Y** | 5 x 5 = 25 **T** |
| 2 x 3 = 6 **B** | 5 x 8 = 40 **E** | 8 x 6 = 48 **T** |
| 6 x 1 = 6 **L** | 4 x 8 = 32 **D** | 2 x 6 = 12 **H** |
| 8 x 2 = 16 **E** | 3 x 7 = 21 **I** | 8 x 9 = 72 **E** |
| 7 x 9 = 63 **R** | 9 x 9 = 81 **O** | 8 x 8 = 64 **R** |
| 4 x 4 = 16 **S** | 3 x 5 = 15 **W** | 2 x 7 = 14 **O** |
| 3 x 4 = 12 **S** | 9 x 4 = 36 **B** | 3 x 9 = 27 **D** |
| 7 x 7 = 49 **P** | 1 x 1 = 1 **C** | 1 x 2 = 2 **C** |
| 5 x 9 = 45 **F** | 4 x 7 = 28 **E** | 8 x 7 = 56 **K** |

___  ___  ___  ___  ___  ___  ___    ___  ___    ___  ___  ___

___  ___  ___  ___

*2 Samuel 22:47*

**5** Read the clues and name the described mystery number.

| 45 | 66 | 72 |
|----|----|----|
| 21 | 32 | 41 |

| 30 | 31 | 33 |
|----|----|----|
| 38 | 35 | 32 |

1. The digits have a sum of 5.
2. One digit is odd, the other is even.
3. The digits have a product of 6.

The mystery number is ____.

1. The digits are both odd.
2. The second digit is smaller than the first.
3. The digits have a product equal to the first digit.

The mystery number is ____.

**6** Draw the indicated figures.

_____    _____    _____

cone         cylinder      sphere




_____         _____              _____

triangular prism   rectangular pyramid   hexagonal pyramid

94 Horizons Math 5, Student Workbook 1

Test 3

**1** Circle the larger number in each pair. 6 pts. total for this exercise.

7,274   7,742

9,612   9,216

10,655   10,556

2,770   2,774

19,682   18,682

174,643   173,643

**2** Round to the indicated place. 9 pts. total for this exercise.

Round to the nearest 10.

5,5<u>7</u>6 _____     3,8<u>9</u>3 _____     4<u>5</u>9 _____

Round to the nearest 100.

5,<u>9</u>41 _____     2,<u>0</u>81 _____     3,<u>7</u>98 _____

Round to the nearest 1,000.

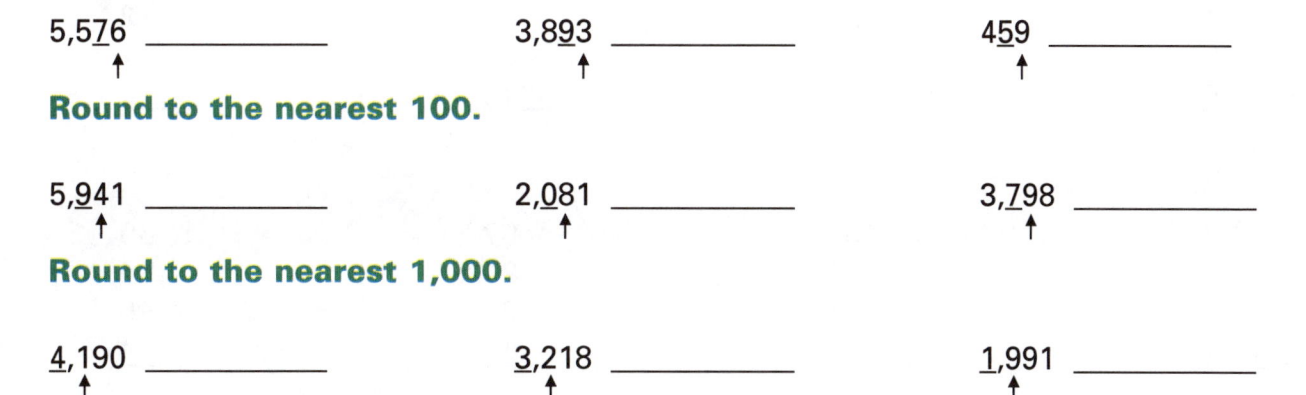

<u>4</u>,190 _____     <u>3</u>,218 _____     <u>1</u>,991 _____

**3** Some of the problems below do not contain enough information to solve them. If a problem is missing necessary information, simply write not enough information. Use a calculator to work the problems that contain enough information to find an answer. 4 pts. total for this exercise.

Sally purchased a new bedroom suite for $1,395.00. She also purchased a comforter set and curtains for the bedroom. How much was her total purchase?

Jim purchased a new car for $25,987.00. He had the car dealership install a new compact disc player and disc changer for an additional $455.00. How much was the total price of the car?

Sabrina sold her old dining room table and chairs for $300.00. She also sold her old china cabinet for $275.00. If she then purchased a new dining room table, chairs, and china cabinet for $985.00, how much additional money was required?

Molly rode her bicycle 10 miles on Monday, 15 miles on Tuesday, and 7 miles on Wednesday. How much further did she ride on Monday than she did on Thursday?

**4** Find the sum. 5 pts. total for this exercise.

| 5,345 | 3,407 | 2,124 | 456 | 718 |
|---|---|---|---|---|
| + 1,949 | + 1,862 | + 571 | + 876 | + 391 |

**5** Find the estimated answer and then find the actual sum.
(Hint: digits smaller than 10 are either rounded to 10 or to 0) 8 pts.

| 44 | 13 | 36 | 12 |
|---|---|---|---|
| 20 | 16 | 34 | 7 |
| + 15 | + 3 | + 45 | + 10 |

| 27 | 56 | 87 | 89 |
|---|---|---|---|
| 12 | 3 | 21 | 81 |
| 11 | 12 | 31 | 45 |
| + 1 | + 2 | + 10 | + 4 |

**6** Find the difference. 8 pts. total for this exercise.

| 56 | 57 | 45 | 80 |
|---|---|---|---|
| − 14 | − 38 | − 23 | − 46 |

| 161 | 193 | 685 | 984 |
|---|---|---|---|
| − 23 | − 25 | − 129 | − 213 |

40 pts. Total

Lesson 31

## Multiplication Tables

Multiplication tables are easy to use. Let's find the product of 5 x 5. Take your finger and place it on the 5 in the darkened first row. Take your finger and place it on the 5 in the other darkened row. Follow the two numbers along the darkened path until they intersect. Those numbers intersect at 25, so 5 x 5 = 25. Find the product of 3 x 3 using the same procedure. The correct answer is 9.

| X | 0 | 1 | 2 | 3 | 4 | 5 |
|---|---|---|---|---|---|---|
| 0 | 0 | 0 | 0 | 0 | 0 | 0 |
| 1 | 0 | 1 | 2 | 3 | 4 | 5 |
| 2 | 0 | 2 | 4 | 6 | 8 | 10 |
| 3 | 0 | 3 | 6 | 9 | 12 | 15 |
| 4 | 0 | 4 | 8 | 12 | 16 | 20 |
| 5 | 0 | 5 | 10 | 15 | 20 | 25 |

(5 x 5 = 25)

Multiplication tables are also helpful in finding patterns in multiplication. The multiples of 3 are 0, 3, 6, 9, 12 and 15. Find the row showing multiples of 2. The multiples are 0, 2, 4, 6, 8, and 10.

**1** Complete the multiplication table below. Several have been done for you.

| X | 0 | 1 | 2 | 3 | 4 | 5 | 6 | 7 | 8 | 9 | 10 |
|---|---|---|---|---|---|---|---|---|---|---|----|
| 0 | | | | | | | | | | | |
| 1 | | | | | | | | | | | |
| 2 | | | | | | | | | | | |
| 3 | | | | | | | | 21 | | | |
| 4 | | | | | | | | | | | |
| 5 | | | | | | | | | | | |
| 6 | | | | | | | | | 48 | | |
| 7 | | | | | | | | 42 | | | |
| 8 | | | | 24 | | | | | | | |
| 9 | | | | | | | | | | | |
| 10 | | | | | | | | | | | |

**2** Use the multiplication table on the previous page to solve.

List the multiples of 4.
_____

List the multiples of 5.
_____

Find the factors of each product:

45 _____        81 _____        4 _____

Find the product of the factors:

2 x 7 _____     5 x 7 _____     4 x 4 _____

**3** The fractions in the highlighted boxes are equivalent to one of the decimals in the row beside them. Find each decimal, and shade the box to find the missing word in the verse from Isaiah 9:6. *For unto us a child is born...and his name shall be called Wonderful Counsellor, The Mighty God, The everlasting Father, The _____ of Peace.*

| | | | |
|---|---|---|---|
| $\frac{1}{10}$ | 0.010  D | 0.1  P | 1.0  L |
| $\frac{2}{100}$ | 0.2  O | 2.02  A | 0.02  R |
| $\frac{13}{100}$ | 13.00  G | 0.13  I | 0.013  L |
| $\frac{99}{100}$ | 0.99  N | 9.9  S | 99.0  M |
| $\frac{70}{100}$ | 0.07  Q | 7.0  T | 0.70  C |
| $2\frac{5}{100}$ | 2.5  B | 0.25  Z | 2.05  E |

Write each letter here (from top to bottom). ___ ___ ___ ___ ___ ___

**4** Add.

```
  12,365        70,934        32,211        79,063        38,921
+ 23,085      + 60,926      + 43,899      + 30,037      + 23,193
```

98  Horizons Math 5, Student Workbook 1

**5** Rewrite these numbers vertically and add.

25 + 132 + 61 + 11 = _____          17 + 9 + 158 + 73 = _____

47 + 4 + 190 + 12 = _____          9 + 77 + 63 + 168 = _____

**6** Find the quotients. Label the first problem with the following words: dividend, divisor, quotient.

_____  3)27  _____

4)36     6)48     9)81     5)15     9)72

6)54     9)63     7)21     4)12

**7** Solve.
Each problem calls for the use of a different operation.
Write the operation next to the answer.

1. Ben must practice the piano for 180 minutes a week. He must practice six days a week. If he practices the same amount of time each day, how many minutes a day will he need to practice?

2. Tickets to Ben's piano recital cost $4.50. If he buys one ticket and gives the cashier a ten dollar bill, how much change will he receive?

3. Ben's piano lessons cost $18.00 a week. How much must he pay each month? (4 weeks in the month)

4. Ben bought three pieces of sheet music at the following prices: $3.50, $4.25, and $2.95. What was the total cost of his music?

## Multiplication

Lesson 32

A **factor** is a number multiplied to become a product. In the illustration, there are two rows of eggs with six eggs in a row. We could write a mathematical sentence to describe the eggs.

$$2 \times 6 = 12$$
Factor   Factor   Product

In this mathematical sentence, there are 2 rows of eggs with an unknown number of eggs in each row. If the product is 10, how many eggs are in each row?

$$2 \times ? = 10$$
Factor   Factor   Product

There are 5 eggs in each row.

Place the missing factors in the circles to equal the product in the top circle.

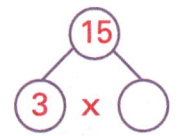

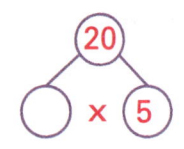

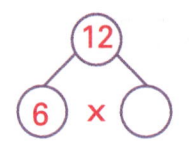

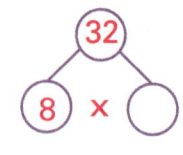

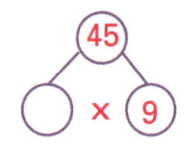

- 15: 3 × ◯
- 20: ◯ × 5
- 12: 6 × ◯
- 32: 8 × ◯
- 45: ◯ × 9

The answers are: 5, 4, 2, 4, and 5.

**1** Write the missing factors in the circles.

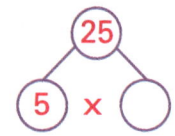

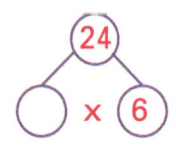

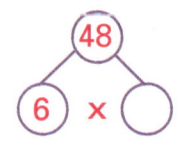

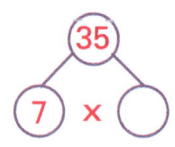

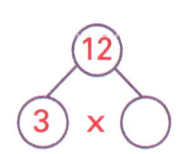

- 25: 5 × ◯
- 24: ◯ × 6
- 48: 6 × ◯
- 35: 7 × ◯
- 12: 3 × ◯

There are several combinations of factors for each product. Find all the possibilities. The first one has been done for you.

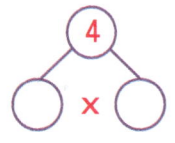

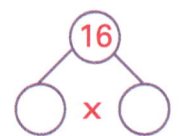

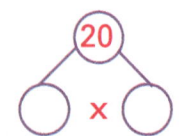

- 4: ◯ × ◯
  1, 4   2, 2
- 16: ◯ × ◯
- 20: ◯ × ◯

② Complete the multiplication table.

| X | 0 | 1 | 2 | 3 | 4 | 5 | 6 | 7 | 8 | 9 | 10 |
|---|---|---|---|---|---|---|---|---|---|---|----|
| 0 |   |   |   |   |   |   |   |   |   |   |    |
| 1 |   |   |   |   |   |   |   |   |   |   |    |
| 2 |   |   |   |   |   |   |   |   |   |   |    |
| 3 |   |   |   |   |   |   |   |   |   |   |    |

③ Solve. Shade the letter to the right of each answer. The remaining letters will complete the verse from Psalms 26:8. *Good and _____ is the Lord: therefore will he teach sinners in the way.*

```
  126      109      631      331
+  45    + 839    + 202    + 427


  170      289      109      712
+ 433    + 689    +  45    + 116
```

| 171 | D |
|-----|---|
| 314 | U |
| 948 | X |
| 833 | L |
| 758 | W |
| 233 | P |
| 100 | R |
| 603 | B |
| 465 | I |
| 341 | G |
| 978 | E |
| 551 | H |
| 709 | T |
| 154 | Y |
| 828 | O |

**4** Find the mystery numbers.

1. I have four digits, and all are different.
2. All of my digits are odd.
3. I have a three in the hundredths' place.
4. I have a seven in the ones' place.
5. The number in the tens' place is less than the number in the tenths' place.
6. None of my digits is 5.
7. I am _____.


1. I have four digits and they are all odd.
2. The number in the hundredths' place is greater than three, it is odd and a factor of 36.
3. The number in the tenths' place is less than four and greater than one.
4. The number in the ones' and tens' place are equal and factors of 49.
5. I am _____.

**5** Find the quotients. Label the first problem with one of the following words: dividend, divisor, quotient.

_____  9)$\overline{36}$  _____

| 6)$\overline{36}$ | 9)$\overline{45}$ | 2)$\overline{16}$ | 5)$\overline{25}$ | 7)$\overline{70}$ |
| 6)$\overline{18}$ | 6)$\overline{24}$ | 7)$\overline{49}$ | 6)$\overline{12}$ | |

**6** Find the sum.

| 57,002 | 30,109 | 90,981 | 38,390 |
| + 12,983 | + 49,037 | + 99,139 | + 17,397 |

Lesson 33

# Prime/Composite

A **prime number** has only two factors, itself and one.
3 x 1 = 3

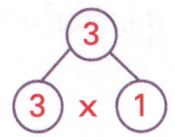

```
    3
   / \
  3 x 1
```

A **composite number** has more than two factors.
6 x 1 = 6   2 x 3 = 6

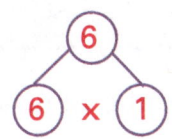

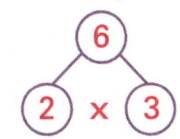

```
    6           6
   / \         / \
  6 x 1       2 x 3
```

The **number 1** has only one factor. It is neither prime or composite.

A composite number is the product of prime numbers. A factor tree can help you find those prime numbers.

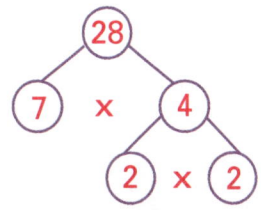

```
    6              28
   / \            /  \
  2 x 3          7 x  4
                     / \
                    2 x 2
```

The prime numbers are 2 and 3.    The prime numbers are 7, 2, and 2.

**1**  Use a factor tree to find prime numbers. Write the missing numbers in the circles.

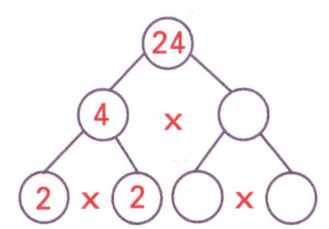

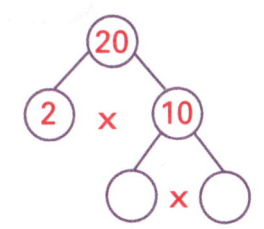

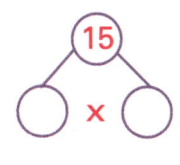

```
      24                20              15
     /  \              /  \             / \
    4 x  ○            2 x 10           ○ x ○
   / \    \                / \
  2 x 2   ○ x ○           ○ x ○
```

**2**  Complete the table.

| x | 2 | 3 | 4 | 5 | 6 | 7 | 8 |
|---|---|---|---|---|---|---|---|
| 5 |   |   |   |   |   |   |   |
| 6 |   |   |   |   |   |   |   |
| 7 |   |   |   |   |   |   |   |
| 8 |   |   |   |   |   |   |   |

**3** Use the term liters, meters, or grams to complete the sentences.

1. I took two _____ of soda to the social.
2. In chemistry class we weighed the sodium in _____ .
3. John ran in a road race. Instead of measuring the distance of the course in feet they used _____ .
4. The paper clips weigh about 15 _____ .
5. The amount of water to fill a fish tank is about 16 _____ .
6. The width of a basketball court is 15 _____ .

**4** Find the sum. Circle the flower pots that match the sum and read the message that completes the verse:
*And the Lord shall guide thee continually, and satisfy thy soul in drought, and make fat thy bones: and thou shall be like a watered garden, and like a spring of water, whose _____ fail not.*
*Isaiah 58:11*

```
  1,367        4,890        9,023        4,952
+ 2,489      + 2,457      + 1,409      + 3,458
```

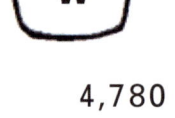

3,856  W
8,347  D 
10,432  A 
8,410  T 

```
  8,903        4,780        7,421        1,365        2,871
+ 3,780      + 4,798      + 2,400      +   609      +    32
```

12,683  E
8,759  A 
9,827  R 
1,973  E 
2,903  S 

104  Horizons Math 5, Student Workbook 1

**5** Find the missing addend.

```
  136        404        592        482        2?3
+ 20?      + 1?3      + ?15      + ?40      + 351
  344        587        907      1,022        614
```

? = \_\_\_\_    ? = \_\_\_\_    ? = \_\_\_\_    ? = \_\_\_\_    ? = \_\_\_\_

**6** Match.

1,000,000,091        one million, ninety-one

34,000,000           one billion, ninety-one

34,000,000,000       thirty-four million

1,000,091            thirty-four billion

3,400,000            three million, four hundred thousand

Lesson 34

## Multiplication

Mrs. Stanley's class is collecting cans for the church pantry. They are averaging 275 cans a week. At that rate, how many cans will they collect at the end of six weeks?
We multiply.

| Multiply the ones. Trade if necessary. | → | Multiply the tens. Add any extra tens. Trade if necessary. | → | Multiply the hundreds. Add any extra hundreds. Trade if necessary. |

```
    3              4 3              4
  27 5           27 5            2 7 5
  ×   6          ×   6           ×   6
      0             5 0          1,6 5 0
```

They will collect about 1,650 cans in 6 weeks.

**1** Multiply.

```
  594        913        933       1,296       5,190
×   7      ×   4      ×   3      ×    8      ×    5
```

**2** Write each ratio as a fraction.

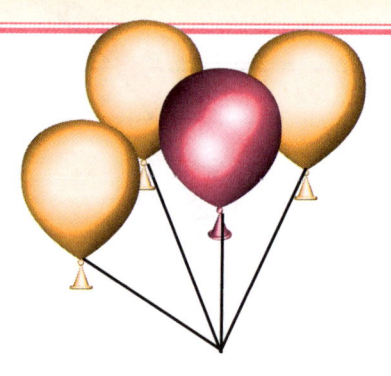

The ratio of: green candy to all candy  _____

The ratio of: orange balloons to all balloons  _____

The ratio of: blue candy to all candy  _____

The ratio of: pink balloons to all balloons  _____

106  Horizons Math 5, Student Workbook 1

**3** Find each difference. Match each digit in the answer with a letter in the code box. Write the letter under each number, and read the message.

| G | L | E | D | A | O | S | I | B |
|---|---|---|---|---|---|---|---|---|
| 1 | 2 | 3 | 4 | 5 | 6 | 7 | 8 | 9 |

```
   3 4 5 6          2 7 8 0          6 4 1 0
 - 3 2 9 2        - 2 6 9 3        -   4 8 7
```

___ ___ ___          ___ ___          ___ ___ ___ ___

**4** Place the numbers and letters in the doves from largest to smallest, and read the message.

| 323,012 | 60,456 | 324,000 | 330,780 | 60,545 |
|---------|--------|---------|---------|--------|
| A | E | E | P | C |

**5** Test each number to see if it is divisible by 2, 5, 10, or 3. Circle the correct responses. The first one has been done for you.

| | | | | |
|---|---|---|---|---|
| 456 is divisible by | (2) | 5 | 10 | (3) |
| 108 is divisible by | 2 | 5 | 10 | 3 |
| 903 is divisible by | 2 | 5 | 10 | 3 |
| 310 is divisible by | 2 | 5 | 10 | 3 |
| 345 is divisible by | 2 | 5 | 10 | 3 |

Horizons Math 5, Student Workbook 1

**6** Use a factor tree to find prime numbers. Write the missing numbers in the circles.

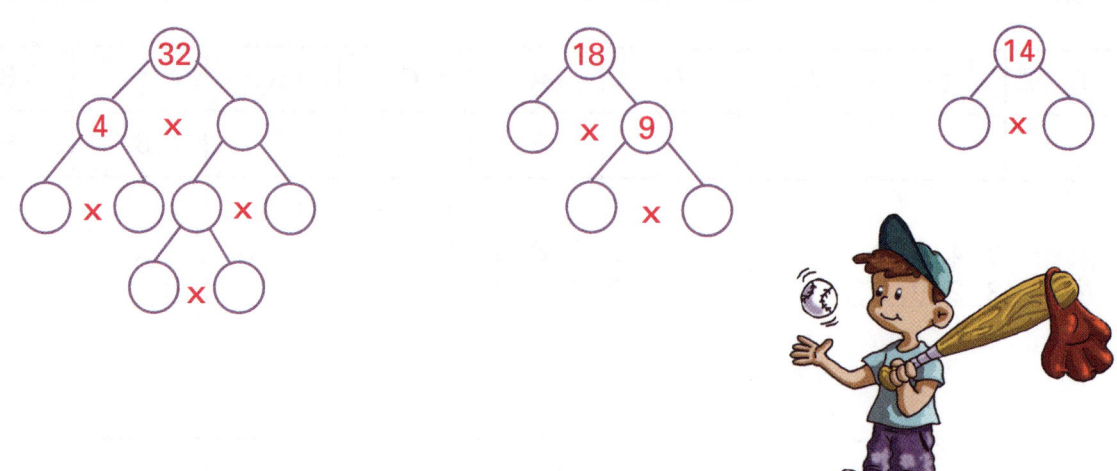

**7** **Finding Prime Numbers**

Eratosthenes invented a way to find prime numbers long ago. Look at the instructions and table to see how it was done. If you would like to do this exercise yourself, use the *Prime and Composite numbers* worksheet.

1. 1 is not a prime. Cross it out.

2. Circle 2. Use skip counting to find all the numbers having 2 as a factor (4, 6, 8, 10.....) Cross out these numbers.

3. Circle 3. Use skip counting to find all the numbers having 3 as a factor (3, 6, 9, 12......) Cross out these numbers.

4. Circle 5, 7, 11, and so on. Use skip counting to find all the numbers having 5, 7, 11, and so on as factors. Cross out these numbers.

5. All the circled numbers are prime.

| 1 | 2 | 3 | 4 | 5 | 6 | 7 | 8 | 9 | 10 |
|---|---|---|---|---|---|---|---|---|----|
| 11 | 12 | 13 | 14 | 15 | 16 | 17 | 18 | 19 | 20 |
| 21 | 22 | 23 | 24 | 25 | 26 | 27 | 28 | 29 | 30 |
| 31 | 32 | 33 | 34 | 35 | 36 | 37 | 38 | 39 | 40 |
| 41 | 42 | 43 | 44 | 45 | 46 | 47 | 48 | 49 | 50 |

**Lesson 35**

# Multiply by 10, 100, and 1,000

How much would it cost to rent a small sailboat for for 4 hours?
4 x 2**0** = 8**0**      4 x 2 **tens** = 8 **tens**
The cost is $80.

How much would it cost to rent a small sailboat for 3 days?
3 x 1**00** = 3**00**     3 x 1 **hundred** = 3 **hundred**
The cost is $300.

How much would it cost to rent a 12 person houseboat for 5 days?
5 x 1**,000** = 5**,000**   5 x 1 **thousand** = 5 **thousand**
The cost is $5,000

**Jim's Marina
Rental Boats and Water Toys**

| | |
|---|---|
| Boogey Boards | $5 an hour |
| Rafts | $10 an hour /$50 day |
| Canoes | $10 an hour /$50 day |
| Pedal Boats | $15 an hour /$70 day |
| Pontoon Boats | $20 an hour /$80 day |
| Small Sailboats | $20 an hour/ $100 day |
| J/24 | $150 a day |
| F27 | $200 a day |
| Seidelman 30 | $300 a day |
| 12 person house boat | $1,000 a day |

**1** Solve the problems. Use the chart above for cost information.

1. Darlene and Ray rented a Seidelman 30 for one week in the Virgin Islands. How much did the boat rental cost them?

2. The Nelson Family and the Davis Family rented the 12 person house boat for 3 days. What was their total cost?

3. Tom rented a canoe for an overnight canoe trip. He had the boat for 34 hours. What was his total cost if he rented by the hour? What was his cost if he rented by the day? Which is the best deal?

4. The Wilson Family rented a F27 for 14 days. What was their total cost?

**2** Find the product.

| | | |
|---|---|---|
| 6 x 10 = | 6 x 100 = | 6 x 1,000 = |
| 8 x 10 = | 8 x 100 = | 8 x 1,000 = |
| 7 x 60 = | 7 x 600 = | 7 x 6,000 = |
| 9 x 30 = | 9 x 300 = | 9 x 3,000 = |

**3** Multiply.

```
  113        237        106        149        544
x   4      x   3      x   8      x   5      x   7
```

**4** Complete the ratio tables.

| sugar | 1 cup | 2 cups | 3 cups | 4 cups | 5 cups |
|---|---|---|---|---|---|
| drink mix | 1 pkg | | | | |

| 1 pkg hot dogs | 2 pkgs hot dogs | 3 pkgs hot dogs | 4 pkgs hot dogs | 5 pkgs hot dogs | 6 pkgs hot dogs |
|---|---|---|---|---|---|
| 8 buns | | | | | |

**5** Write the numbers in numeral form, and order them from least to greatest in the rocket. The letters beside each number will spell a message.

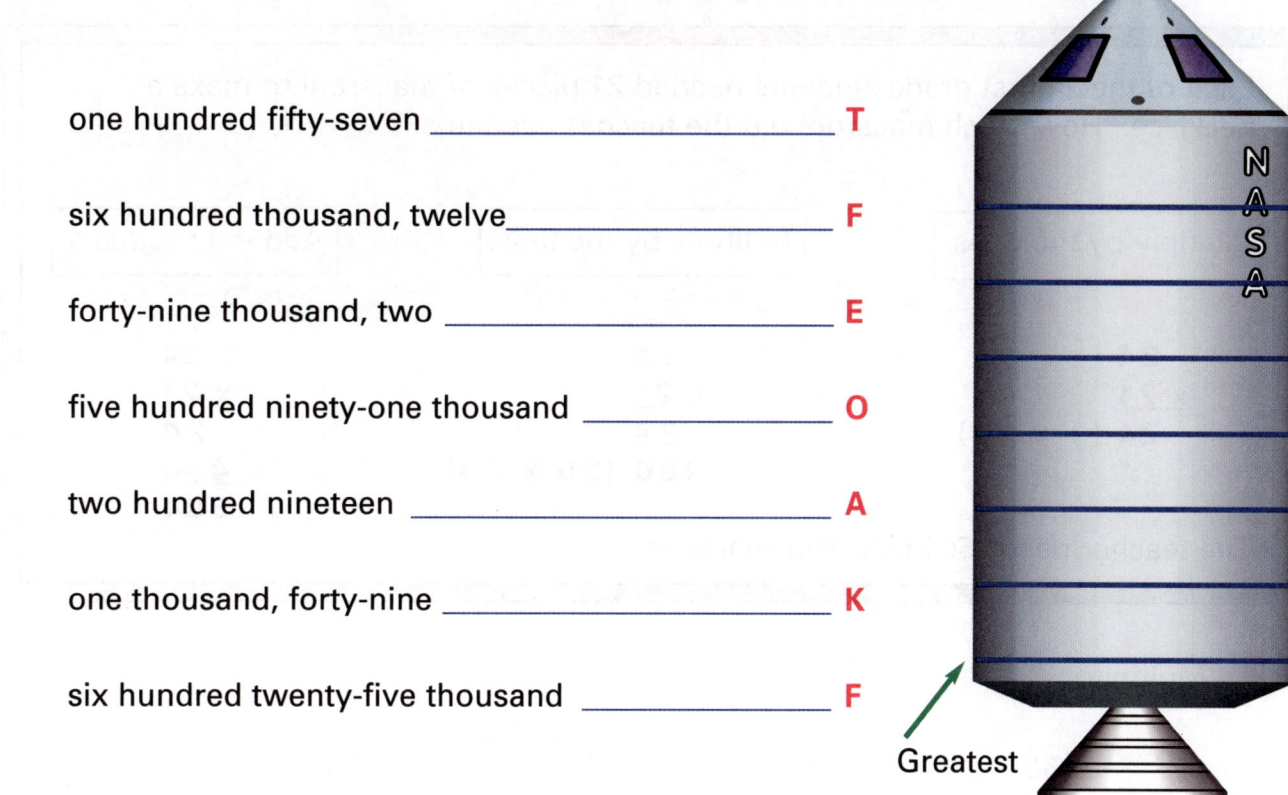

one hundred fifty-seven _____ T

six hundred thousand, twelve _____ F

forty-nine thousand, two _____ E

five hundred ninety-one thousand _____ O

two hundred nineteen _____ A

one thousand, forty-nine _____ K

six hundred twenty-five thousand _____ F

Greatest

**6** Shade all prime numbers to find the MYSTERY message. (There are 27)

| 2 | 20 | 5 | 15 | 43 | 31 | 37 | 9 | 7 | 5 | 3 |
| 4 | 3 | 16 | 45 | 47 | 12 | 24 | 6 | 11 | 8 | 10 |
| 10 | 11 | 35 | 36 | 5 | 13 | 50 | 8 | 13 | 17 | 23 |
| 6 | 13 | 6 | 14 | 11 | 14 | 20 | 4 | 8 | 6 | 29 |
| 14 | 41 | 12 | 80 | 13 | 19 | 3 | 12 | 3 | 17 | 19 |

**7** Use a factor tree to find prime numbers. Write the missing numbers in the circles.

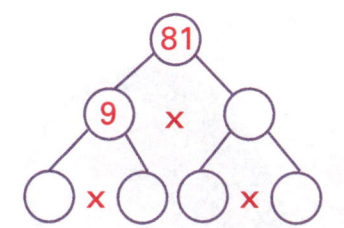

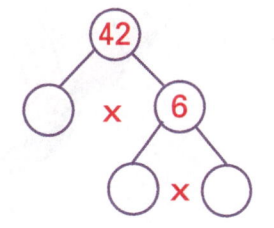

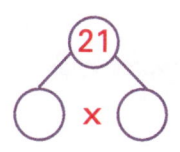

81
9 × ◯
◯ × ◯    ◯ × ◯

42
◯ × 6
◯ × ◯

21
◯ × ◯

Horizons Math 5, Student Workbook 1   111

**Lesson 36**

## Multiplication by a Two-Digit Factor

Each of the 24 first grade students needed 21 pieces of macaroni to make a necklace. How much macaroni did the teacher need in all?

| Multiply by the ones. | Multiply by the tens. | Add the products. |
|---|---|---|
| 24<br>x 21<br>24 (1 x 24) | 24<br>x 21<br>24<br>480 (20 x 24) | 24<br>x 21<br>24<br>+ 480<br>504 |

The teacher needs 504 pieces of macaroni.

**1** Multiply.

| 63 | 99 | 89 | 259 | 191 |
|---|---|---|---|---|
| x 21 | x 13 | x 28 | x 32 | x 36 |

**2** Find the missing number.

| 367 | 811 | 500 | 301 | 2?8 |
|---|---|---|---|---|
| − 10? | − 4?9 | − ?89 | − ?90 | − 109 |
| 259 | 322 | 111 | 11 | 149 |

? = ____    ? = ____    ? = ____    ? = ____    ? = ____

**3** Solve.

27 − (3 × 3) = _____     11 + (8 ÷ 4) = _____     (36 ÷ 4) − 2 = _____

(9 × 9) + 19 = _____     (24 + 6) − 10 = _____     21 ÷ (12 − 9) = _____

Make the statement true by adding parentheses in the proper place.

3 × 9 + 5 = 32     8 × 13 − 4 = 72     12 ÷ 3 + 8 = 12

**4** Find the product.

3 × 10 =          3 × 100 =         3 × 1,000 =

21 × 10 =         21 × 100 =        21 × 1,000 =

77 × 60 =         77 × 600 =        77 × 6,000 =

92 × 30 =         92 × 300 =        92 × 3,000 =

**5** Use a factor tree to find prime numbers.

[Factor trees for 36, 45, and 25]

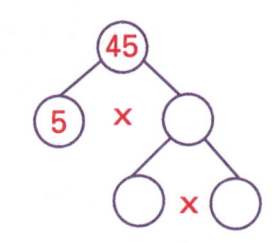

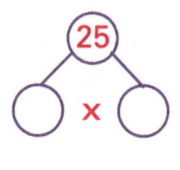

**6** If the number is composite, write the prime factors. If the number is prime, shade in the letter box. The shaded boxes will solve the riddle: **What animal keeps the best time?**

The first two have been done for you.

| 3  | W |       | 24 | H |  |
|----|---|-------|----|---|--|
| 6  | L | 2 x 3 | 7  | D |  |
| 5  | A |       | 10 | B |  |
| 9  | A |       | 21 | R |  |
| 37 | T |       | 19 | O |  |
| 40 | C |       | 8  | G |  |
| 12 | L |       | 17 | G |  |
| 16 | D |       | 25 | A |  |
| 29 | C |       | 32 | A |  |
| 4  | L |       | 4  | I |  |
| 11 | H |       | 14 | N |  |

**7** Find the products.

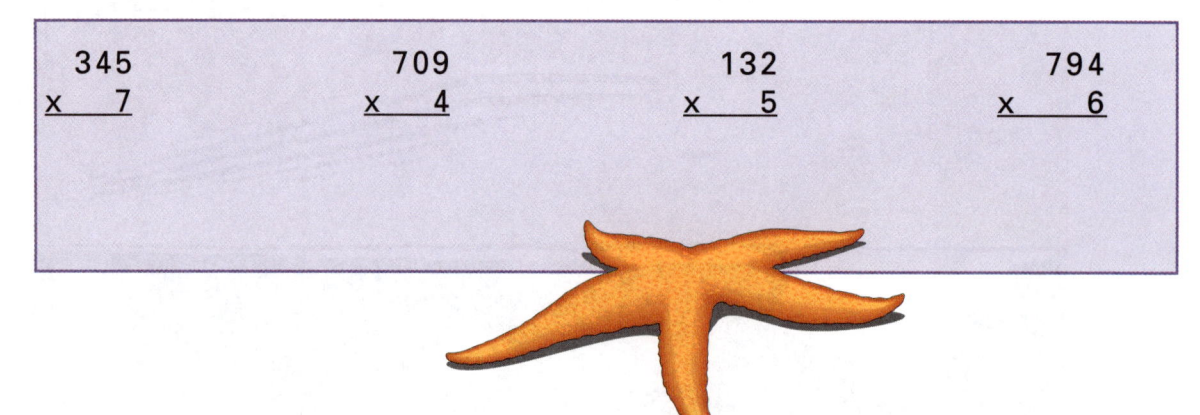

```
  345        709        132        794
x   7      x   4      x   5      x   6
```

114 Horizons Math 5, Student Workbook 1

**Lesson 37**

## Multiplication by a Three-Digit Factor

Magic Mac's Hamburger stand sells, on the average, 237 hamburgers a day. At this rate, how many hamburgers will he sell in a year (365 days)?

| Multiply by the ones. | Multiply by the tens. | Multiply by the hundreds. | Add the products. |
|---|---|---|---|

(237 x 5)     (237 x 60)     (237 x 300)

```
    237         237         237         237
  x 365       x 365       x 365       x 365
  1,185       1,185       1,185       1,185
             14,220      14,220      14,220
                         71,100      71,100
                                     86,505
```

Magic Mac will sell 86,505 hamburgers in a year at the given rate.

**1** Multiply. Find the answer in the data bank and the corresponding letter. Place the letter under each product to solve the riddle: **What do you call bread in a bank?**

| 305,805 U | 67,640 D | 79,272 H | 76,680 O | 125,222 G |

```
    356         360         703         493         216
  x 190       x 213       x 435       x 254       x 367
```

___  ___  ___  ___  ___

**2** Find the product.

```
     63          59          32          19          28
   x 35        x 73        x 45        x 27        x 49
```

**3** Find each sum.

| 34,992 | 103,947 | 813,089 | 23,568 |
|---|---|---|---|
| + 13,987 | + 389,268 | + 209,352 | + 56,909 |

**4** Find each sum. Label the first problem.

| 6 _____ | 5 | 7 | 9 | 6 | 3 | 2 |
|---|---|---|---|---|---|---|
| + 7 _____ | + 7 | + 8 | + 9 | + 8 | + 7 | + 9 |

**5** Multiply.

| 504 | 416 | 933 | 296 | 190 |
|---|---|---|---|---|
| x 8 | x 4 | x 3 | x 8 | x 5 |

**6** Find the product.

3 x 5 =

3 x 50 =

3 x 500 =

3 x 5,000 =

30 x 50 =

30 x 500 =

300 x 500 =

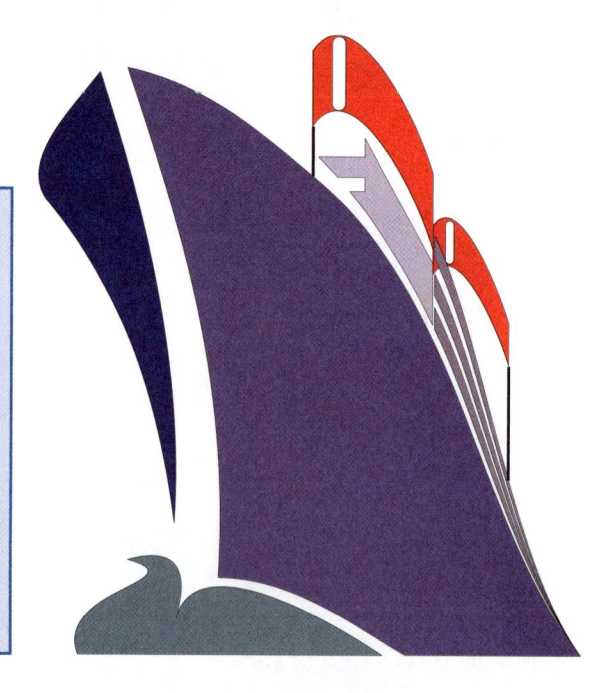

**7** Match each number with its prime factors. Place the letter next to the correct answer in the boxes below to solve the riddle, *What works best when there is something in its eye?* Use factors trees to help you.

1. The prime factors of 9.
   - 2 x 2 — T
   - 2 x 2 x 5 x 5 — B
   - 3 x 3 — A
   - 3 x 3 x 2 — T

2. The prime factors of 12.
   - 2 x 3 x 3 — M
   - 2 x 5 — I
   - 2 x 3 — E
   - 2 x 2 x 3 — N

3. The prime factors of 20.
   - 2 x 2 x 5 — E
   - 3 x 7 — C
   - 2 x 5 — H
   - 2 x 2 x 3 — B

4. The prime factors of 21.
   - 3 x 7 — E
   - 2 x 3 x 5 — B
   - 5 x 5 — T
   - 2 x 2 x 2 — N

5. The prime factors of 18.
   - 2 x 3 x 3 — D
   - 2 x 3 x 5 — A
   - 2 x 3 x 7 — I
   - 2 x 2 x 3 — R

6. The prime factors of 30.
   - 2 x 3 x 5 — L
   - 2 x 5 — N
   - 2 x 3 x 3 — D
   - 5 x 5 — B

7. The prime factors of 15.
   - 2 x 5 — U
   - 3 x 3 x 5 — T
   - 3 x 5 — E
   - 5 x 5 — D

   A   N   E   E   D   L   E
   1   2   3   4   5   6   7

**Lesson 38**

## Estimating Products

We often estimate or approximate answers for everyday problems in life.
For example, Amy wanted to buy 4 boxes of macaroni and cheese for $0.89 apiece.
What is her total cost?

$$4 \times \mathbf{89} =$$

To estimate, round the 89 to 90.

$$4 \times \mathbf{90} = 360$$

It will cost approximately $3.60 to buy 4 boxes of macaroni and cheese.

**1** Estimate by rounding two-digit numbers to the nearest ten and three-digit numbers to the nearest hundred.

| | | | |
|---|---|---|---|
| 3 × 562 = | 7 × 69 = | 8 × 484 = | 2 × 482 = |
| 11 × 48 = | 18 × 78 = | 48 × 302 = | 57 × 597 = |

**2** Find the product.

2 × 6 =

2 × 60 =

2 × 600 =

2 × 6,000 =

20 × 60 =

20 × 600 =

200 × 600 =

**3** Find the products. Beside each answer is a letter. Place that letter in the puzzle above the corresponding product. (For example: 12 x 4 = 48 = M, an M has been placed over the number 48.)

| 304<br>x 45<br>= L | 310<br>x 176<br>= W | 913<br>x 421<br>= Y | 423<br>x 218<br>= D | 276<br>x 302<br>= K |
|---|---|---|---|---|
| 93<br>x 47<br>= H | 52<br>x 18<br>= E | 78<br>x 60<br>= F | 34<br>x 24<br>= N | 25<br>x 42<br>= O |
| 18<br>x 9<br>= S | 63<br>x 7<br>= R | 45<br>x 5<br>= U | 29<br>x 2<br>= T | 25<br>x 3<br>= A |

___  ___  ___  ___  ___
75  816  92,214  384,373  936

___  ___  ___  ___
162  4371  75  13,680 13,680

___  ___  ___  ___
83,352  816  1,050  54,560

___  ___  ___
58  4371  936

___  ___  ___  ___  ___  ___  ___  ___  ___  ___  ___
58  441  225  58  4,371  75  816  92,214  58  4,371  936

___  ___  ___  ___  ___  ___  ___  ___  ___  ___
58  441  225  58  4,371  162  4,371  75  13,680 13,680

**M** ___  ___  ___  ___  ___  ___  ___  ___  ___  ___ !
48  75  83,352  936  384,373  1,050  225  4,680  441  936  936

*John 8:32*

**4** Find the difference. Label the first problem.

| 16<br>− 7<br>___ | 15<br>− 7 | 17<br>− 8 | 19<br>− 9 | 16<br>− 8 | 13<br>− 7 | 12<br>− 9 | 14<br>− 7 |
|---|---|---|---|---|---|---|---|

**5** Subtract. Find the answer and the corresponding letter in the data bank. There are some answers in the data bank that will not be used. Write the letter in the space provided under each problem to complete the verse: *Be not forgetful to entertain strangers: for thereby some have entertained _____ unawares.  Hebrews 13:2.*

| 380 B | 348 L | 193 S | 22,801 T | 10,101 N |
|---|---|---|---|---|
| 20,046 G | 608 P | 1,359 E | 22,818 A | |

$$\begin{array}{r} 35{,}798 \\ -\ 12{,}980 \end{array} \quad \begin{array}{r} 39{,}002 \\ -\ 28{,}901 \end{array} \quad \begin{array}{r} 71{,}095 \\ -\ 51{,}049 \end{array} \quad \begin{array}{r} 8{,}251 \\ -\ 6{,}892 \end{array} \quad \begin{array}{r} 9{,}436 \\ -\ 9{,}088 \end{array} \quad \begin{array}{r} 12{,}094 \\ -\ 11{,}901 \end{array}$$

**6** Solve the equations and check.

$n + 33 = 75$

Check

$n + 53 = 99$

Check

$n + 68 = 197$

Check

$n + 44 = 131$

Check

$n + 27 = 129$

Check

$n + 113 = 246$

Check

**Lesson 39**

## Multiplication Equations

A number sentence which contains an equal sign is called an **equation**.
A **variable** is a letter that stands for a number.

$n \times 4 = 8$
$\div 4 = \div 4$
$n = 2$

1. To solve an equation the variable ($n$) must be alone on one side. On the left side $n$ is multiplied by 4, so we must divide by 4 to eliminate it.
2. Whatever is done to one side of the equation, must be done to the other. Also divide the right side by 4.
3. $n = 2$

**Check**
$n \times 4 = 8$
$2 \times 4 = 8$

1. Plug the answer back into the original problem to check.

**1** Solve the equations and check.

$n \times 9 = 81$
$\div \qquad \div$

Check

$n \times 7 = 56$
$\div \qquad \div$

Check

$n \times 3 = 36$
$\div \qquad \div$

Check

$n \times 9 = 72$
$\div \qquad \div$

Check

$n \times 10 = 90$
$\div \qquad \div$

Check

$n \times 6 = 36$
$\div \qquad \div$

Check

**2** Estimate by rounding two-digit numbers to the nearest ten and three-digit numbers to the nearest hundred.

| 7 x 580 = | 9 x 169 = | 3 x 448 = | 2 x 122 = |
| 19 x 98 = | 12 x 28 = | 49 x 702 = | 97 x 597 = |

**3** Define the polygons using the following names: square, decagon, pentagon, octagon, and hexagon.

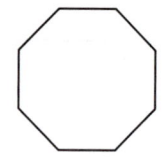

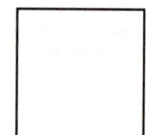

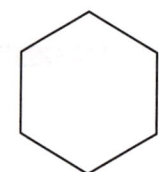

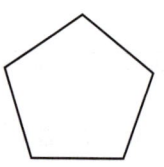

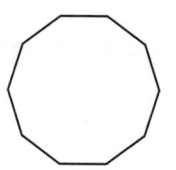

_____   _____   _____   _____   _____

**4** Solve the equations and check.

$n - 31 = 69$
+        +
_____

Check

$n - 83 = 104$
+        +
_____

Check

$n - 68 = 97$
+        +
_____

Check

$n - 14 = 31$
+        +
_____

Check

$n - 26 = 79$
+        +
_____

Check

$n - 33 = 46$
+        +
_____

Check

5. Multiply. Follow the products through the maze from the smallest to largest number.

Finish ↓

| 8 x 5 | 6 x 8 | 9 x 11 | 4 x 9 | 9 x 9 | 8 x 9 |
| --- | --- | --- | --- | --- | --- |
| 9 x 4 | 9 x 5 | 9 x 10 | 5 x 9 | 7 x 8 | 6 x 7 |
| 11 x 3 | 8 x 4 | 6 x 5 | 9 x 8 | 6 x 8 | 8 x 8 |
| 9 x 6 | 5 x 7 | 9 x 3 | 5 x 5 | 6 x 4 | 5 x 7 |
| 8 x 2 | 6 x 3 | 4 x 5 | 7 x 3 | 11 x 2 | 4 x 10 |
| 3 x 5 | 7 x 2 | 3 x 4 | 6 x 7 | 6 x 6 | 4 x 7 |
| 6 x 5 | 4 x 7 | 2 x 5 | 9 x 1 | 4 x 2 | 3 x 2 |
| 3 x 3 | 7 x 7 | 7 x 6 | 4 x 5 | 2 x 2 | 5 x 1 |
| 2 x 4 | 9 x 1 | 1 x 1 | 2 x 1 | 3 x 1 | 9 x 2 |
| 7 x 7 | 6 x 8 | 2 x 0 | 4 x 1 | 8 x 1 | 7 x 1 |

Start ↑

6. Find the products. Place the numbers in order from smallest to largest. The corresponding letter will spell a word that solves the riddle: **What animal needs to wear a wig?** The first one has been done for you.

|  45  |  38  |  94  |  53  |  28  |
| --- | --- | --- | --- | --- |
| x 78 | x 80 | x 14 | x 67 | x 73 |
| 3,510 = L | = A | = A | = D | = B |

|  341  |  808  |  403  |  392  |  310  |
| --- | --- | --- | --- | --- |
| x 210 | x 411 | x 291 | x 128 | x 931 |
| = A | = E | = G | = E | = L |

_____ _____ _____ _L_ _____   _____ _____ _____ _____ _____
1,316  2,044  3,040  3,510  3,551   50,176  71,610  117,273  288,610  332,088

# Exponents

Lesson 40

**Exponents** show how many times a number is used as a factor. It is expressed by placing a small number next to the number that is the base.

This number is called the base. → $10^2$ ← This number is called the exponent.

| | | | |
|---|---|---|---|
| 10 squared, or 10 to the second power | $10^2$ | 10 x 10 | = 100 |
| 10 cubed, or 10 to the third power | $10^3$ | 10 x 10 x 10 | = 1,000 |
| 10 to the fourth power | $10^4$ | 10 x 10 x 10 x 10 | = 10,000 |
| 10 to the fifth power | $10^5$ | 10 x 10 x 10 x 10 x 10 | = 100,000 |

Here are some other numbers with exponents.

$7^3$ = 7 x 7 x 7 = 343    $4^2$ = 4 x 4 = 16    $3^4$ = 3 x 3 x 3 x 3 = 81

**1** Complete the table.

| | Factors | Product | Exponent | Number of Zeros |
|---|---|---|---|---|
| $10^2$ | | | | |
| $10^3$ | | | | |
| $10^4$ | | | | |
| $10^5$ | | | | |
| $10^6$ | | | | |

**2** Solve the equations and check.

| $n$ x 5 = 40 | $n$ x 7 = 56 | $n$ x 9 = 54 |
|---|---|---|
| ÷       ÷ | ÷       ÷ | ÷       ÷ |
| Check | Check | Check |

**3** Estimate by rounding two-digit numbers to the nearest ten and three-digit numbers to the nearest hundred.

| 2 x 430 = | 9 x 119 = | 3 x 821 = | 2 x 122 = |
|---|---|---|---|
| 11 x 91 = | 19 x 78 = | 89 x 582 = | 97 x 231 = |

**4** Match the picture, definition, and name of the shapes.

| Cone | All points are the same distance from the center. |
| Cylinder | 2 parallel bases that are not polygons; curved sides. |
| Pyramid | This figure has curved sides. The base is not a polygon. |
| Sphere | All faces are triangles that meet at a point. |
| Prism | All faces are rectangles with two parallel polygon bases. |

**5** Find the products.

| 398 | 815 | 402 | 311 | 298 |
|---|---|---|---|---|
| x  38 | x 107 | x 125 | x 309 | x 302 |

**6** Find the products.

| x | 5 | 6 |
|---|---|---|
| 3 |   |   |
| 4 |   |   |
| 5 |   |   |

| x | 5 | 9 |
|---|---|---|
| 0 |   |   |
| 1 |   |   |
| 7 |   |   |

| x | 2 | 3 |
|---|---|---|
| 5 |   |   |
| 6 |   |   |
| 7 |   |   |

**7** Shade the prime numbers to see the answer to the riddle: *What creature is a big grouch?*

| 37 | 3  | 11 | 20 | 5  | 47 | 41 | 10 | 32 | 7  | 5  | 3  | 10 | 17 | 41 | 45 |
|----|----|----|----|----|----|----|----|----|----|----|----|----|----|----|----|
| 31 | 16 | 21 | 4  | 7  | 4  | 43 | 12 | 45 | 19 | 4  | 5  | 12 | 11 | 35 | 43 |
| 19 | 18 | 60 | 14 | 13 | 3  | 30 | 14 | 30 | 17 | 11 | 7  | 16 | 7  | 41 | 25 |
| 17 | 8  | 6  | 24 | 11 | 6  | 17 | 15 | 25 | 13 | 22 | 2  | 18 | 5  | 12 | 5  |
| 5  | 23 | 29 | 12 | 2  | 8  | 4  | 7  | 42 | 11 | 6  | 3  | 42 | 3  | 3  | 14 |

126  Horizons Math 5, Student Workbook 1

Test 4

**1** Find the difference. 8 pts. total for this exercise.

| 7,470 | 842,098 | 1,748 | 13,572 |
|---|---|---|---|
| − 2,082 | − 434,132 | − 962 | − 12,835 |

| 4,953 | 25,045 | 66,324 | 647,081 |
|---|---|---|---|
| − 1,790 | − 8,438 | − 26,275 | − 179,000 |

**2** Estimate by rounding to the indicated place. 9 pts. total for this exercise.

Nearest 10

| 44 | 92 | 136 |
|---|---|---|
| − 27 | − 28 | − 87 |

Nearest 100

| 526 | 1,397 | 1,807 |
|---|---|---|
| − 376 | − 765 | − 498 |

Nearest 1,000

| 7,697 | 21,203 | 8,437 |
|---|---|---|
| − 2,876 | − 9,783 | − 1,129 |

**3** Find the sum or difference. 8 pts. total for this exercise.

| $235.97 | $571.21 | $890.71 | $667.09 |
|---|---|---|---|
| − 183.22 | − 42.29 | − 599.22 | − 432.55 |

| $5.98 | $17.54 | $4.16 | $19.78 |
|---|---|---|---|
| + 8.18 | + 10.25 | + 4.03 | + 2.99 |

**4** Use the Four Steps to a Solution to solve these problems. Remember to look for key words to help you know which operation to use. 3 pts. total for this exercise.

How Many?   How Much?   Difference?

1. Mrs. Jones' class opened a school store. Suzanne bought a notebook for $5.00, a dozen pencils for $2.00, and one package of notebook paper for $1.50. How much money did Suzanne spend?

2. Steve purchased 12 erasers and gave away 3. Then he bought 2 more. How many erasers did he have then?

3. Ashley spent $4.50 on folders and $3.00 on notebook paper. If she had a $10.00 bill how much money does she still have?

**5** Complete the factor trees. 6 pts. total for this exercise.

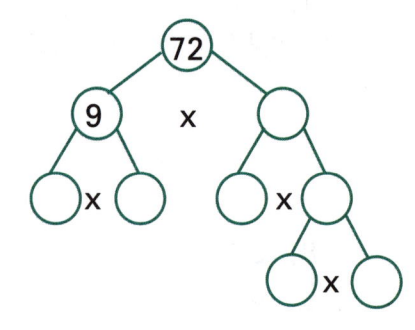

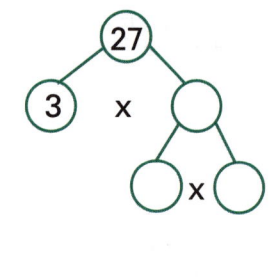

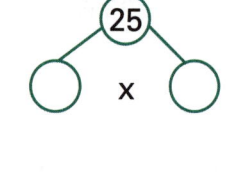

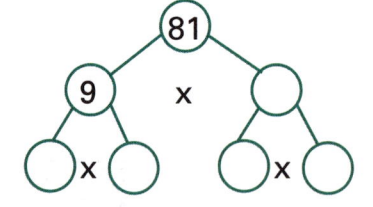

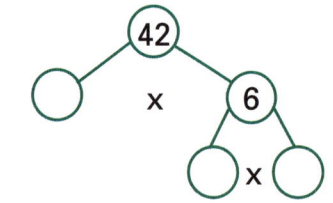

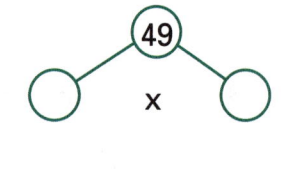

[Factor tree for 72: 9 × __; with further branches]
[Factor tree for 27: 3 × __; with further branches]
[Factor tree for 25: __ × __]

[Factor tree for 81: 9 × __; with further branches]
[Factor tree for 42: __ × 6; with further branches]
[Factor tree for 49: __ × __]

**6** Find the product. 5 pts. total for this exercise.

| 50 | 900 | 30 | 600 | 4,000 |
|---|---|---|---|---|
| × 20 | × 20 | × 80 | × 50 | × 700 |

39 pts. Total

**Lesson 41**

## Division

Sandy had 38 pieces of candy to put into 9 plastic Easter eggs for the annual Easter egg hunt. If she placed an equal amount in each bag, how many pieces of candy will be in each bag? How many pieces will be left over?

We divide:

$$\begin{array}{r} 4\ \text{R}2 \\ 9\overline{)38} \\ -36 \\ \hline 2 \end{array}$$

Subtract → 
9 x 4

Sandy will put 4 pieces of candy in each egg. There will be 2 pieces left over.

Check to see that the remainder is less than the divisor. If it is not, recheck the problem for errors.

We check:

$$\begin{array}{r} 4 \\ \times\ 9 \\ \hline 36 \\ +\ 2 \\ \hline 38 \end{array}$$

To check, multiply the quotient by the divisor. Add the remainder.

The sum should equal the dividend.

**1** Divide and check.

$6\overline{)25}$    $5\overline{)32}$    $4\overline{)17}$    $3\overline{)20}$    $6\overline{)38}$

**2** Find the sum.

| 23 | 561 | 89 | 451 | 781 | 25 |
|---|---|---|---|---|---|
| + 31 | + 250 | + 15 | + 108 | + 312 | + 10 |

**3** Use a factor tree to find prime numbers. Write the missing numbers in the circles.

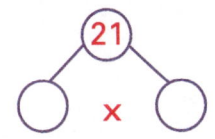

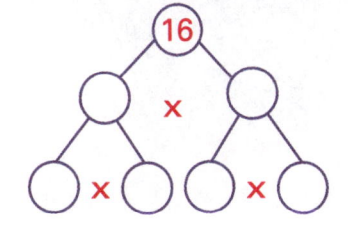

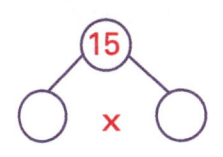

21     16     15

4. Write the correct english unit of measure.

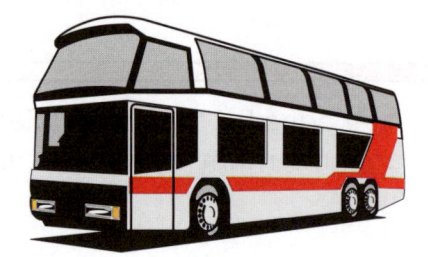

The bus weighs 12 ____.

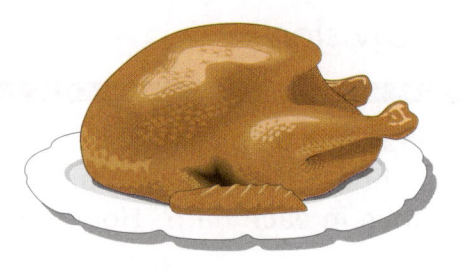

The turkey weighs 9 ____.

The can weighs 12 ____.

5. Write the temperature in Fahrenheit degrees.

Water freezes at ____.

Normal body temperature is ____.

Water boils at ____.

**6** Name the century in which each year would belong.

1867 \_\_\_\_\_

1905 \_\_\_\_\_

987 \_\_\_\_\_

1256 \_\_\_\_\_

1598 \_\_\_\_\_

**7** Label the missing information and multiply.

5
x 6

4
x 7

3
x 2

9
x 5

2
x 10

6
x 8

7
x 8

Lesson 42

# Division – One- and Two-Digit Quotients

There are 178 boxes of crackers to be packed and shipped from the factory to the Sim's Grocery Store. Each large box holds 6 cartons of crackers. How many boxes will be needed to hold all 178 boxes of crackers? How many cartons will be left over?

We Divide:

Think: 17 ÷ 6      Think: 58 ÷ 6

Multiply
   6 × 2 = 12 ⟶ 2
              6)178

Subtract
   17 − 12 = 5 ⟶ 5
             −12

         29 R 4
        6)178
          −12
           58
          −54
            4

Multiply
   6 × 9 = 54

Subtract
   58 − 54 = 4

The factory will need 29 boxes. There will be 4 cartons left over.

Some students find that memorizing the steps used in division is helpful. One class made this saying for easy memorization. See how it works using the problem above.

| **D**o | **D**IVIDE - How many 6s are in 17? |
| **M**any | **M**ULTIPLY - Multiply 2 × 6. |
| **S**tudents | **S**UBTRACT - Subtract 12 from 17. |
| **C**ollect | **C**HECK - Is 4 less than the divisor? |
| **B**ugs? | **B**RING DOWN - Bring down the 8. |

**1** Rewrite each problem. Divide and check. The first one is done for you.

            15 R2
47 ÷ 3 = 3)47
             3
            17
            15
             2

55 ÷ 3 =       68 ÷ 5 =

137 ÷ 8 =      148 ÷ 9 =

132 Horizons Math 5, Student Workbook 1

**2** Divide and check.

$89 \div 9 =$     $56 \div 9 =$     $43 \div 7 =$     $33 \div 4 =$

$27 \div 5 =$     $11 \div 4 =$     $43 \div 5 =$     $21 \div 6 =$

**3** Find the answers in the puzzle below. Color each answer shape red and reveal a picture.

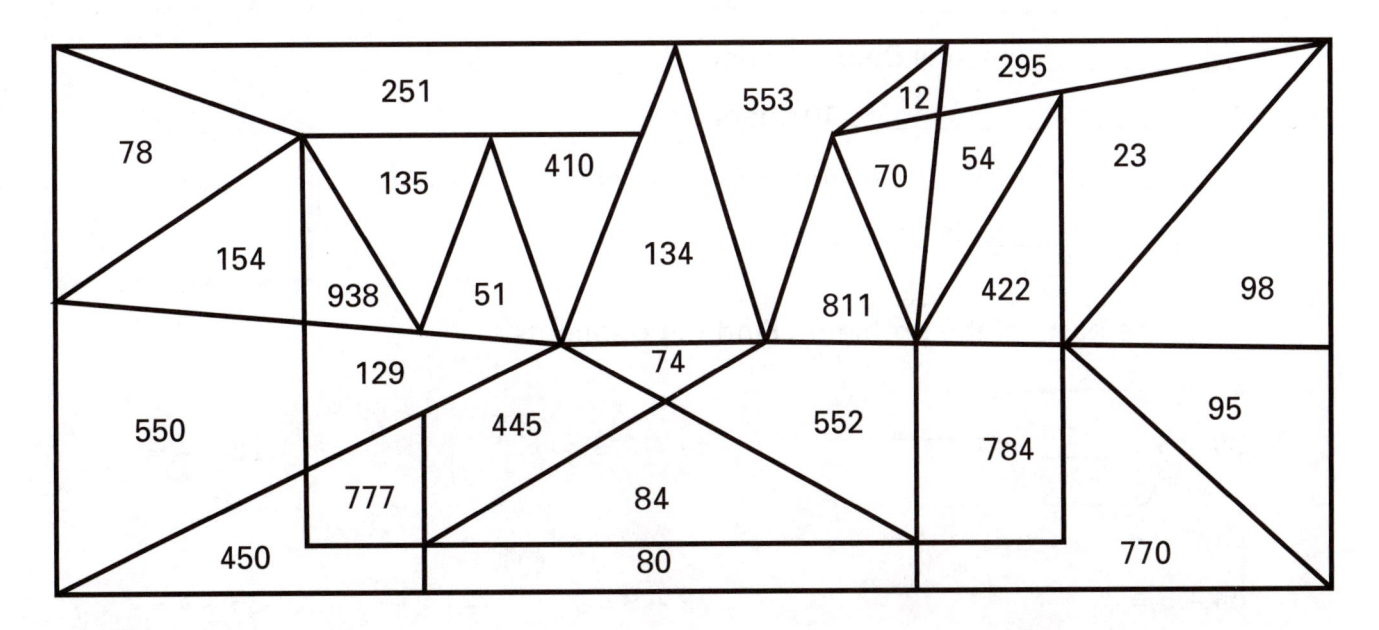

| 53 | 75 | 224 | 39 | 141 | 321 |
|---|---|---|---|---|---|
| + 21 | + 54 | + 198 | + 12 | + 304 | + 231 |

| 784 | 61 | 89 | 570 | 634 | 456 |
|---|---|---|---|---|---|
| + 154 | + 23 | + 45 | + 241 | + 143 | + 328 |

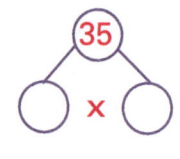

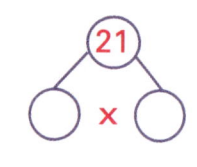

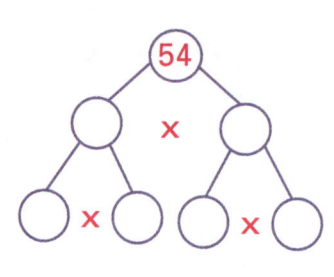

**4** Write in the missing factors on each factor tree.

**5** Look at the following items. Would each one be measured in feet, yards, or miles?

The small room was 7 _____ long. (feet, yards, or miles)

The ceiling was 8 _____ tall. (feet, yards, or miles)

The house was 10 _____ from town. (feet, yards, or miles)

The football field was 120 _____ long. (feet, yards, or miles)

Complete.

6 yd = _____ ft          2 miles = _____ yd          24 yd = _____ ft

220 yd = _____ ft        24 ft = _____ yd

**6** Fill in the blanks.

A _____ is 100 years.

_____ means Before Christ.

A _____ is 10 years.

_____ means *anno Domini* or *in the year of our Lord*

A _____ is 1,000 years.

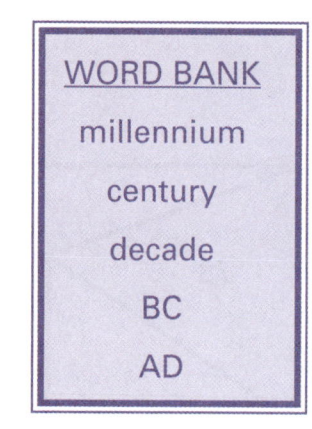

WORD BANK
millennium
century
decade
BC
AD

**7** Label the parts of the problem. Find the quotients.

30 ÷ 5 = _____          48 ÷ 8 =          28 ÷ 4 =

54 ÷ 9 =                72 ÷ 9 =          36 ÷ 4 =

# Lesson 43

## One- and Two-digit Quotient Division

Money is divided in the same way as any larger number. The only additional step is to line up the decimal point before you begin to divide. Look at the example below.

A package of four pens cost $3.72. How much are you paying for each pen?

**We divide:**

```
        $0.93
    4 )$3.72
      - 3 6
          12
        - 12
           0
```

Put the decimal point in the quotient over the decimal point in the dividend.

**Don't Forget**
1. Divide
2. Multiply
3. Subtract
4. Check
5. Bring Down

Each pen costs $ .93.

Five pieces of candy costs $ .35. How much does one cost?

**We divide:**

```
        $0.07
    5 )$0.35
       - 35
          0
```

When a quotient is less than ten cents, put a zero in the tenths' place.

Each piece of candy costs $ .07.

**1** Find the quotient.

9)$ .72    4)$4.32    5)$10.15    2)$1.60

**2** Find the quotient.

7)194    6)63    8)279    4)37    9)75

**3** Find the sum.

| | | | | |
|---|---|---|---|---|
| 154,891 | 12,891 | 2,451 | 1,003 | 165,781 |
| + 345,005 | + 1,087 | + 1,887 | + 2,543 | + 154,008 |

**4** Color the prime numbers yellow if they are larger than 50.
Color the prime numbers brown if they are smaller than 50.
Color the composite numbers green.

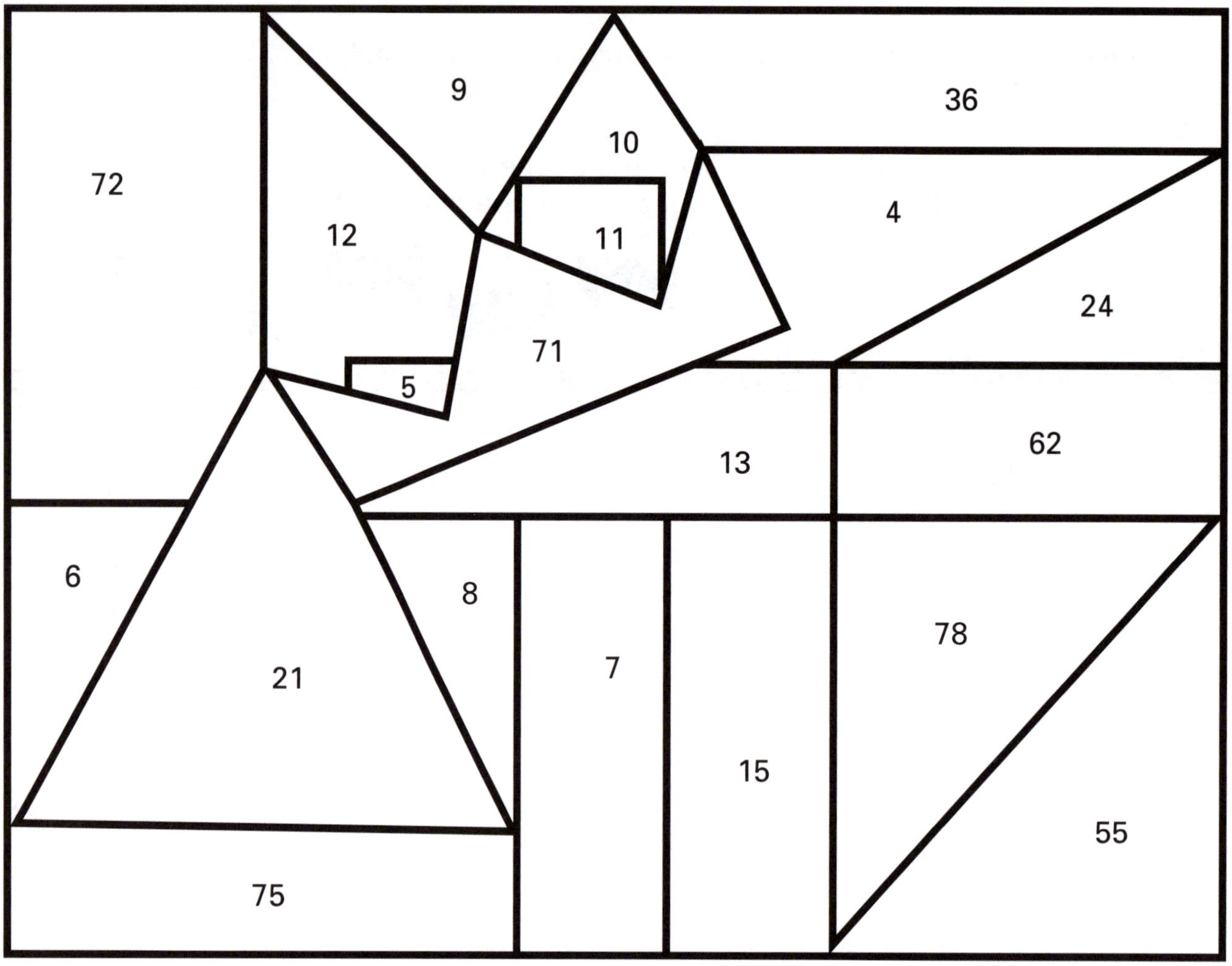

72
9
10
36
12
11
4
24
71
5
13
62
6
8
21
7
78
15
55
75

**5** Solve.

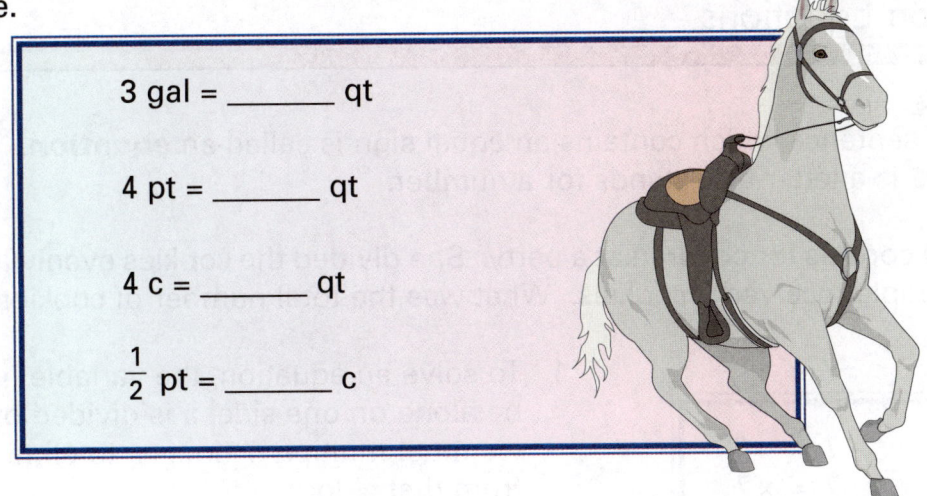

3 gal = _____ qt

4 pt = _____ qt

4 c = _____ qt

$\frac{1}{2}$ pt = _____ c

**6** Find the missing addends.

```
   ?        10         ?        98         ?        50
 + 8       + ?       + 45       + ?       + 5       + ?
  13        25         68       118        18        95
```

**7** Find the products.

$3^2$  $4^2$  $5^2$

$2^3$  $10^2$

# Lesson 44

## Division Equations

**Equations**
A number sentence which contains an equal sign is called an **equation**. A **variable** is a letter that stands for a number.

Susan had cookies for children at a party. She divided the cookies evenly and each of the 7 people received 2 cookies. What was the total number of cookies?

$$n \div 7 = 2$$
$$\times 7 = \times 7$$
$$n = 14$$

1. To solve an equation, the variable ($n$) must be alone on one side. $n$ is divided by 7, so we must multiply 7 times $n$ to eliminate it from that side.

2. Whatever is done to one side of the equation must be done to the other. Multiply 7 times the right side, also.

3. $n = 14$. There were 14 cookies total.

**Check:**

$n \div 7 = 2$
$14 \div 7 = 2$

1. Plug the answer back into the original problem to check.

**1** Solve the equations and check.

$n \div 3 = 9$      $n \div 5 = 5$      $n \div 7 = 5$
× × × × × ×

Check      Check      Check

$n \div 4 = 5$      $n \div 5 = 9$      $n \div 8 = 9$
× × × × × ×

Check      Check      Check

## 2. Find the quotient.

5)$7.25   3)$18.48   8)$51.20   4)$8.08

## 3. Find the quotient.

9)589   7)487   6)475   4)123

## 4. Match the problem and the answer.

406 x 7 =        5,832

361 x 3 =        2,842

263 x 4 =        1,083

729 x 8 =        1,052

**5** Circle the problems with the incorrect answers. Then correct them.

|  6,909 | 536,250 | 582,731 | 68,214 | 80,342 |
|---|---|---|---|---|
| + 1,828 | + 236,695 | + 48,046 | + 1,850 | + 19,517 |
|  8,737 | 770,845 | 637,707 | 70,064 | 89,588 |

**6** Give the digit that holds the specified place value in the number below.

226,504,825,986

_____ Thousands      _____ Hundred millions

_____ Hundreds       _____ Hundred billions

_____ Ten thousands  _____ Tens

_____ Ten millions   _____ Billions

**7** Find the missing addend and reveal the message.

| ? P | ? O | ? A | 13 | ? A |
|---|---|---|---|---|
| + 6 | + 7 | + 7 | + ? A | + 20 |
| 14 | 14 | 16 | 18 | 41 |

| 11 | ? H | 21 | ? E | ? G |
|---|---|---|---|---|
| + ? M | + 4 | + ? L | + 30 | + 25 |
| 21 | 17 | 46 | 80 | 100 |

___ ___ ___ ___ ___ & ___ ___ ___ ___ ___
21  25  8  13  9      7  10  50  75  5

**Revelation 22: 12a & 13**

Lesson 45

## Two- and Three-digit Quotient Division

The Crown Chewing Gum Company had 6,646 sticks of gum that needed to be packaged. If each package can hold 9 sticks of gum, how many packages will there be? Will there be any extra sticks left over?

**Don't Forget**
1. Divide
2. Multiply
3. Subtract
4. Check
5. Bring Down

We Divide:

### STEP 1

Think: 66 ÷ 9

Multiply
$9 \times 7 = 63$ ⟶ 7
$\phantom{00}$ 9)6,646
Subtract $\phantom{0}$ − 6 3
$66 - 63 = 3$ $\phantom{000}$ 3

### STEP 2

Think: 34 ÷ 9

$\phantom{00}$ 73 ⟵ Multiply
9)6,646 $\phantom{000}$ $9 \times 3 = 27$
− 6,3
$\phantom{0}$ 34
− 27 ⟵ Subtract
$\phantom{00}$ 7

### STEP 3

Think: 76 ÷ 9

$\phantom{00}$ 738 R4 ⟵ Multiply
9)6,646 $\phantom{000}$ $9 \times 8 = 72$
− 6 3
$\phantom{0}$ 34
− 27
$\phantom{0}$ 76 $\phantom{00}$ Subtract
− 72 ⟵ $\phantom{00}$ $76 - 72 = 4$
$\phantom{00}$ 4

The factory will need 738 packages. There will be 4 sticks left over.

**1** Find the quotient.

$\phantom{00}$ 7)2,385 $\phantom{0000000}$ 7)3,223 $\phantom{0000000}$ 6)4,183

**2** Match the problem and the answer.

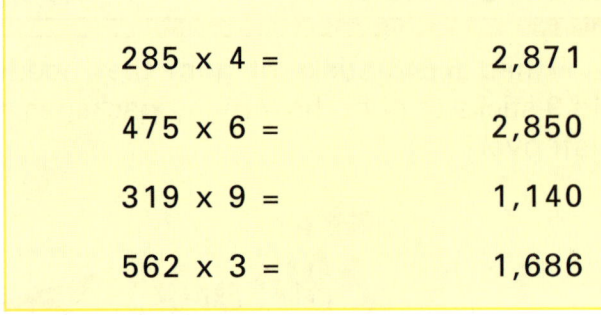

| | |
|---|---|
| 285 x 4 = | 2,871 |
| 475 x 6 = | 2,850 |
| 319 x 9 = | 1,140 |
| 562 x 3 = | 1,686 |

**3** Find the quotient amount.

$3\overline{)\$1.83}$   $6\overline{)\$25.56}$   $4\overline{)\$23.88}$

$5\overline{)\$55.00}$   $4\overline{)\$1.68}$

**4** Match the remainder with the appropriate answer.

$6\overline{)207}$   $7\overline{)394}$   $6\overline{)167}$   $5\overline{)394}$

R 4   R 2   R 3   R 5

**5** Find the difference. Order the answers from smallest to largest to reveal a message.

| 439 | 75 | 93 | 981 | 44 |
|---|---|---|---|---|
| − 367 | − 17 | − 48 | − 457 | − 21 |
| **C** | **A** | **R** | **E** | **G** |

___  ___  ___  ___  ___

**Proverbs 3:34**

142 Horizons Math 5, Student Workbook 1

**6** Solve.

Write the greatest number possible with 5 in the hundred thousands' place using the digits in 347,325,623.

_____

Write the smallest number possible with 1 in the hundred millions' place using the digits in 185,295,237.

_____

Write the largest number possible with 8 in the tens' place using the digits in 638,453,521.

_____

**7** Sunday School Attendance for April

1. What was the difference in the total attendance for the entire month of April in 1996 and 1997?

2. Look at week 1 and week 4. What was the total difference in attendance between these two weeks in 1996? In 1997?

3. What is the difference in attendance for each week in 1996 and each week in 1997?

**Lesson 46**

# Division with Zeros in the Quotient

Zeros in the Quotient

**Don't Forget**

1. Divide
2. Multiply
3. Subtract
4. Check
5. Bring Down

There are 153 students preparing for field day. The students need to be put into groups of seven. How many groups of seven will there be? Are there any students left over who will form a smaller group?

**We divide:**

```
      20 R3
   ┌──────
 7 │ 143
   − 14
   ─────
      03
    −  0
   ─────
       3
```

Be careful when there are zeros in the quotient.

There will be 20 groups of seven on field day. Three students will form a smaller group.

**1** Find the quotient. Watch out for the zeros!

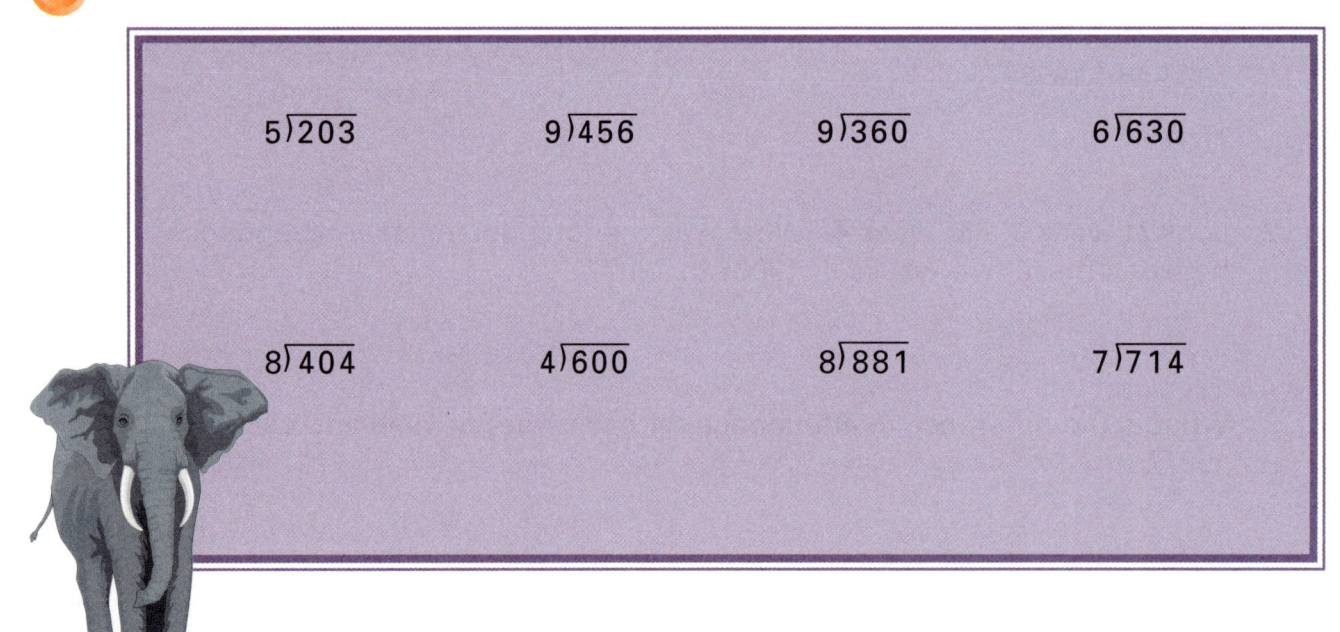

5)203   9)456   9)360   6)630

8)404   4)600   8)881   7)714

144 Horizons Math 5, Student Workbook 1

**2** Find the quotient.

$8\overline{)3{,}627}$  $\qquad$ $5\overline{)3{,}947}$  $\qquad$ $4\overline{)1{,}558}$

**3** Find the product.

| 53 | 39 | 86 | 75 | 62 |
|---|---|---|---|---|
| x 47 | x 68 | x 74 | x 33 | x 57 |

**4** Match the problem with the appropriate answer.

$9\overline{)\$7.92}$

$4\overline{)\$23.88}$

$8\overline{)\$37.68}$

$6\overline{)\$25.56}$

5. Find the sum. Place the answers in order from the largest to the smallest to reveal a message.

| 10  E | 21  L | 56  E | 19  F | 17  E |
|---|---|---|---|---|
| + 12 | + 9 | + 15 | + 20 | + 8 |

| 80  R | 10  I | 61  S | 42  S | 31  T |
|---|---|---|---|---|
| + 5 | + 52 | + 0 | + 21 | + 11 |

___ ___ ___ ___ ___ ___ & ___ ___ ___ ___

**James 4:7**

6. Solve.

Kristen purchased a bicycle for $67.98, a tire pump for $15.78, and an extra bicycle reflector for $1.00. How much change did she receive from a $100.00 bill?

There are 725 seats on the ground floor in the sanctuary of Loganville First Baptist Church. There are 75 seats in the choir loft, 60 more seats in an additional overflow room, and 150 children in children's church. If every seat was full for 3 Sundays in a row, and children's church was full all 3 Sundays, how many people attended church on those Sundays combined?

**Lesson 47**

## Estimating Quotients

Kathy types 65 words per minute. About how long will it take her to type a report with 629 words?

We often use estimation when we are finding approximate answers. The word "about" lets you know that an estimated answer is sufficient. Round the divisor and dividend and then complete the problem. Look below.

We round:   Think:   65 rounds to 70
629 rounds to 630

$$\begin{array}{r} 9 \\ 70\overline{)630} \\ -630 \\ \hline 0 \end{array}$$ ←—Think: 7 × 9 = 63 so 70 × 9 = 630

It will take Kathy about 9 minutes to type the report.

**1** Estimate the quotients by rounding three-digit numbers to the nearest 10 and four-digit numbers to the nearest 100.

148 ÷ 3 =      556 ÷ 7 =      2,357 ÷ 6 =      4,856 ÷ 7 =

**2** Find the quotient.

3)904      5)54      6)965      5)549

2)812      7)729      3)916

**3** Find the missing number.

| 3? | 5? | ?6 |
|---|---|---|
| x 40 | x 67 | x 40 |
| 1,280 | 3,350 | 1,840 |

**4** Find the difference.

$$93 - 41 \qquad 174 - 97 \qquad 833 - 260 \qquad 641 - 278 \qquad 39 - 25$$

**5** Find the products.

$6^2$ $\qquad$ $2^3$ $\qquad$ $10^3$

$4^3$ $\qquad$ $3^2$

**6** Label each part. Solve.

$n + 25 = 50$ _____

$n + 75 = 100$ $\qquad$ $n + 125 = 200$ $\qquad$ $n + 4 = 9$

**7** Follow the numbers in order from the largest to the smallest to find your way through the maze.

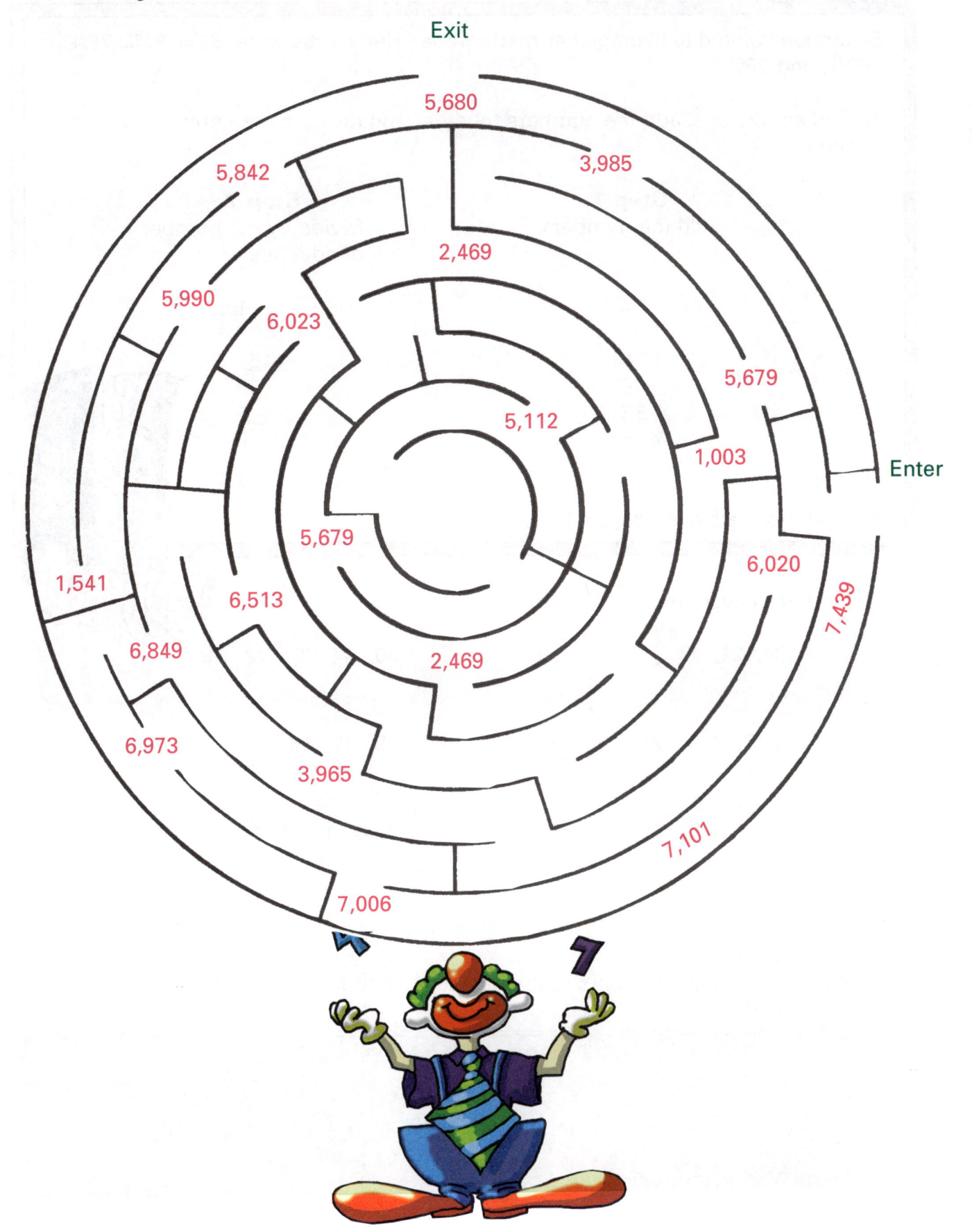

Exit

5,680
5,842    3,985
    2,469
5,990  6,023
            5,679
        5,112  1,003    Enter
    5,679
1,541        6,020
  6,513           7,439
6,849
    2,469
6,973
  3,965
        7,101
    7,006

**Lesson 48**

## Averaging

Savannah wanted to average her math grade. Her scores were: 84%, 97%, 79%, 100%, and 95%.

To find an average, add the numbers together and divide by the number of addends.

**Step 1**
Add the numbers.

```
   84
   97
   79
  100
 + 95
  455
```

**Step 2**
Divide by the number of addends.

```
      91%
    _____
  5 ) 455
     - 45
      ___
       05
      - 5
      ___
        0
```

Savannah's math average is a 91%.

**1** Find each average.

34, 21, 17          39, 44, 27, 22, 18

6, 7, 6, 4, 2       19, 29, 15

26, 37, 32, 25      3, 8, 12, 7, 10

**2** Estimate the quotient.
Round three-digit numbers to the nearest 10 and four-digit numbers to the nearest 100.

5)247     9)272     8)404     5)449     9)7,195

150 Horizons Math 5, Student Workbook 1

**3** Fill in each quotient and remainder on the division wheel.

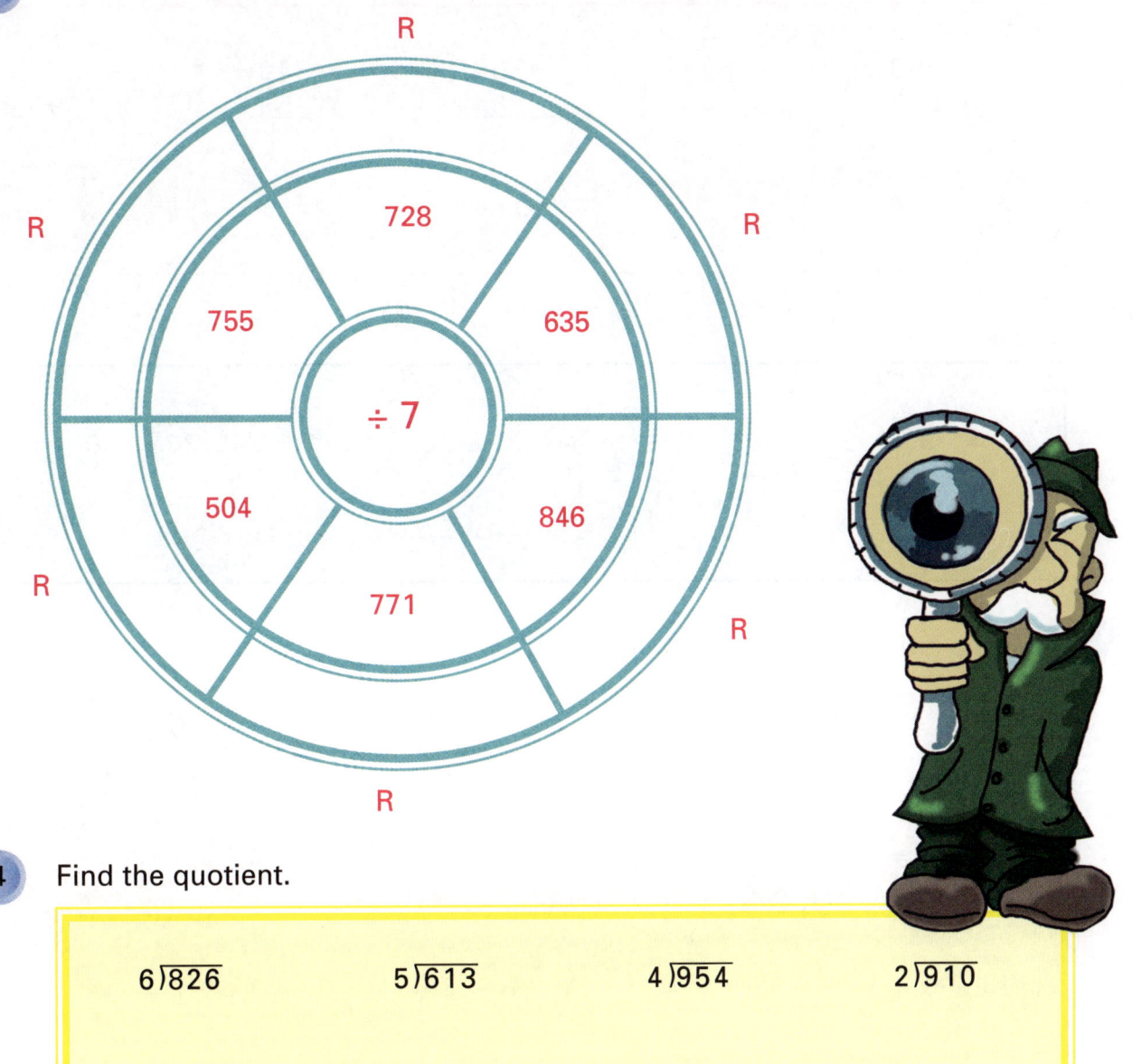

Division wheel: ÷ 7
- 728 R
- 635 R
- 846 R
- 771 R
- 504 R
- 755 R

**4** Find the quotient.

$6\overline{)826}$   $5\overline{)613}$   $4\overline{)954}$   $2\overline{)910}$

**5** Find the difference. Order the answers from largest to smallest to reveal a message.

16,206 **U**      7,003 **S**      37,037 **S**      156,000 **E**      237,008 **J**
− 11,893         − 3,736          − 22,440          − 53,665             − 112,616

___  ___  ___  ___  ___

*Colossians 1:13-14*

**6** Find the product.

| 183 | 622 | 355 | 340 | 538 |
|---|---|---|---|---|
| x 542 | x 445 | x 864 | x 759 | x 189 |

**7** Solve.

$n + 15 = 30$  $n + 45 = 90$  $n + 26 = 41$  $n + 33 = 66$

**8** Find the difference.

3 − 1 =     4 − 2 =     25 − 3 =    10 − 5 =

11 − 5 =    20 − 9 =    6 − 5 =     15 − 1 =

45 − 0 =    7 − 4 =     8 − 3 =     12 − 7 =

**Lesson 49**

## Averaging

While visiting the Grand Canyon, Chet and Lori decided to hike into the canyon. One of the hiking areas, Bright Angel Trail to Indian Garden, had 4 different paths they could follow. All 4 of the paths had elevation changes. The first trail changed by 1,140 feet, the second by 1,941, the third by 3,060, and the last by 3,100. What was the average elevation change for all four trails?

To find an average, add the numbers and divide by the number of addends. If you have a remainder, round to the nearest whole number.

### Step 1
Add the numbers.

```
  1,141
  1,940
  3,060
+ 3,100
  9,241
```

### Step 2
Divide by the number of addends.

```
       2,310 R1
    4)9,241
     - 8
       1 2
     - 1 2
         04
        - 4
          01
         - 0
           1
```

### Step 3
Write the remainder in fractional form by placing the remainder over the divisor.

$$2,310\frac{1}{4}$$
$$4)\overline{9,241}$$

### Step 4:
Round the fraction to the nearest whole number. If the fraction is $\frac{1}{2}$ or greater, round the fraction to the next higher whole number. If the fraction is less than $\frac{1}{2}$, the whole number remains the same.

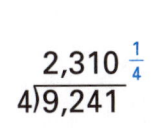

$$2,310\frac{1}{4}$$
$$4)\overline{9,241}$$

This fraction is less than $\frac{1}{2}$, so the number remains the same.

The average height of the four hikes is 2,310 ft.

---

Try this problem with a calculator. The remainder is in decimal form. Use your knowledge of decimals and rounding to round to the nearest whole number.

### Step 1
Add the numbers.

```
  1,141
  1,940
  3,060
+ 3,100
  9,241
```

This decimal is less than .5, so the number remains the same.

### Step 2
Divide by the number of addends.

$$2,310.25$$
$$4)\overline{9,241}$$

$$2,310.25$$
$$4)\overline{9,241}$$

### Step 3
Round the decimal to the nearest whole number.

If the decimal is .50 or greater, round the fraction to the next higher whole number.

If the decimal is less than .50, the whole number remains the same.

The average height of the four hikes is 2,310 ft.

*Horizons Math 5, Student Workbook 1* 153

**1** Find the average. Use your calculator and round remainders to the nearest whole number.

46, 17, 34, 50                86, 51, 13, 17, 91

**2** Use paper and pencil to find the average. Round the fractional remainder to the nearest whole number.

71, 36, 64, 15        43, 26, 76, 9, 21, 80        85, 74, 28, 49

**3** Estimate by rounding three-digit numbers to the nearest 10 and four-digit numbers to the nearest 100.

7)5,573        8)2,351        6)543        3)266

**4** Find the missing numbers.

```
     2?8              70 R2            109
4)8??             3)?12            ?)654
 - 8               - ?1             - 6
 ───               ───              ───
  03                02               05
 - 0               - 0              - 0
 ───               ───              ───
  32                 2               5?
 -32                                - 5?
 ───                                ───
   0                                  0
```

**5** Find the difference.

9 − 6 =        11 − 5 =        14 − 8 =        7 − 7 =

9 − 8 =        11 − 9 =        10 − 1 =        14 − 7 =

10 − 3 =       13 − 4 =        15 − 8 =        6 − 2 =

**6** Solve.

**Five Highest Mountain Peaks of the World**
| | |
|---|---|
| Everest | 29,108 |
| Goodwin Austen (K2) | 29,064 |
| Kanchenjunga | 28,208 |
| Lhotse | 27,890 |
| Makalu | 27,790 |

The tallest mountain in the world is Mount Everest. How much taller is it than Mount Makalu?

How much taller is Goodwin Austen (K2) than Lhotse?

What is the combined height of Mount Everest and Goodwin Austen (K2).

Which height difference is greater, the difference between Kanchenjunga and K2, or the difference between K2 and Everest?

**7** Round to the specified place.

Nearest 10

45     72     193

Nearest 100

345     671     1,589

Nearest 1,000

12,937     6,523     2,003

**8** Solve.

$$13 - n = 4 \qquad 20 - n = 5 \qquad 78 - n = 60$$

$$100 - n = 50 \qquad 45 - n = 20 \qquad 6 - n = 3$$

Lesson 50

## Interpreting Answers

When working problem solving solutions, you need to carefully examine and interpret each answer. Look at the example below.

Amy had 749 pencils to package for the festival school supply booth. How many bags will Amy fill if there are 5 pencils in each bag?

We Divide:

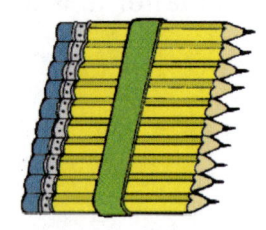

```
        149 R4       ← Remember: 4/5
    5)749
     - 5
      24
     -20
       49
     - 45
        4
```

**DON'T FORGET**
1. Divide
2. Multiply
3. Subtract
4. Check
5. Bring Down

**Interpretation 1:**

$\frac{4}{5}$ is larger than $\frac{1}{2}$ so round up. If Amy needs to package every pencil, she will need 150 bags. 149 bags will have 5 pencils and 1 bag will only have 4 pencils.

Always make sure your response is completely answering the question being asked, and double check to see if you are interpreting the answer correctly.

Look at this example:
Sabrina and Trish ate lunch together. The total bill for lunch was $15.75. They decided to split the bill evenly. How much will each girl have to pay?

```
        $ 7.87 R1     ← 1/2 is the same as .50
    2)$15.75
      -14
       17
      -16
        15
       -14
         1
```

Normally, we would just round the remainder up and each girl would need to pay $7.88. This will not work when paying a bill. The restaurant needs to be paid $15.75. If each girl pays $7.88 the restaurant will be paid $15.76, a penny extra. What does this mean?

**Interpretation 1:**
It means that each girl needs to pay $7.88 to pay the same amount and still cover the total price of the bill. The restaurant will be paid $15.76, one cent extra.

**Interpretation 2:**
Or the girls will not pay the exact same price. One girl will need to pay $7.87 and one will need to pay $7.88, which totals to $15.75, the exact price of the bill. This is the easiest way to solve the problem.

**1** Solve and interpret each answer.

Kathy, Bill, and Craig ate lunch together and split the bill evenly among the three of them. If the bill was $27.98 how much did each person have to pay?
(Hint: round decimal answers to the nearest penny)


A florist has 145 flowers to place in 6 different table arrangements for the wedding reception. How many flowers will go in each arrangement?

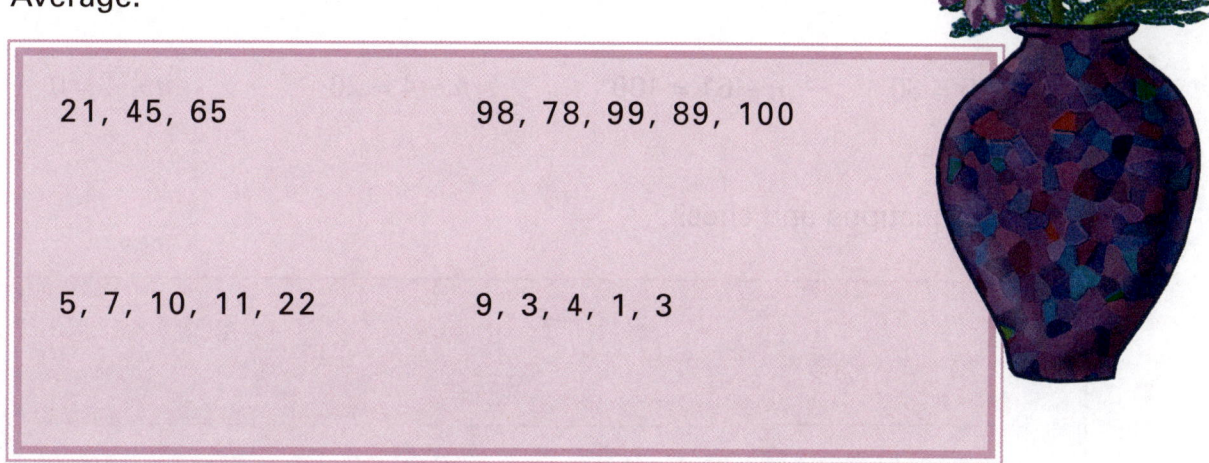

**2** Average.

| | |
|---|---|
| 21, 45, 65 | 98, 78, 99, 89, 100 |
| 5, 7, 10, 11, 22 | 9, 3, 4, 1, 3 |

**3** Estimate by rounding three-digit numbers to the nearest ten and four-digit numbers to the nearest hundred.

| | | | |
|---|---|---|---|
| 718 ÷ 8 = | 352 ÷ 7 = | 119 ÷ 6 = | 6,363 ÷ 8 = |
| 4,480 ÷ 5 = | 3,562 ÷ 9 = | 358 ÷ 6 = | 2,058 ÷ 3 = |

**4** Complete the table. The first one is done for you.

|  | Factors | Product | Exponent | Number of Zeros |
|---|---|---|---|---|
| $10^2$ | 10 x 10 | 100 | 2 | 2 |
| $10^3$ |  | 1,000 |  |  |
|  | 10 x 10 x 10 x 10 |  |  |  |
|  | 10 x 10 x 10 x 10 x 10 |  |  |  |
| $10^6$ |  | 1,000,000 |  |  |

**5** Solve.

$n - 15 = 30$     $n - 61 = 100$     $n - 4 = 20$     $n - 4 = 0$

**6** Solve the equations and check.

$n \times 9 = 54$     $n \times 7 = 49$     $n \times 3 = 15$

Check     Check     Check

$n \times 5 = 45$     $n \times 10 = 100$     $n \times 6 = 42$

Check     Check     Check

**Test 5**

**1** Find the product. 10 pts. total for this exercise.

| 53 | 90 | 89 | 259 | 191 |
|---|---|---|---|---|
| × 21 | × 13 | × 30 | × 52 | × 26 |

| 791 | 409 | 343 | 192 | 818 |
|---|---|---|---|---|
| × 657 | × 727 | × 411 | × 221 | × 255 |

**2** Estimate by rounding two-digit numbers to the nearest ten and three-digit numbers to the nearest hundred. 8 pts. total for this exercise.

3 × 462 =         3 × 69 =         8 × 434 =         2 × 582 =

11 × 48 =        18 × 98 =        48 × 302 =       37 × 597 =

**3** Solve the equations and check. 6 pts. total for this exercise.

$n \times 9 = 81$          $n \times 7 = 49$          $n \times 3 = 39$
____ ÷ ____ ÷ ____        ____ ÷ ____ ÷ ____        ____ ÷ ____ ÷ ____

Check                      Check                      Check

$n \times 8 = 72$          $n \times 10 = 70$         $n \times 8 = 64$
____ ÷ ____ ÷ ____        ____ ÷ ____ ÷ ____        ____ ÷ ____ ÷ ____

Check                      Check                      Check

Horizons Math 5, Student Workbook 1

**4** Complete the table. 14 pts. total for this exercise.

|  | Factors | Product | Exponent | Number of Zeros |
|---|---|---|---|---|
| $10^3$ | 10 x 10 x 10 | 1,000 | 3 | 3 |
| $10^4$ |  |  |  |  |
| $10^5$ |  | 100,000 |  |  |
| $10^6$ | 10 x 10 x 10 x 10 x 10 x 10 |  |  |  |
| $10^7$ |  |  |  |  |

**5** Find the quotient. 8 pts. total for this exercise.

$3\overline{)51}$     $4\overline{)56}$     $6\overline{)843}$     $2\overline{)415}$     $4\overline{)2{,}182}$

$8\overline{)3{,}500}$     $5\overline{)\$4.90}$     $7\overline{)\$17.29}$

**6** Solve the equations and check. 6 pts. total for this exercise.

$n \div 3 = 7$       $n \div 5 = 5$       $n \div 7 = 8$

___ x ___ x ___       ___ x ___ x ___       ___ x ___ x ___

Check       Check       Check

$n \div 4 = 12$       $n \div 6 = 9$       $n \div 8 = 9$

___ x ___ x ___       ___ x ___ x ___       ___ x ___ x ___

Check       Check       Check

52 pts. total

**Lesson 51**

## Dividing by Tens

Shawn has 287 pamphlets advertising the community carnival. If 30 of his friends help him pass them out, how many will each person get? How many will be left over?
Divide 287 by 30.

1. Decide where to put the first digit in the quotient.

   $\phantom{30)}?\phantom{287}$  $\phantom{30)}\phantom{2}?\phantom{87}$  $\phantom{30)}\phantom{28}?$
   $30\overline{)287}$   $30\overline{)287}$   $30\overline{)287}$

   No since 30 > 2.   No since 30 > 28.   Yes since 30 < 287.

2. Divide.

   Think.... $3\overline{)28}$ is about 9, so $30\overline{)287}$ is about 9.

   $\phantom{30)}9$
   $30\overline{)287}$

3. Multiply and subtract.

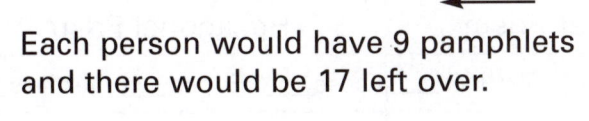

   $\phantom{30)}9$
   $30\overline{)287}$
   $\phantom{30)}\underline{-270}$      9 × 30
   $\phantom{30)2}17$ ←

   Each person would have 9 pamphlets and there would be 17 left over.

4. Check.

   $\phantom{30)}9$ R 17
   $30\overline{)287}$

   9 × 30 = 270
   270 + 17 = 287

**1** Divide and check.

$70\overline{)210}$   $50\overline{)350}$   $40\overline{)87}$   $60\overline{)255}$   $80\overline{)498}$

$60\overline{)475}$  $50\overline{)339}$  $80\overline{)725}$  $20\overline{)170}$  $90\overline{)638}$

**2** Use a factor tree to find prime numbers. Write the missing numbers in the circles.

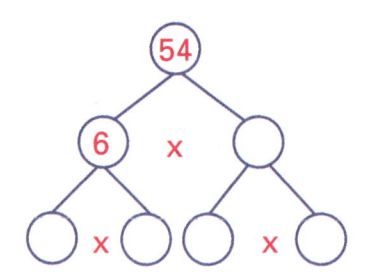

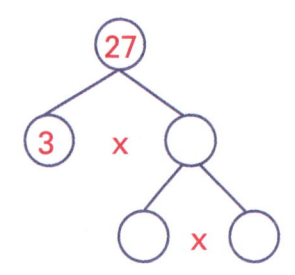

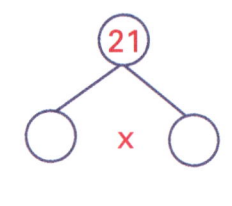

**3** Many solid figures have faces, edges, and vertices.

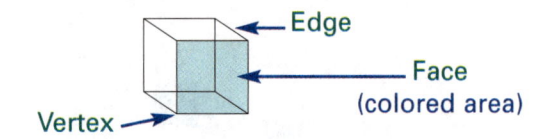

The cube has 6 **faces**.
It has 12 **edges**.
It has 8 **vertices**.

Give the number of faces, edges and vertices.

| Triangular Prism | Rectangular Prism | Hexagonal Prism |
|---|---|---|
| Faces____ Edges____ Vertices____ | Faces____ Edges____ Vertices____ | Faces____ Edges____ Vertices____ |

**4** Solve.

1. Colleen has 450 pennies to put in penny rolls. 50 pennies go in each roll. How many rolls will she have in all? _____

2. Colleen has 650 dimes. 50 dimes go in each roll. How many rolls will she have in all? _____

3. Colleen has 129 quarters. 40 quarters go in each roll. How many rolls will she have in all? How many coins will be left over? _____

4. Colleen has 312 nickels. 40 nickels go in each roll. How many rolls will she have in all? How many coins will be left over? _____

5. Complete the blanks with the following words: meters, liters, or grams.

   1. John's mother bought 2 _____ of soda for the party.

   2. Amy's room measured 12 _____ by 14 _____ .

   3. The scientist weighed the sodium in _____ .

6. Match.

   square

   hexagon

   octagon

   dodecagon

   pentagon

7. Multiply. Find the product in the boxes and shade. The unshaded boxes will spell the solution to the riddle:

   **What are the strongest creatures in the sea?**

   | 7 | 9 | 8 | 3 | 2 |
   |---|---|---|---|---|
   | x 4 | x 8 | x 7 | x 9 | x 7 |

   | 6 | 5 | 3 | 2 | 9 |
   |---|---|---|---|---|
   | x 3 | x 5 | x 8 | x 4 | x 9 |

   | 4 | 6 | 8 | 1 | 9 |
   |---|---|---|---|---|
   | x 5 | x 9 | x 8 | x 5 | x 0 |

   | 13 | 28 | 72 | 56 | 27 | 15 | 14 | 18 | 12 | 6 | 25 |
   |----|----|----|----|----|----|----|----|----|---|----|
   | M | T | R | D | V | U | A | Y | S | S | L |
   | 24 | 8 | 81 | 20 | 54 | 4 | 64 | 5 | 0 | 50 | 49 |
   | X | O | N | P | Z | E | K | P | B | L | S |

Lesson 52

## Division – One-Digit Quotients

There are 352 pieces of candy to be packaged in candy bags. If there are 44 pieces of candy in each bag, how many candy bags will there be in all?

Divide 352 by 44.

1. **Decide where to put the first digit in the quotient.**

   $$\begin{array}{r}?\phantom{00}\\44\overline{)352}\end{array} \qquad \begin{array}{r}?\phantom{0}\\44\overline{)352}\end{array} \qquad \begin{array}{r}?\\44\overline{)352}\end{array}$$

   No since 44 > 3.   No since 44 > 35.   Yes since 44 < 352.

2. **Round the divisor and estimate.**

   Think . . . 44 rounds to 40.   $4\overline{)35}$ is about 8,

   So $40\overline{)352}$ is about 8.

3. **Divide.**
   $$44\overline{)352}^{\,8}$$

4. **Multiply and subtract.**

   $$\begin{array}{r}8\phantom{0}\\44\overline{)352}\\-352\\\hline 0\end{array} \quad 8 \times 44$$

   There will be 8 full bags of candy.

5. **Check.**
   $$44\overline{)352}^{\,8}$$

   $8 \times 44 = 352$

**1** Find the quotients.

$36\overline{)89}$     $43\overline{)98}$     $63\overline{)156}$     $31\overline{)162}$

$88\overline{)225}$  $62\overline{)387}$  $49\overline{)127}$  $81\overline{)630}$

**2**  Find the quotients.

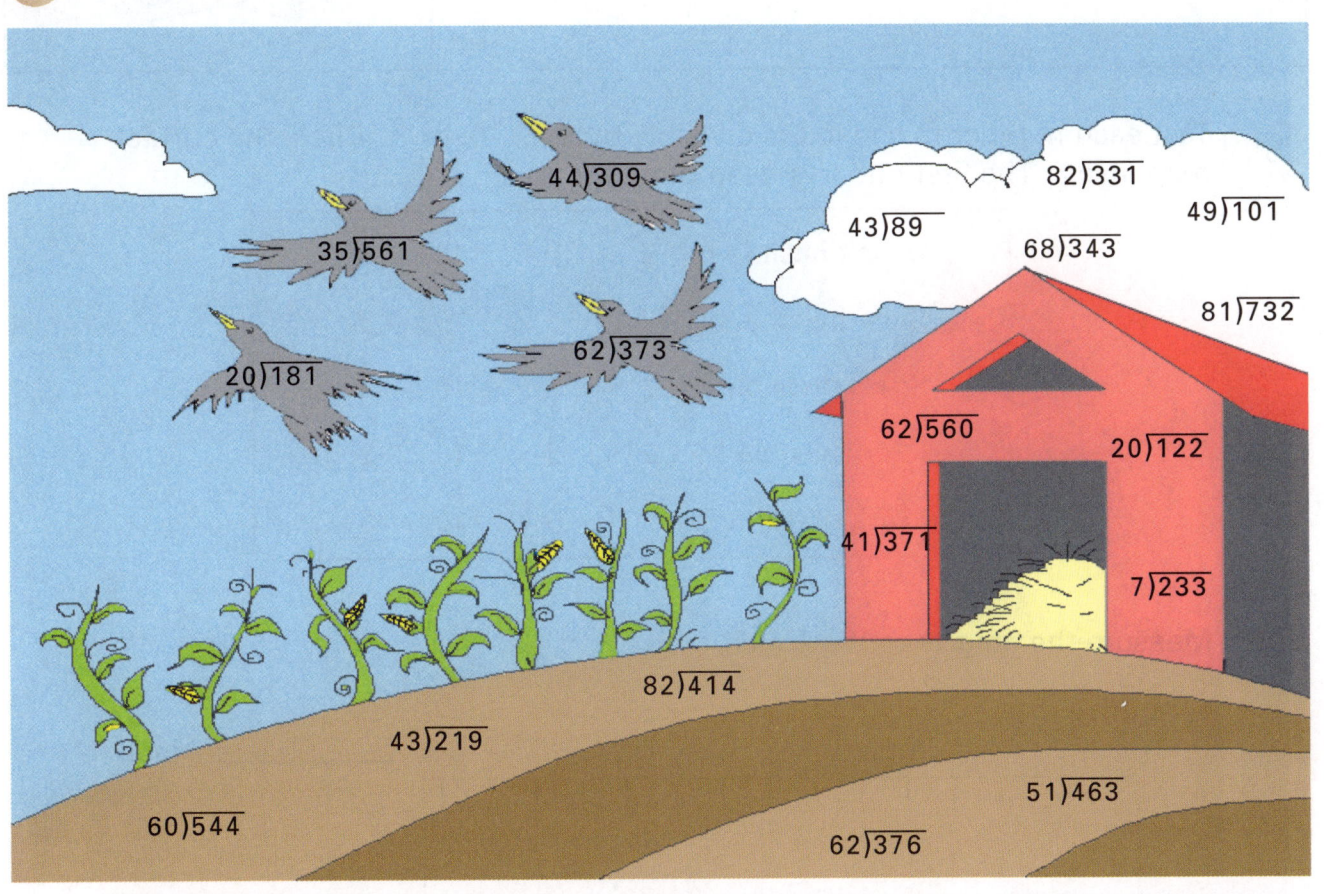

$44\overline{)309}$
$35\overline{)561}$
$82\overline{)331}$
$43\overline{)89}$
$49\overline{)101}$
$68\overline{)343}$
$20\overline{)181}$
$62\overline{)373}$
$81\overline{)732}$
$62\overline{)560}$
$20\overline{)122}$
$41\overline{)371}$
$7\overline{)233}$
$82\overline{)414}$
$43\overline{)219}$
$60\overline{)544}$
$62\overline{)376}$
$51\overline{)463}$

**Consider the ravens, for they neither sow nor reap; and they have no store room nor barn; and yet God feeds them; how much more valuable you are than the birds!**

**Luke 12:24**

**3**  Use a factor tree to find prime numbers. Write the missing numbers in the circles.

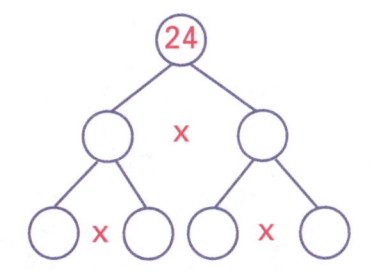

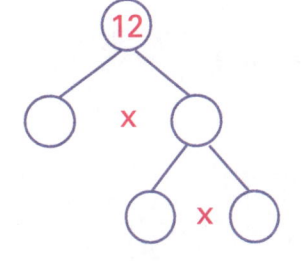

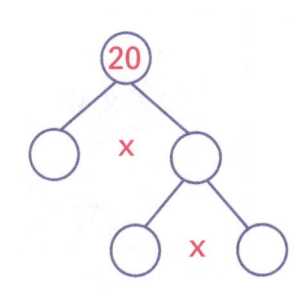

24

12

20

**4** Give the number of faces, edges and vertices.

| Triangular Pyramid | Rectangular Pyramid | Cube |
|---|---|---|
| Faces____ Edges____ Vertices____ | Faces____ Edges____ Vertices____ | Faces____ Edges____ Vertices____ |

**5** Test each number to see if it is divisible by 2, 5, 10, or 3. Circle the correct responses. The first one has been done for you.

45 is divisible by  2  ⑤  10  ③
80 is divisible by  2  5  10  3
120 is divisible by  2  5  10  3
63 is divisible by  2  5  10  3
912 is divisible by  2  5  10  3

**6** Measure the objects to the $\frac{1}{4}$ inch.

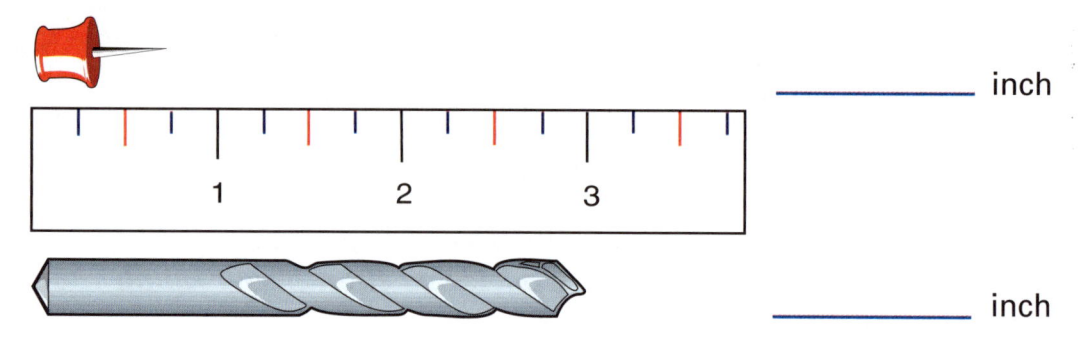

_____ inch

_____ inch

**7** Find each quotient and label the first problem.

_____ 3)15      _____ 3)12      4)16      5)20

3)9      2)12      7)49      8)32

9)81      6)42      3)18      6)24

166 Horizons Math 5, Student Workbook 1

**Lesson 53**

# Division – Two-Digit Quotients

Adam has 148 eggs to put in egg cartons. If there are 12 eggs in each carton, how many full cartons will he have? How many eggs will be left over?

Divide 148 by 12.

1. **Decide where to put the first digit in the quotient.**

    $\phantom{12)}?$  $\qquad\qquad$  $\phantom{12)1}?$
    $12\overline{)148}$ $\qquad\qquad$ $12\overline{)148}$

    No since 12 > 1. $\qquad$ Yes since 12 < 14.

2. **Divide.**

    Think … 12 rounds to 10. $\qquad$ Think … 12 rounds to 10.

    $10\overline{)14}$ is about 1. $\qquad\qquad$ $10\overline{)28}$ is about 2.

    $\phantom{12)1}1$ $\qquad\qquad\qquad\qquad$ $\phantom{12)1}12\ \ R4$
    $12\overline{)148}$ $\qquad\qquad\qquad\qquad$ $12\overline{)148}$
    $\underline{-12}\phantom{0}$ $\qquad\qquad\qquad\qquad$ $\underline{-12}\phantom{0}$
    $\phantom{-1}28$ $\qquad\qquad\qquad\qquad\phantom{11}$ $28$
    $\qquad\qquad\qquad\qquad\qquad\phantom{111}$ $\underline{-24}$
    $\qquad\qquad\qquad\qquad\qquad\phantom{1111}$ $4$

    There are 12 full egg cartons and 4 eggs left over.

**1** Find the quotients.

$68\overline{)778}$ $\qquad\qquad$ $45\overline{)566}$ $\qquad\qquad$ $23\overline{)487}$

$35\overline{)1{,}173}$ $\qquad\qquad$ $54\overline{)3{,}892}$ $\qquad\qquad$ $41\overline{)3{,}581}$

**2** Solve. Find the remainders on the picture below. Connect the remainders in order of the problems to create a picture. The first two have been done for you.

$$\overset{7 \quad R8}{12\overline{)92}} \quad \overset{42 \quad R1}{38\overline{)1{,}597}} \quad 28\overline{)681} \quad 12\overline{)957}$$

$$31\overline{)458} \quad 7\overline{)41} \quad 21\overline{)562} \quad 5\overline{)98}$$

$$8\overline{)66} \quad 8\overline{)76} \quad 14\overline{)893} \quad 18\overline{)642}$$

$$6\overline{)47} \quad 25\overline{)360} \quad 9\overline{)43} \quad 15\overline{)103}$$

*Matthew 3:16-17:* And Jesus, when he was baptized, went up straightway out of the water: and, lo, the heavens were opened unto him, and he saw the Spirit of God descending like a dove, and lighting up on him: And lo a voice from heaven, saying, This is my beloved Son, in whom I am well pleased.

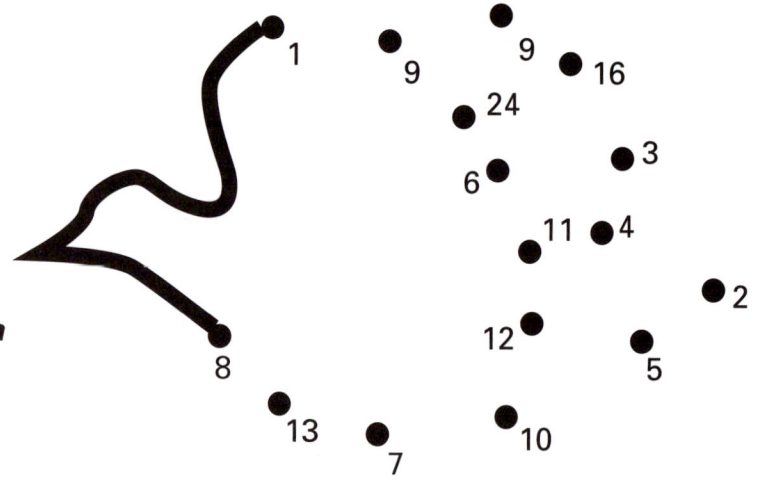

**3** Find each quotient.

$$3\overline{)18} \quad 3\overline{)27} \quad 4\overline{)28} \quad 5\overline{)45} \quad 9\overline{)81}$$

168 Horizons Math 5, Student Workbook 1

**4** Find your way through the maze with prime numbers. You may move vertically, horizontally, or diagonally, but you must connect all of the prime numbers.

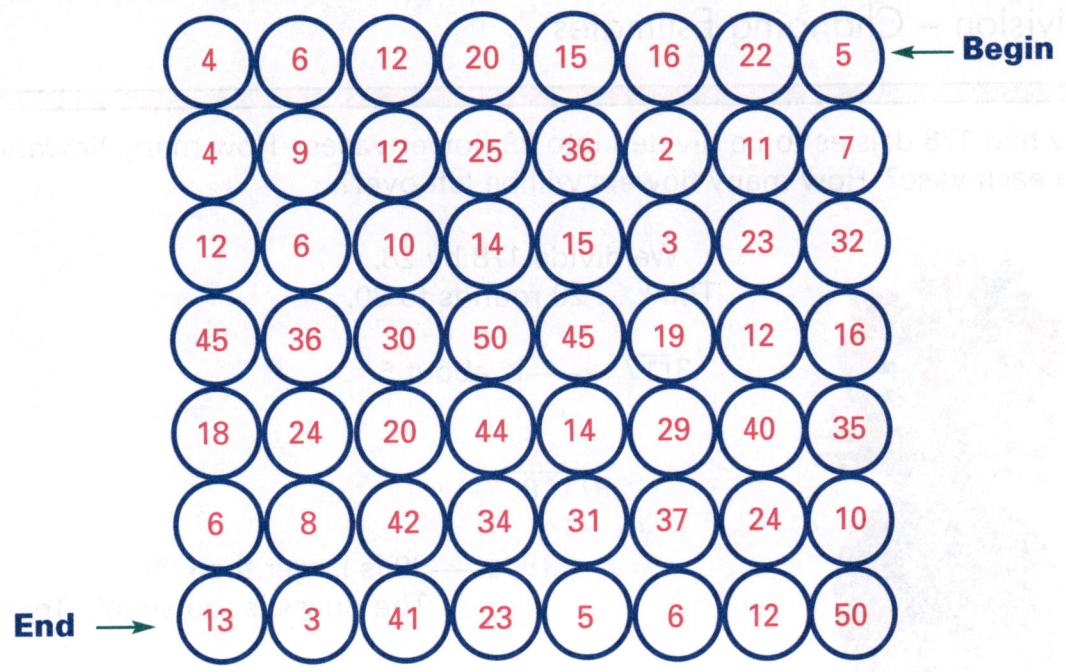

| 4 | 6 | 12 | 20 | 15 | 16 | 22 | 5 | ← Begin |
|---|---|---|---|---|---|---|---|---|
| 4 | 9 | 12 | 25 | 36 | 2 | 11 | 7 | |
| 12 | 6 | 10 | 14 | 15 | 3 | 23 | 32 | |
| 45 | 36 | 30 | 50 | 45 | 19 | 12 | 16 | |
| 18 | 24 | 20 | 44 | 14 | 29 | 40 | 35 | |
| 6 | 8 | 42 | 34 | 31 | 37 | 24 | 10 | |
| 13 | 3 | 41 | 23 | 5 | 6 | 12 | 50 | |

End →

**5** Test each number to see if it is divisible by 2, 5, 10, or 3. Circle the correct responses. The first one has been done for you.

| | | | | |
|---|---|---|---|---|
| 75 is divisible by | 2 | ⑤ | 10 | ③ |
| 100 is divisible by | 2 | 5 | 10 | 3 |
| 150 is divisible by | 2 | 5 | 10 | 3 |
| 21 is divisible by | 2 | 5 | 10 | 3 |
| 522 is divisible by | 2 | 5 | 10 | 3 |

**6** Measure the objects to the $\frac{1}{4}$ inch.

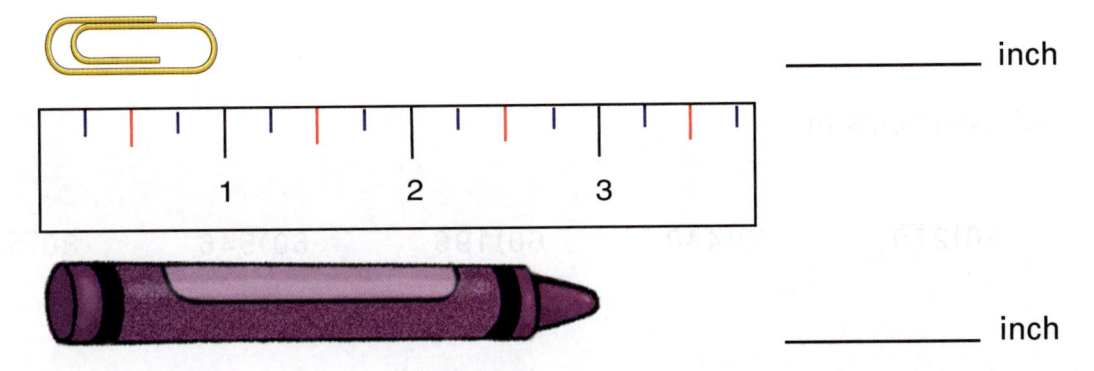

_____ inch

_____ inch

## Lesson 54

### Division – Changing Estimates

Macy had 178 daisies to be divided into 28 flower vases. How many flowers will be in each vase? How many flowers will be left over?

We divide 178 by 28.
Think … 28 rounds to 30.

3)17̄ ⟵ is about 5.

```
        5
28)178
   -140
     38  ⟵ 38 is larger than 28
            The guess is too small. Try 6
```

```
        6
28)178
   -168
     10  ⟵ is less than 28.
            This guess is correct.
```

There will be 6 flowers in each vase. There will be 10 flowers left over.

Sometimes our guess is too large or too small, and we need to adjust it up or down.

**1** Find each quotient. Many of your original guesses may be incorrect.

46)324̄     68)404̄     78)628̄     72)634̄     43)330̄

**2** Find each quotient.

50)270̄     70)440̄     60)196̄     60)546̄     80)632̄

**3** Beside each number write prime or composite. If the number is composite, find the prime factors. The first one has been done for you.

1. 12     composite     2, 2, 3
2. 3     _____     _____
3. 9     _____     _____
4. 25     _____     _____
5. 24     _____     _____
6. 17     _____     _____
7. 40     _____     _____
8. 55     _____     _____

**4** Find the missing addends.

16, 45, 23, ? = 96

25, 13, 17, ? = 80

**5** Find the sum.

$$13{,}489 + 12{,}603$$

$$23{,}709 + 35{,}931$$

$$15{,}290 + 48{,}981$$

$$39{,}131 + 3{,}084$$

**6** Use the bar graph to answer the questions.

### Profits from Games at the Community Festival

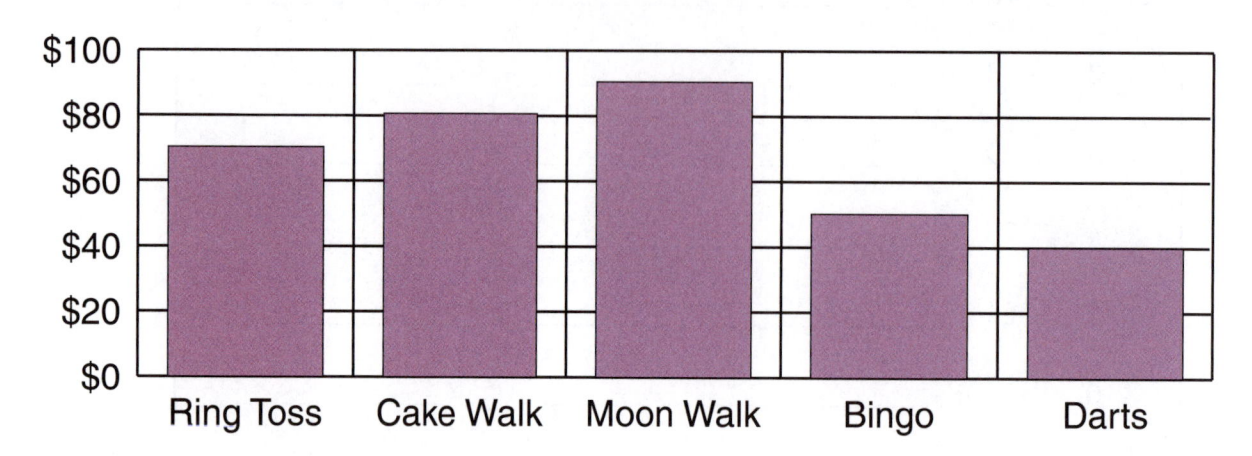

1. How much money was made from the Ring Toss? _____
2. What game brought twice as much profit as the Dart game? _____
3. What was the total profit from the Community Festival? _____
4. What game brought the most profit? _____
5. What game brought the least profit? _____
6. If each person paid $0.50 to play Bingo, how many people played the game? _____
7. How much less did the Ring Toss make than the Moon Walk? _____
8. What game brought half the profit of the Cake Walk? _____

**7** Complete the magic square. Each row and column must have the same sum.

| $\frac{1}{10}$ | $\frac{6}{10}$ |  |
| --- | --- | --- |
| $\frac{7}{10}$ |  |  |
| $\frac{1}{10}$ |  | $\frac{6}{10}$ |

172 Horizons Math 5, Student Workbook 1

**Lesson 55**

## Division – Three-Digit Quotients

Karl drives 6,780 miles a year. About how far does he drive each month?

We divide 6,780 by 12.

1. Decide where to start. Divide the hundreds.

    ```
         5
    12)6,780
       -6 0
         7
    ```

2. Divide the tens.

    ```
         56
    12)6,780
       -6 0
         78
        -72
          6
    ```

3. Divide the ones.

    ```
         565
    12)6,780
       -6 0
         78
        -72
         60
        -60
          0
    ```

Karl drives about 565 miles a month.

**1** Find each quotient.

27)3,576    37)4,890    45)7,902    23)14,763

42)6,527    31)5,992    77)8,790    55)7,429

**2** Find each product and place it in the puzzle. There is only one solution.

| 3 | 6 | 82 | 10 | 49 |
|---|---|----|----|----|
| x 7 | x 8 | x 7 | x 9 | x 3 |

| 698 | 909 | 9,927 | 794 | 4,027 |
|-----|-----|-------|-----|-------|
| x 8 | x 7 | x 9 | x 6 | x 2 |

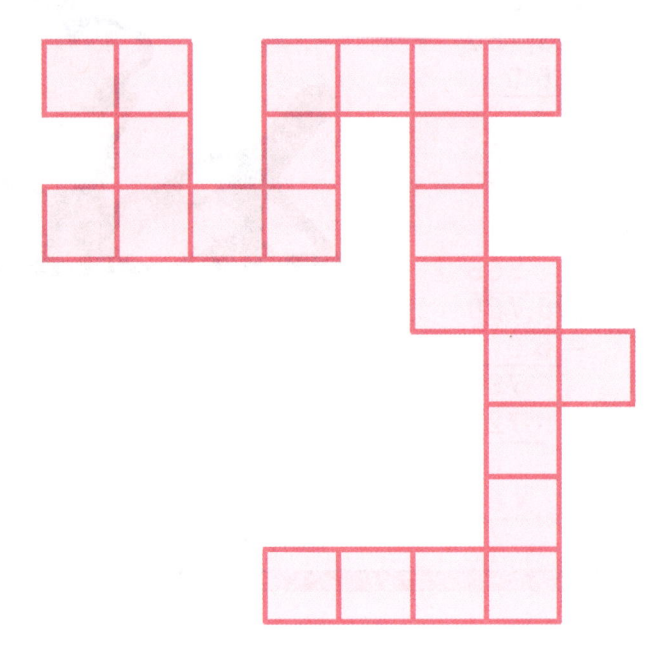

**3** Find the missing addends.

```
  ☐3 5           6☐ 9           2 7 9
+  2 5 8       +  3 7 9       + ☐2 5
   7 9 3          9 9 8        1,2 0 4


                   6 0 3         ☐4☐
                +  ☐4 8       +  2 4 7
                  1,0 5 1         8 9 6
```

**4** Find each quotient.

$13\overline{)927}$        $24\overline{)850}$        $38\overline{)758}$        $69\overline{)964}$

**5** Find the difference.

479 − 46 = _____        209 − 37 = _____

981 − 492 = _____        793 − 304 = _____

**6** Write each number in numeric form in the boxes above the letters. Circle the boxes that contain the number one (1) to read the solution to the riddle:

**On what horse would you get all wet riding?**

| Number in words | | | | | | | | |
|---|---|---|---|---|---|---|---|---|
| Three hundred ten million, nine hundred fifty-two thousand, nine hundred and sixty-three. | | | | | | | | |
| | M | A | J | K | N | N | O | Y | R |
| Fifty-seven million, two | | | | | | | | |
| | T | U | N | C | S | E | R | I | S |
| Three hundred twenty-one million, five hundred eighteen thousand, one hundred two. | | | | | | | | |
| | F | H | S | U | E | J | A | L | T |
| Two hundred ninety-nine million, six hundred thousand, eighty-eight. | | | | | | | | |
| | F | B | C | T | W | D | A | W | L |
| Two hundred million, one hundred ten thousand, six hundred ninety-eight. | | | | | | | | |
| | O | T | E | H | O | U | S | E | O |
| Eight hundred seventeen million, one hundred thousand. | | | | | | | | |
| | F | R | E | S | H | K | L | I | P |
| Nine hundred million, ten | | | | | | | | |
| | T | D | R | W | A | L | K | E | R |

# Lesson 56

## Division – Zeros in the Quotient

It is easy to make mistakes when working with zeros in the quotient. Make sure your columns are straight, and carefully follow the division formula.

**Division Formula**
- Divide
- Multiply
- Subtract
- Compare

```
        3                30              305
   18)5,490          18)5,490        18)5,490
    - 5 4             - 5 4           - 5 4
        0                 09              09
                        -  0            -  0
                           9              90
                                        - 90
                                           0
```

**1** Find the quotients.

29)5,220     15)6,105     13)2,704     45)8,550

72)7,776     63)25,326    82)49,938    97)13,580

**2** Find the sum.

| 34 | 67 | 89 | 90 | 13 |
| 21 | 99 | 43 | 71 | 19 |
| 93 | 80 | 27 | 37 | 64 |
| + 88 | + 61 | + 94 | + 44 | + 37 |

**3** Find the quotient.

$69\overline{)208}$  $67\overline{)529}$  $77\overline{)1,386}$

$38\overline{)350}$  $84\overline{)1,632}$  $63\overline{)4,197}$

**4** Match.

| | |
|---|---|
| 54,000,000 | one hundred twenty-six million |
| 126,000 | one hundred twenty-six thousand |
| 100,026 | five thousand, four hundred |
| 126,000,000 | fifty-four million |
| 540,000 | five hundred forty thousand |
| 5,400 | one hundred thousand, twenty-six |

**5** Solve.

3 + (2 x 4) =   (17 − 6) + 8 =   4 x (6 + 9) =

(64 ÷ 8) + 39 =   16 + (49 − 13) =   (7 x 9) + 12 =

**6** Find the products. Circle the blocks where the product is divisible by 2. The shaded letters complete the verse in Psalms 116:1-2. *I love the Lord because he hears my prayers and answers them. Because he bends down and listens...* (Hint: The answer is another way of saying as long as I am alive and my lungs are working.)

| 9 x 9 =<br>**B** | 12 x 3 =<br>**I** | 6 x 6 =<br>**W** | 2 x 4 =<br>**I** | 4 x 4 =<br>**L** | 1 x 3 =<br>**N** | 7 x 6 =<br>**L** |
|---|---|---|---|---|---|---|
| 2 x 7 =<br>**P** | 9 x 1 =<br>**L** | 6 x 8 =<br>**R** | 8 x 4 =<br>**A** | 5 x 5 =<br>**K** | 1 x 8 =<br>**Y** | 6 x 7 =<br>**A** |
| 12 x 6 =<br>**S** | 3 x 4 =<br>**L** | 6 x 3 =<br>**O** | 9 x 7 =<br>**D** | 2 x 6 =<br>**N** | 4 x 5 =<br>**G** | 8 x 8 =<br>**A** |
| 6 x 4 =<br>**S** | 6 x 7 =<br>**I** | 4 x 7 =<br>**B** | 5 x 6 =<br>**R** | 7 x 3 =<br>**O** | 8 x 7 =<br>**E** | 9 x 2 =<br>**A** |
| 9 x 6 =<br>**T** | 3 x 5 =<br>**R** | 7 x 7 =<br>**M** | 8 x 10 =<br>**H** | 11 x 3 =<br>**B** | 9 x 2 =<br>**E** | 5 x 7 =<br>**L** |

**7** Find each product. Use the code to find the letter that stands for each answer. Put the letter in the box next to the problem and find the answer to the riddle:

**What is the strongest creature in the sea?**

| S | L | M | U | A | E |
|---|---|---|---|---|---|
| 600 | 832 | 266 | 4984 | 352 | 504 |

16 x 22 = ☐

14 x 19 = ☐

56 x 89 = ☐

50 x 12 = ☐

40 x 15 = ☐

28 x 18 = ☐

26 x 32 = ☐

# Lesson 57

## Division – Estimate Quotients

If a family used 42,831 liters of water last year, about how much water did they use a week? (There are 52 weeks in a year.)

To solve this problem, we need to estimate 42,831 ÷ 52.

1. Round the divisor and the dividend to the first digit.   50)40,000
2. Divide to find the first digit in the quotient.

$$50 \overline{)40,000}$$
with quotient 8, −40 0, remainder 0.

3. Place zeros above the other digits in the dividend.

$$50 \overline{)40,000}$$
with quotient 800, −40 0, remainder 0.

They used about 800 liters of water a week.

**1** Round the dividend and divisor to estimate each quotient.

54)392        28)882        82)4,241        32)61,899

**2** Find each quotient.

36)184        12)1,560        62)1,279        52)17,689

**3** Find each sum. Match your answer with an answer in one of the boxes. Write the corresponding letter in the blank next to the answer space. You will solve this riddle. *John was bored waiting for his dad to arrive by boat in the harbor. He tied his watch to a nearby pigeon. He did this because he wanted to...*

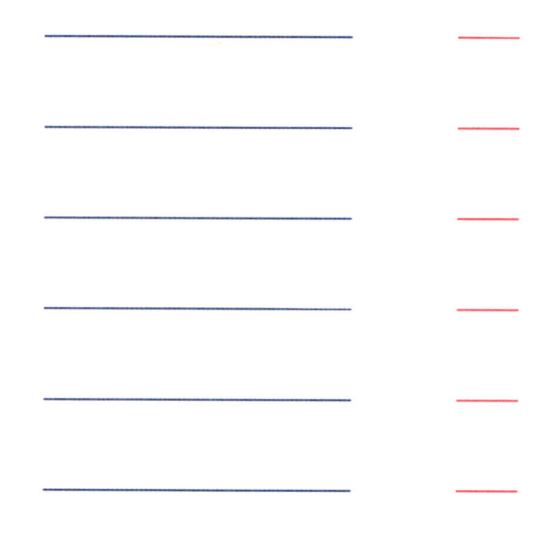

```
   4        8        9        4        3
  +7       +8       +9       +6       +9
  ___      ___      ___      ___      ___

  10        2        0        1
  +8       +3       +7       +7
  ___      ___      ___      ___

   8        6        7
  +1       +9       +7
  ___      ___      ___
```

| 5 | 7 | 8 | 9 | 10 | 11 | 12 | 14 | 15 | 16 | 18 |
|---|---|---|---|----|----|----|----|----|----|----|
| I | M | E | F | C  | W  | H  | Y  | L  | A  | T  |

**4** Place these numbers and their corresponding letter on the lines from least to greatest. If your answers are correct, the letters will answer the riddle: *What animal isn't trustworthy?*

890,000 **H**   8,900 **T**   345 **C**   1,900 **E**   98,000 **A**   809 **H**   5,000 **E**

___ ___
___ ___
___ ___
___ ___
___ ___
___ ___
___ ___

180 Horizons Math 5, Student Workbook 1

**5** Find each quotient.

$91\overline{)86{,}366}$   $74\overline{)56{,}539}$   $62\overline{)48{,}962}$   $56\overline{)75{,}632}$

**6** Place the parentheses in the problem so the statement is true.

5 + 6 x 4 = 29      2 + 8 − 6 = 4      25 − 5 + 7 = 27

56 − 9 x 2 = 38      12 x 12 − 12 = 132      30 ÷ 2 x 3 = 45

**7** Solve each equation.

6 x $n$ = 18      5 x $n$ = 25      $n$ x 8 = 72      $n$ x 3 = 21

$n$ x 2 = 20      4 x $n$ = 32      6 x $n$ = 36      $n$ x 5 = 15

**Lesson 58**

## Division – Money

Carl gets $432.00 a year for delivering newspapers. How much does he make a month?

We divide $432.00 by 12.

```
        $ 36.00
   12)$432.00
       - 36
         72
       - 72
          0
        - 0
          0
```

Don't forget to place the decimal point in the quotient above the decimal point in the dividend.

Carl makes $36.00 a month.

**1** Find the quotients. Don't forget decimal points and dollar signs in your quotient.

13)$26.39   15)$45.60   27)$378.00

45)$40.95   68)$53.72   75)$42.00

**2** Find the products. The first one has been done for you.

$10^2$ = 10 × 10 = 100

$6^2$ = _____     $7^3$ = _____

$10^5$ = _____     $2^4$ = _____

182 Horizons Math 5, Student Workbook 1

**3** Find the quotients.

$23\overline{)9{,}296}$     $32\overline{)9{,}600}$     $13\overline{)2{,}717}$     $200\overline{)13{,}600}$

**4** Solve the equations and check.

| $n + 33 = 69$ | $n + 93 = 134$ | $n + 18 = 97$ |
|---|---|---|
| −    − | −    − | −    − |
| Check | Check | Check |

| $n + 14 = 71$ | $n + 29 = 79$ | $n + 33 = 146$ |
|---|---|---|
| −    − | −    − | −    − |
| Check | Check | Check |

**5** Find the sums. Color the sums divisible by 10 red. Color the sums divisible by 3 blue. Color the sums divisible by 2 green.

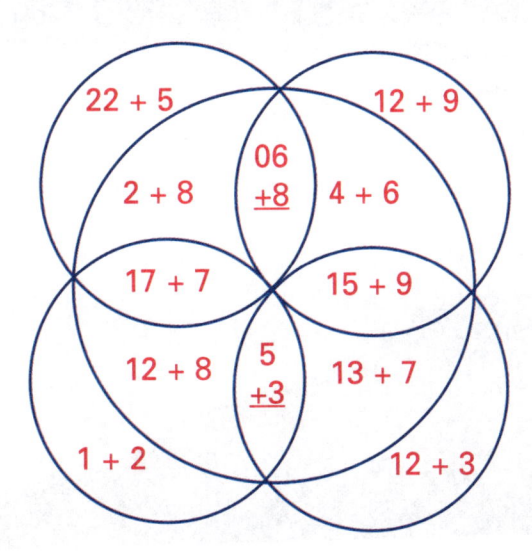

22 + 5     12 + 9

2 + 8     06 +8     4 + 6

17 + 7     15 + 9

12 + 8     5 +3     13 + 7

1 + 2     12 + 3

**6** Match.

| | |
|---|---|
| 1,000,002 | three thousand, eight hundred ninety |
| 456,900 | four million, five hundred sixty-nine thousand |
| 3,890 | four hundred fifty-six thousand, nine hundred |
| 1,002 | one million, two |
| 389,000 | one thousand, two |
| 4,569,000 | three hundred eighty-nine thousand |

**7** Complete the magic square. Each row and column must have the same sum.

| 18 | 2 | |
|---|---|---|
| | 1 | |
| 6 | 16 | |

# Divisibility

**Lesson 59**

**A number is divisible by another number when the remainder is 0.**
For instance 4 **is** divisible by 2. 4 ÷ 2 = 2, there is no remainder. 4 **is not** divisible by 3. 4 ÷ 3 = 1 **R1**, there is a remainder.

Use the rules below to determine whether one number is divisible by another.

1. A number is divisible by 2 if its **last** digit is 0, 2, 4, 6, or 8. For instance, 40, 12, 44, 96, and 78 are all divisible by 2, because their last digit meets the requirements.

2. A number is divisible by 5 if its last digit is 0 or 5. For instance 4,095, and 490 are divisible by 5, because their last digit meets the requirements.

3. A number is divisible by 10 if its last digit is a zero. For instance 30, 7,000 and 600,000 are all divisible by 10, because their last digit meets the requirements.

4. A number is divisible by 3 if the sum of its digits are divisible by 3. Is 726 divisible by 3? 7 + 2 + 6 = 15. We know 15 is divisible by 3, so we know 726 is also divisible by 3.

**1** Test each number to see if it is divisible by 2, 5, 10, or 3. Circle the correct responses. The first one has been done for you.

| | | | | |
|---|---|---|---|---|
| 48 is divisible by | **(2)** | 5 | 10 | **(3)** |
| 920 is divisible by | 2 | 5 | 10 | 3 |
| 8,430 is divisible by | 2 | 5 | 10 | 3 |
| 6,000 is divisible by | 2 | 5 | 10 | 3 |
| 3,024 is divisible by | 2 | 5 | 10 | 3 |

**2** Find the quotients. Don't forget to place your decimal point and dollar sign in the quotient.

15)$180.00    21)$406.56    42)$509.46    89)$1,562.84

**3** Find the sum or difference.

| $295.97<br>+ 183.32 | $481.21<br>+ 42.49 | $999.71<br>+ 599.22 | $287.19<br>+ 402.40 |
|---|---|---|---|
| $105.37<br>− 25.10 | $271.22<br>− 50.40 | $890.71<br>− 100.29 | $267.09<br>− 188.80 |

**4** Solve the equations and check.

| $n + 13 = 16$<br>—————<br>Check | $n + 27 = 114$<br>—————<br>Check | $n + 98 = 102$<br>—————<br>Check |
|---|---|---|
| $n + 24 = 75$<br>—————<br>Check | $n + 127 = 179$<br>—————<br>Check | $n + 13 = 176$<br>—————<br>Check |

**5** Find each average.

| 34, 21, 17 | 40, 44, 28, 24, 19 |
|---|---|
| 6, 3, 6, 5 | 19, 29, 15 |
| 22, 33, 31, 26 | 3, 8, 12, 7, 10 |

**6** Work each problem and circle the correct letter. Place the letters you circled on the blanks under the riddle.

| Problem | If the answer is: | Circle | If the answer is: | Circle |
|---|---|---|---|---|
| 29 + 37 = | 66 | A | 68 | T |
| 78 + 51 = | 137 | B | 129 | S |
| 76 + 89 = | 159 | L | 165 | W |
| 37 + 111 = | 148 | A | 152 | E |
| 28 + 234 = | 262 | L | 260 | T |
| 134 + 167 = | 299 | E | 301 | L |
| 347 + 489 = | 836 | O | 846 | R |
| 514 + 619 = | 1,133 | W | 1,033 | E |

What bird is always eating ?

___  ___ ___ ___ ___ ___ ___

**Lesson 60**

# Problem Solving – Too Much? Too Little?

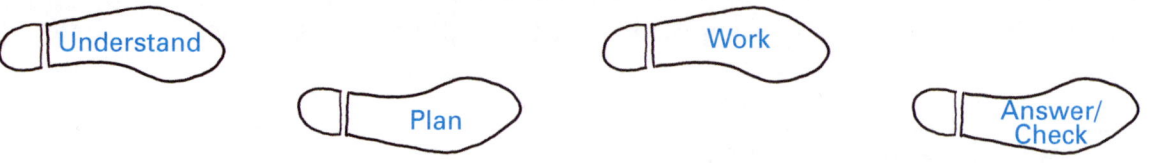

Understand  Plan  Work  Answer/Check

Some problems give you too little information to solve a problem, others give you additional data that you don't need. Look at these examples.

## Too Much Information

Steven made $16.00 last week mowing lawns.

He made $12.00 last week washing cars.

He made $632.00 last year on his paper route.

How much money did Steven earn last week?

**Facts not needed:**

The money he made on his paper route last year.

**Facts needed:**

$16.00 mowing lawns
$12.00 washing cars.

$16.00 + $12.00 = $28.00

Steven earned $28.00 last week.

## Too Little Information

Suzanne and Molly are making pies for a bake sale.

It cost $3.74 to make one apple pie.

How much will it cost to make all the pies for the bake sale?

**Missing Facts**

How many pies are needed in all?

You cannot solve this problem without more information.

**1** Some problems have information that is not needed. Underline the data that is not needed. Solve the problems.

1. John bought a slice of pizza for $2.50 and a soft drink for $ .95. He purchased a watch for $12.95. How much did John's lunch cost?

2. Tim bought a burger for $2.75, fries for $ .95, and a soft drink for $ .95. How much did Tim's lunch cost?

3. Tom bought lunch for $5.65 on Tuesday, and he spent $6.95 on Wednesday. On Friday he spent $9.50. How much more did he spend on Friday than Tuesday?

4. Gary spent $120.00 a month for eating lunch at at restaurant. If he ate out 20 times, about how much did it cost him each day?

## 2  Find the quotients.

$32\overline{)\$136.00}$    $50\overline{)\$447.50}$    $62\overline{)\$76.26}$    $95\overline{)\$1{,}170.40}$

## 3  Find the difference.

| 13 | 8 | 9 | 12 | 11 | 17 |
|---|---|---|---|---|---|
| − 8 | − 2 | − 7 | − 9 | − 8 | − 6 |

| 15 | 18 | 13 | 9 | 12 | 7 |
|---|---|---|---|---|---|
| − 7 | − 9 | − 6 | − 8 | − 4 | − 6 |

## 4  Solve the equations and check.

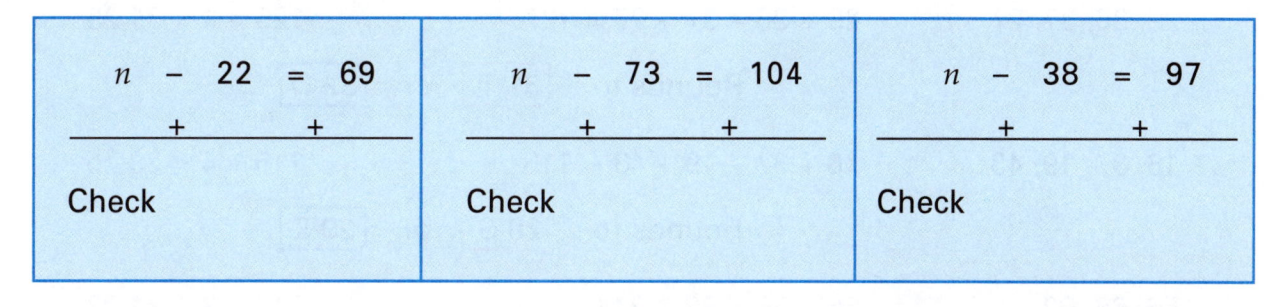

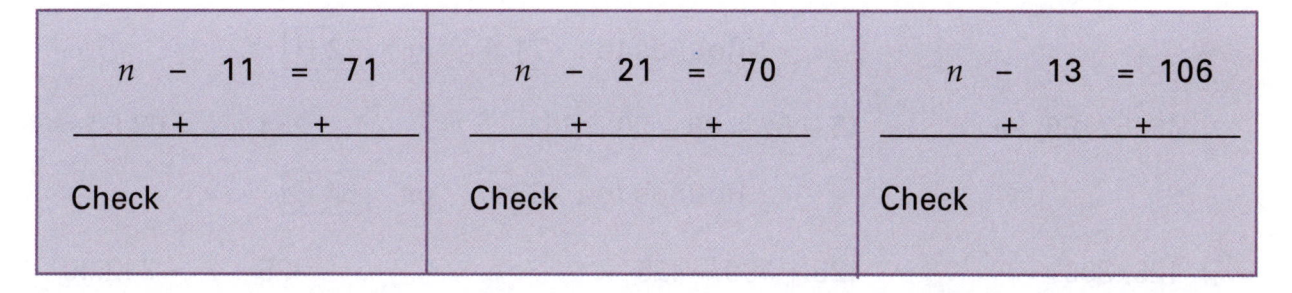

$n - 22 = 69$
+     +
Check

$n - 73 = 104$
+     +
Check

$n - 38 = 97$
+     +
Check

$n - 11 = 71$
+     +
Check

$n - 21 = 70$
+     +
Check

$n - 13 = 106$
+     +
Check

**5** Color the numbers divisible by 2 black. Color the numbers divisible by 3 red. Color the prime numbers yellow.

| | 47 | | 67 | | 23 | | 31 | | 7 | | 5 |
|---|---|---|---|---|---|---|---|---|---|---|---|
| 3 | 4 | 15 | 20 | 45 | 14 | 9 | 60 | 54 | 10 | 39 | 76 |
| | 43 | | 13 | | 11 | | 17 | | 41 | | 19 |
| 33 | 98 | 69 | 8 | 57 | 44 | 75 | 22 | 4 | 26 | 93 | 28 |

**6** Pauline averaged these numbers. She wrote the remainders as fractions. Decide if the whole number should be rounded up or down. Circle the correct answer.

13, 12, 25, 22     13 + 12 + 25 + 21 = 71     $4\overline{)71}$ = 17 R3 = $17\frac{3}{4}$

Rounds to: 17 or 18

29, 45, 72     29 + 45 + 72 = 146     $3\overline{)146}$ = 48 R2 = $48\frac{2}{3}$

Rounds to: 48 or 49

**7** Joanna used a calculator to average these numbers. She needs help rounding to the nearest whole number. Use the information you know about rounding, and circle the correct answer. If your answers are correct, they will complete the scripture:

_____ me Thy way, O lord; I will walk in thy truth.
**Psalms 86:11a**

25, 36, 37, 27     25 + 36 + 37 + 27 = 127     125 ÷ 4 = 31.25

Rounds to : 31 T or 32 O

16, 37, 19, 43     16 + 37 + 19 + 43 = 115     115 ÷ 4 = 28.75

Rounds to : 28 S or 29 E

56, 66, 92     56 + 66 + 92 = 214     214 ÷ 3 = 71.33

Rounds to : 71 A or 72 H

45, 52, 66, 90     45 + 52 + 66 + 90 = 254     254 ÷ 4 = 63.50

Rounds to : 63 O or 64 C

125, 300     125 + 300 = 425     425 ÷ 2 = 212.50

Rounds to : 212 W or 213 H

**Test 6**

**1** Find the quotient. Watch out for the zeros! 8 pts. total for this exercise.

$5\overline{)206}$     $9\overline{)456}$     $9\overline{)450}$     $6\overline{)631}$

$8\overline{)304}$     $4\overline{)589}$     $8\overline{)781}$     $7\overline{)514}$

**2** Estimate the quotients by rounding three-digit numbers to the nearest 10 and four-digit numbers to the nearest 100. 4 pts. total for this exercise.

$3\overline{)208}$     $7\overline{)626}$     $6\overline{)2,357}$     $6\overline{)4,156}$

**3** Find the average. Use your calculator to check. 5 pts. total for this exercise.

46, 15, 34, 50         86, 51, 23, 17, 91

71, 36, 64, 15         44, 26, 76, 11, 21, 80

85, 74, 28, 49

**4** Solve and interpret each answer. 2 pts. total for this exercise.

Lisa, Lori, and Kathryn went in together and purchased one nice wedding gift for a friend. They split the bill evenly among the three of them. If the bill was $96.56 how much did each person pay?

A caterer had 166 people to seat at 15 different tables for a wedding reception. How many people should be seated at each table?

## 5. Divide and check. 10 pts. total for this exercise.

$70\overline{)280}$  $50\overline{)450}$  $40\overline{)88}$  $50\overline{)255}$  $80\overline{)498}$

$70\overline{)475}$  $40\overline{)339}$  $80\overline{)725}$  $20\overline{)193}$  $90\overline{)641}$

## 6. Find the quotients. 7 pts. total for this exercise.

$88\overline{)235}$  $62\overline{)287}$  $49\overline{)127}$  $67\overline{)652}$

$35\overline{)1{,}073}$  $44\overline{)3{,}892}$  $41\overline{)3{,}578}$

## 7. Estimate the quotients by first guessing. Many of your original guesses will be incorrect. Then find the actual answer. 8 pts. total for this exercise.

$46\overline{)224}$  $68\overline{)444}$  $78\overline{)628}$  $72\overline{)640}$

$43\overline{)330}$  $12\overline{)6{,}780}$  $11\overline{)4{,}865}$  $15\overline{)9{,}803}$

44 pts. Total

**Lesson 61**

# Time Definitions

In 597 B.C. King Nebuchadnezzar looted the Jewish temple and took Judean captives to Babylon (2 Chronicles 36).

Below is Donald's baptismal certificate. Look closely at the wording on the certificate.

> This is to certify that **Donald C. Crump** was baptized at
> **Center Hill Baptist Church**
> on **February 13th** in the year of our Lord,
> **1998**.

Many times you will see information such as the statements listed above. Some may not understand what the abbreviation B.C., or the statement *in the year of our Lord,* means. Both of these are time definitions, or units for measuring time. Below you will find a chart which lists many of the time definitions you need to know.

| B.C. | = | Before Christ |
| A.D. | = | Anno Domini (after Christ's birth–*in the year of our Lord*) |
| 10 years | = | a decade |
| 100 years | = | a century |
| 1,000 years | = | a millennium |

**1** Complete.

Lori graduated from school 9 years ago. That is almost one _____ .

The United States of America is over two _____ old.

When Christ returns to Earth He will reign for 1,000 years, or a _____ .

James graduated in 1990 _____ .

In 168 _____ , Antiochus Epiphanes desecrated the temple altar by sacrificing a pig to the mythological god Zeus.

**2** Find the quotient.

9)56    3)11    7)15    5)21    4)15

**3** Use the clues to find the Mystery Number.

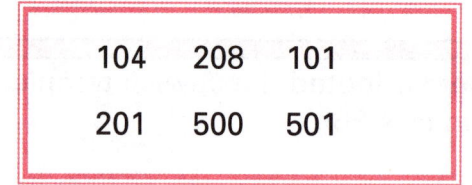

| 104 | 208 | 101 |
| 201 | 500 | 501 |

1. This number has 2 odd digits.
2. This number has a 0 in the tens' place.
3. This number has a prime digit in the hundreds' place.
4. The sum of this number's digits is 6.

   What is the number? _____

| 6,020 | 7,008 | 5,679 |

1. This number has a 0 in the hundreds' column.
2. This number is even.
3. This number is divisible by 2, 5 and 10.

   What is the number? _____

**4** Label each polygon as a pentagon, hexagon, heptagon, octagon, or decagon.

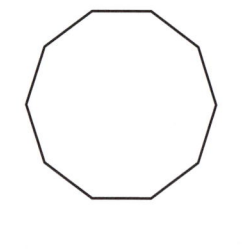

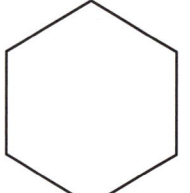

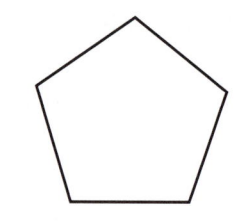

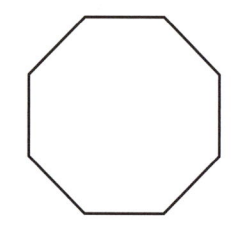

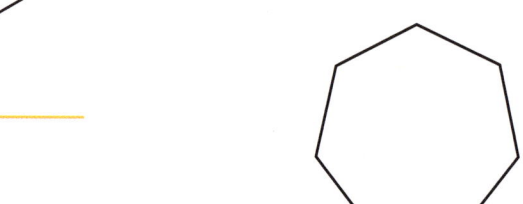

## 5  Complete.

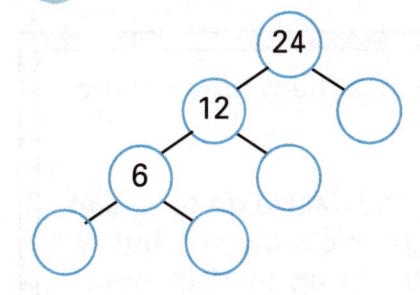

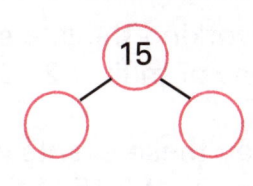

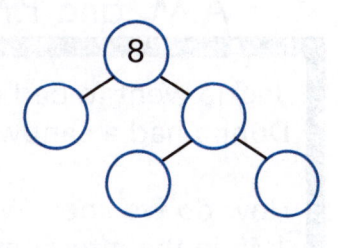

(factor trees: 24 → 12, __ ; 12 → 6, __ ; 6 → __, __ ; 15 → __, __ ; 8 → __, __ )

## 6  Solve.

$n + 5 = 26$

$n + 7 = 17$

$n + 67 = 100$

$n + 5 = 3 + 7$

$4 + n = 12 + 1$

$7 + n = 5 + 6$

## 7  Label and find the product.

```
    3  _____
  x 5  _____
   15  _____
```

$10 \times 10 =$

$12 \times 4 =$

$6 \times 9 =$

$5 \times 8 =$

$4 \times 7 =$

$9 \times 5 =$

**Lesson 62**

## A.M. and P.M.

Jackie went to bed at 1:45 after working the late shift at the local hamburger stand. Donna had a sandwich and a glass of milk at 2:45.

How do we know what time of day these events occurred? Did Jackie go to bed at 1:45 in the afternoon? Did Donna eat at 2:45 in the morning? Probably not, but how could we know for sure? It is simple. **Times from midnight up to 12:00 noon are labeled** A.M. **Times from 12:00 noon up to 12:00 midnight are labeled** P.M.

For example, we have labeled each of the following events and times as either A.M. or P.M.

| Breakfast | Dinner | Sunday School | Piano Lessons |
|---|---|---|---|
| 7:15 A.M. | 6:30 P.M. | 9:30 A.M. | 4:30 P.M. |

**1** Write A.M. or P.M.

Activity:
Eating Breakfast

Time _____

Watching the news

Time _____

Eating an early lunch

11:27  A.M.
       P.M.

Time _____

Ending the school day

2:50  A.M.
      P.M.

Time _____

196 Horizons Math 5, Student Workbook 1

**2** Give the number of faces, edges, and vertices for each space figure.

_____ faces
_____ vertices
_____ edges

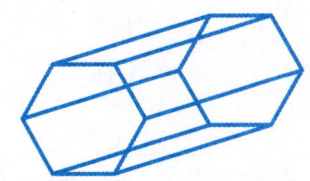

_____ faces
_____ vertices
_____ edges

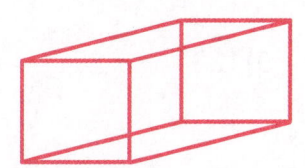

_____ faces
_____ vertices
_____ edges

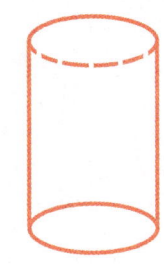

_____ faces
_____ vertices
_____ edges

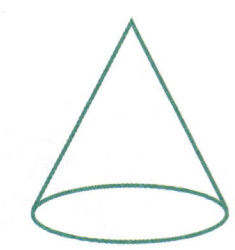

_____ faces
_____ vertices
_____ edges

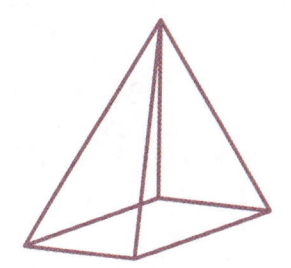

_____ faces
_____ vertices
_____ edges

**3** Use the graph to answer the following questions.

**Record Daily Temperatures**

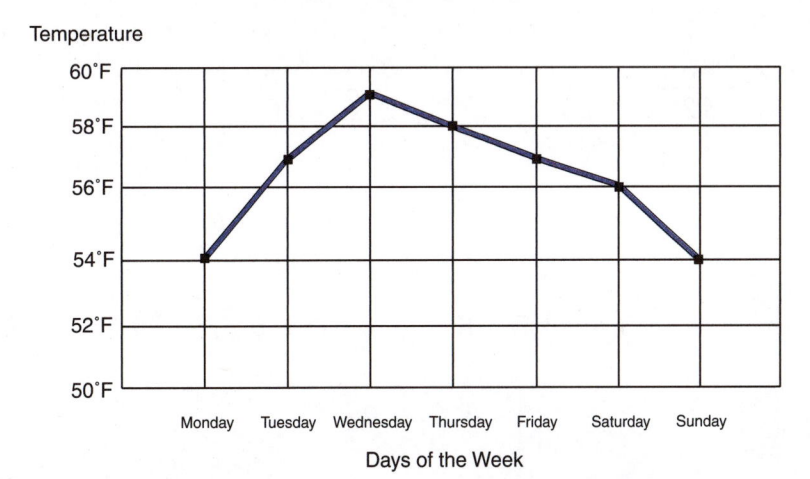

Which day(s) had the highest temperature for the week? _____

Which day(s) had the lowest temperature for the week? _____

What was the temperature difference between Wednesday and Sunday? _____

**4** Find the quotient.

$9\overline{)123}$  $\quad\quad$ $4\overline{)62}$  $\quad\quad$ $7\overline{)135}$  $\quad\quad$ $5\overline{)400}$  $\quad\quad$ $3\overline{)111}$

**5** Complete.

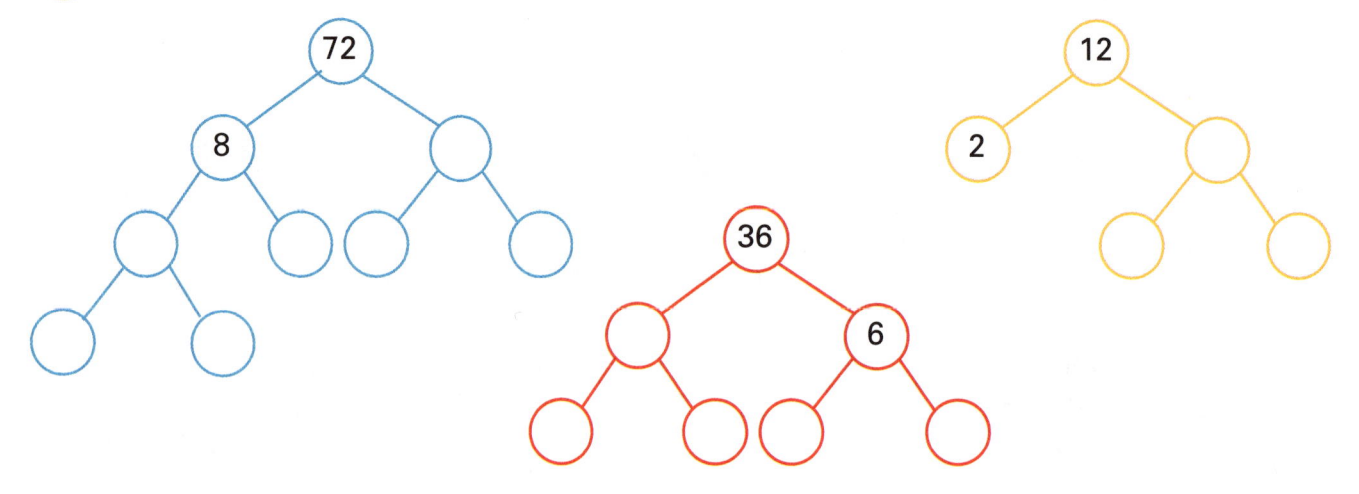

(factor tree with 72 at top, 8 on one branch)

(factor tree with 36 at top, 6 on one branch)

(factor tree with 12 at top, 2 on one branch)

**6** Circle the incorrect answers and correct them.

$$\begin{array}{r} 4 \\ \times\ 5 \\ \hline 25 \end{array} \quad\quad \begin{array}{r} 9 \\ \times\ 7 \\ \hline 60 \end{array} \quad\quad \begin{array}{r} 1 \\ \times\ 9 \\ \hline 1 \end{array}$$

$$\begin{array}{r} 7 \\ \times\ 6 \\ \hline 42 \end{array} \quad\quad \begin{array}{r} 3 \\ \times\ 5 \\ \hline 16 \end{array} \quad\quad \begin{array}{r} 10 \\ \times\ 3 \\ \hline 30 \end{array}$$

**7** Solve.

$4 + 3 = 1 + n$

$3 + n = 5 + 8$

$15 - 5 = 5 + n$

$6 + n = 14 - 4$

198 Horizons Math 5, Student Workbook 1

**Lesson 63**

## Century

What is a Century? A century is a time period of 100 years. We now live in the 21st Century. People who lived in the year 1864 lived in the 19th Century. Look at the chart below. This chart shows all the dates and centuries up to the present.

| | | | |
|---|---|---|---|
| 0 A.D. | to | 99 A.D. | 1st Century |
| 100 A.D. | to | 199 A.D. | 2nd Century |
| 200 A.D. | to | 299 A.D. | 3rd Century |
| 300 A.D. | to | 399 A.D. | 4th Century |
| 1800 A.D. | to | 1899 A.D. | 19th Century |
| 1900 A.D. | to | 1999 A.D. | 20th Century |
| 2000 A.D. | to | 2099 A.D. | 21st Century |

If you look closely you will notice that the beginning digits of the year, 1864, and the beginning digits of the century, 19th Century are one number off. This is an easy way to remember what century a year is in. Look at the first two digits of the year and then add one. For example: 1598 is in the 16th Century, 1768 is in the 18th Century, and 2012 is in the 21st Century.

**1** State the century for each year.

1394 = _____

1437 = _____

1989 = _____

1776 = _____

2201 = _____

987 = _____

② Label each angle as obtuse, acute or right.

_____   _____   _____

_____   _____

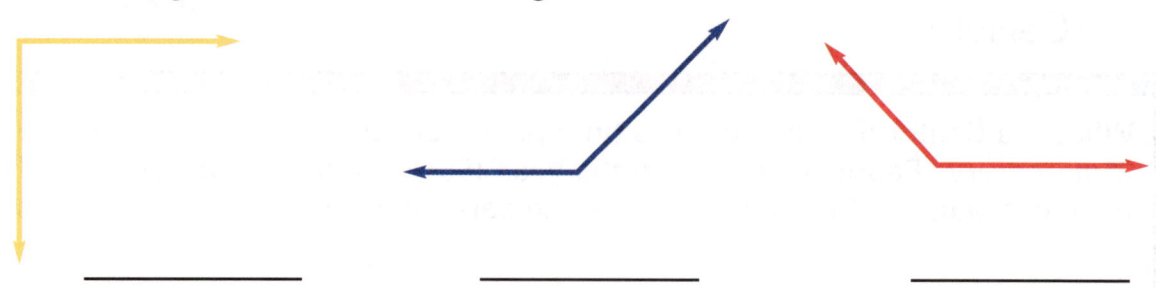

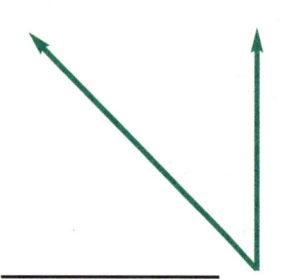

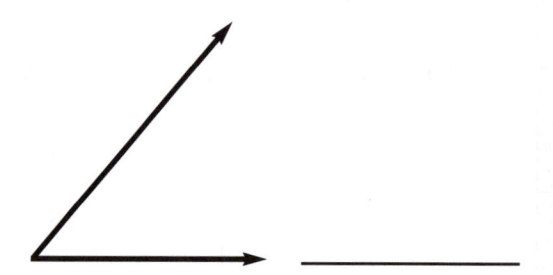

③ Answer the questions using the graph below.

**Electronic Equipment Sold in One Month**

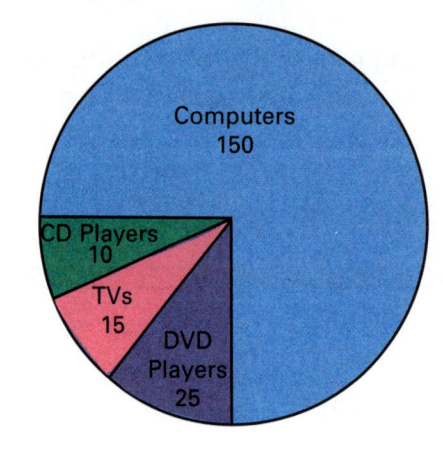

- Computers 150
- CD Players 10
- TVs 15
- DVD Players 25

How many DVD players were sold in one month? _____

Were more computers or more CD players sold in this month? How many more/less?

_____

How many electronic devices were sold in all?

_____

How many TVs and DVD players were sold?

_____

**4** Find the missing information and solve the message.

$$7\overline{)755} \dfrac{107 \text{ R } \square}{} \text{ O} \qquad 3\overline{)932} \dfrac{310 \text{ R } \square}{} \text{ R} \qquad 6\overline{)407} \dfrac{67 \text{ R } \square}{} \text{ P}$$

$$5\overline{)903} \dfrac{180 \text{ R } \square}{} \text{ W} \qquad 5\overline{)684} \dfrac{136 \text{ R } \square}{} \text{ E}$$

___  ___  ___  ___  ___
 5    6    3    4    2

**5** Use the alphabet code to add the numerical values of each word. Which word has a numerical value that is a prime number?

| | | | |
|---|---|---|---|
| A = 1 | I = 9 | Q = 17 – 12 | Y = 24 – 21 |
| B = 2 | J = 10 – 4 | R = 18 – 9 | Z = 25 – 20 |
| C = 3 | K = 11 – 2 | S = 19 – 12 | |
| D = 4 | L = 11 – 9 | T = 20 – 14 | |
| E = 5 | M = 13 – 7 | U = 21 – 13 | |
| F = 6 | N = 14 – 7 | V = 22 – 18 | |
| G = 7 | O = 15 – 7 | W = 23 – 17 | |
| H = 8 | P = 16 – 9 | X = 0 | |

JAMES _____ = _____

JOHN _____ = _____

ANDREW _____ = _____

SIMON PETER _____ = _____

**6** Fill in the missing information. Use the number 2 for "?" in the divisor and the number 5 for any "?" in the dividend. Find the quotient.

$?\overline{)16}$     $7\overline{)21}$     $3\overline{)1?}$     $9\overline{)4?}$

**Lesson 64**

## Time Equivalents

Tom needed to tape a 1½ hour TV show for school. When he went to buy a blank video tape at the store all of the video tape lengths were labeled in minutes, not hours. How many minutes of tape would he need in order to tape a 1½ hour movie?

This problem can easily be solved if Tom knows his time equivalents. The chart below shows these time equivalents.

| 1 minute | = | 60 seconds |
|---|---|---|
| 1 hour | = | 60 minutes |
| 1 day | = | 24 hours |

Tom would need a 90 minute tape in order to have enough tape to record his TV show.

How long of a tape would be needed to record a 2 hour show? 120 minutes. If there are 60 minutes in 1 hour, then 60 minutes + 60 minutes = 120 minutes.

**1** Match.

_____ 1 hour         A. 300 seconds

_____ 90 seconds     B. 3 days

_____ 24 hours       C. 60 minutes

_____ 72 hours       D. 2 hours

_____ 120 Minutes    E. 1½ minutes

_____ 5 minutes      F. 1 day

**2** Find the quotient.

2)802          8)856          2)441          3)571

**3** Fill in the bar graph with the given information.

Faye hiked 25 miles
Lori hiked 30 miles
Cindy hiked 20 miles
Lisa hiked 10 miles

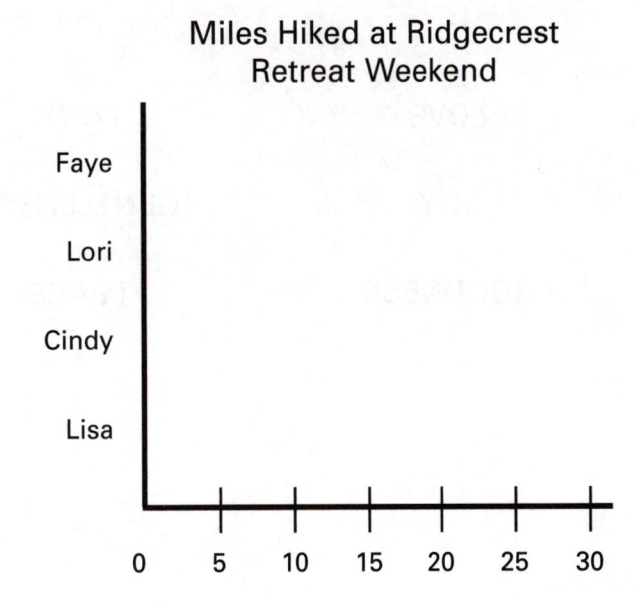

Miles Hiked at Ridgecrest Retreat Weekend

Faye
Lori
Cindy
Lisa

0   5   10   15   20   25   30

**4** Find the perimeter.

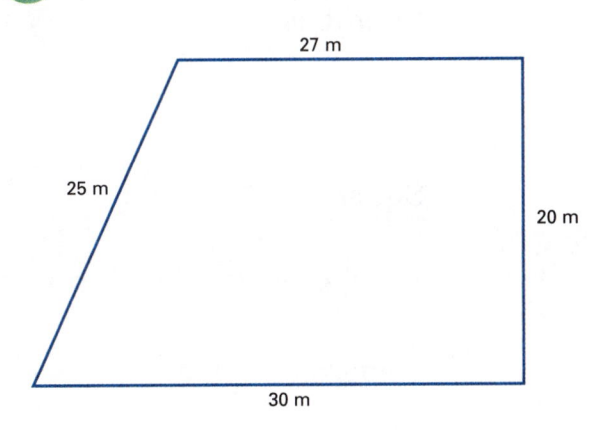

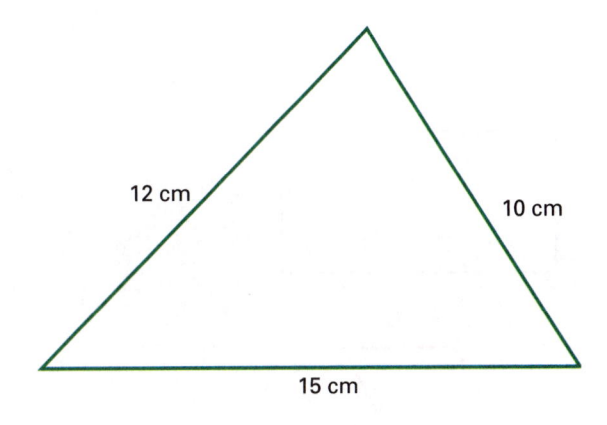

27 m
25 m
20 m
30 m

12 cm
10 cm
15 cm

Perimeter = _____     Perimeter = _____

**5** Find the quotient. Every number has a corresponding letter above it. Put the **dividends** in order from smallest to largest to reveal a message.

V    A
54 ÷ 6 =

L    O
72 ÷ 9 =

E    I
16 ÷ 8 =

I    S
63 ÷ 9 =

6. Count the number of letters in each word. Circle the words with a prime number of letters.

| LOVE | FAITH | PATIENCE |
| JOY | GENTLENESS | KINDNESS |
| GOODNESS | PEACE | SELF-CONTROL |

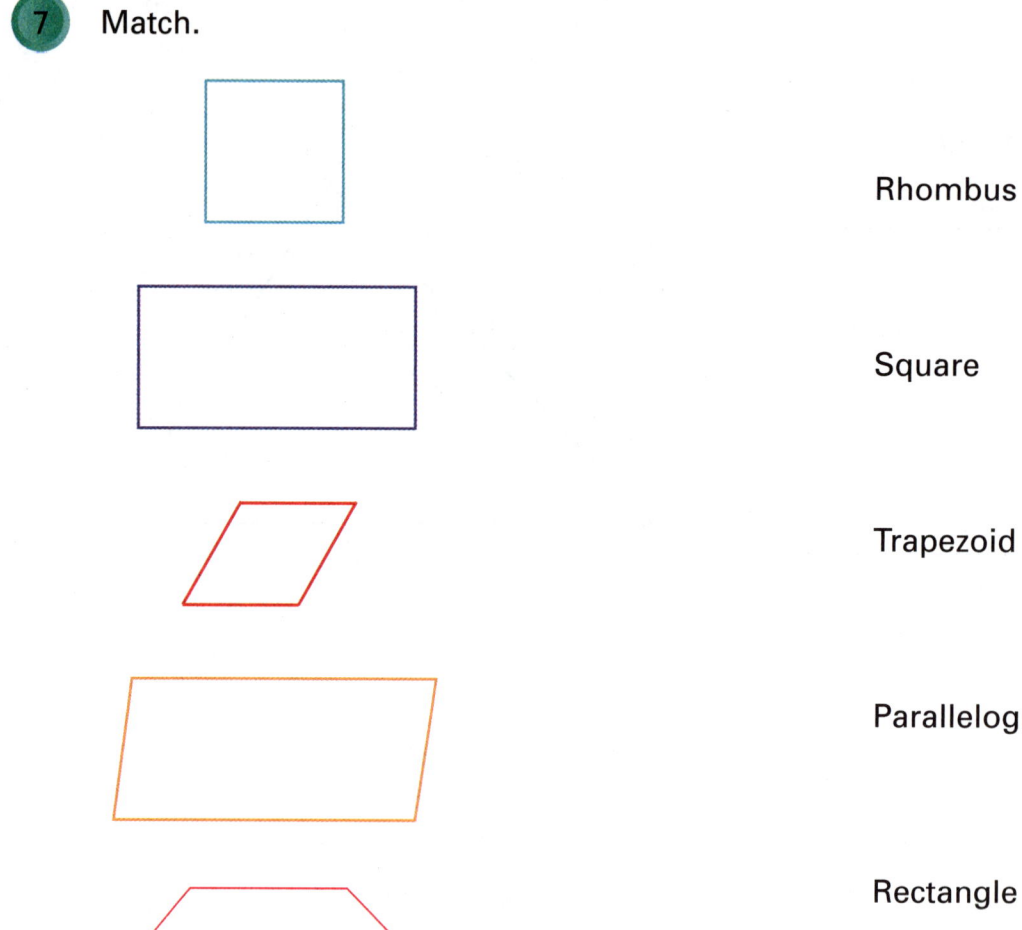

7. Match.

square — Rhombus

rectangle — Square

rhombus — Trapezoid

parallelogram — Parallelogram

trapezoid — Rectangle

**Lesson 65**

# Elapsed Time

| Current Time | Plane Destination | Departure Time |
|---|---|---|
| (clock showing 8:00) | San Francisco, CA | 9:00 |
| | Denver, CO | 8:35 |
| | Miami, FL | 8:20 |
| (8:00) | Jackson Hole, WY | 8:45 |

In how many minutes will the plane leave for Miami, Florida?

If it is now 8:00 (according to the clock), count by five to find the number of minutes from 8: to 8:20 when the Miami plane leaves.

The plane bound for Miami will leave in 20 minutes.

The plane bound for Jackson Hole, Wyoming stops 2 hours and 30 minutes into the flight for a connection in Salt Lake City. What time will it be then? (Do not adjust for any time zone changes)

$$8:45 \; + \; 2 \text{ hours} \; + \; 30 \text{ minutes} \; = 11:15$$
$$(8:45) \quad (9:45, 10:45) \quad (11:15)$$

These examples have shown how to calculate elapsed time, or the passing of time.

**1** Find the elapsed time. Write the new time on the blank clock.

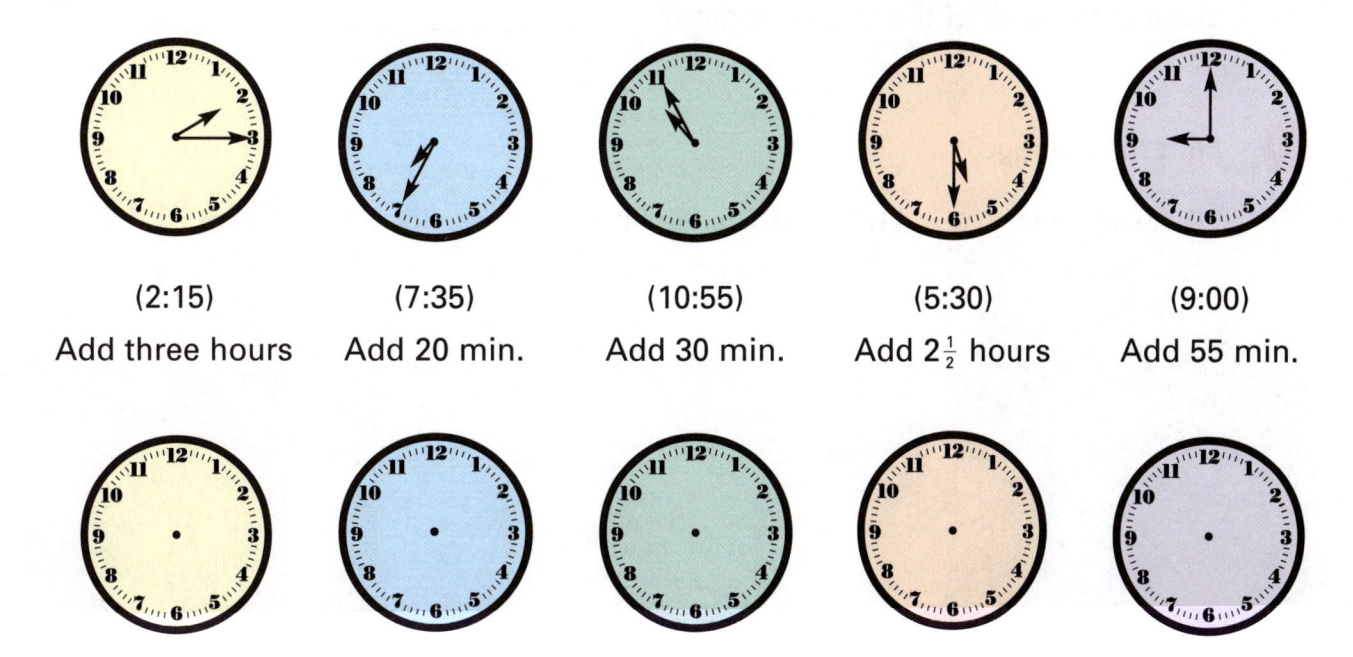

| (2:15) | (7:35) | (10:55) | (5:30) | (9:00) |
|---|---|---|---|---|
| Add three hours | Add 20 min. | Add 30 min. | Add $2\frac{1}{2}$ hours | Add 55 min. |

**2** Match.

| | |
|---|---|
| 3 minutes | 1 minute |
| 2 days | 60 minutes |
| 1 hour | 48 hours |
| 60 seconds | 180 seconds |

**3** Find the area.

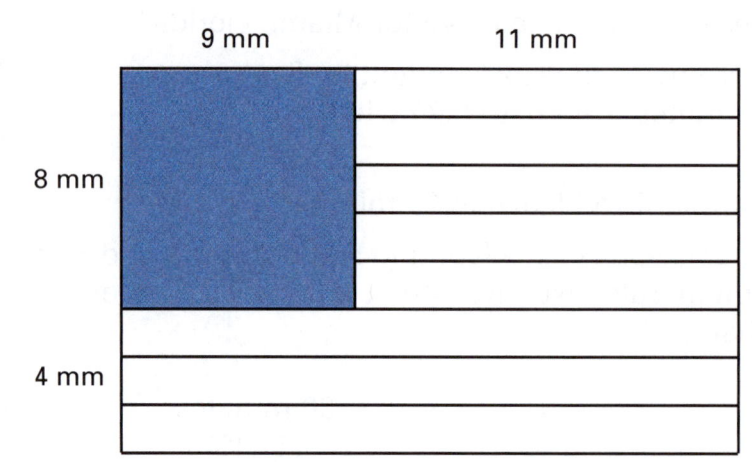

9 mm    11 mm

8 mm

4 mm

What is the area of the blue region? _____

What is the total area of the flag? _____

What is the area of the striped region? _____

**4** Find the average.

16, 20, 80, 14

41, 50, 70, 35, 90, 55, 60, 75, 30, 35

50, 26, 75, 25

**5** Find the product.

```
  472        319            562
x   6      x   3          x   5
```

```
  570            543
x   4          x   2
```

**6** Find the sum.

```
  65         42        248        363        725
+ 27       + 51      + 103      + 321      +  56
```

**7** Solve.

$891 + n = 1{,}496$

$46 + n = 78$

$193 + n = 290$

$23 + n = 50$

### Lesson 66

## Calendar

Every April, several Canadian geese fly into the pond behind the Fowler's house. They stay for about 6 months. At that time they leave for warmer weather. In what month do the birds leave?

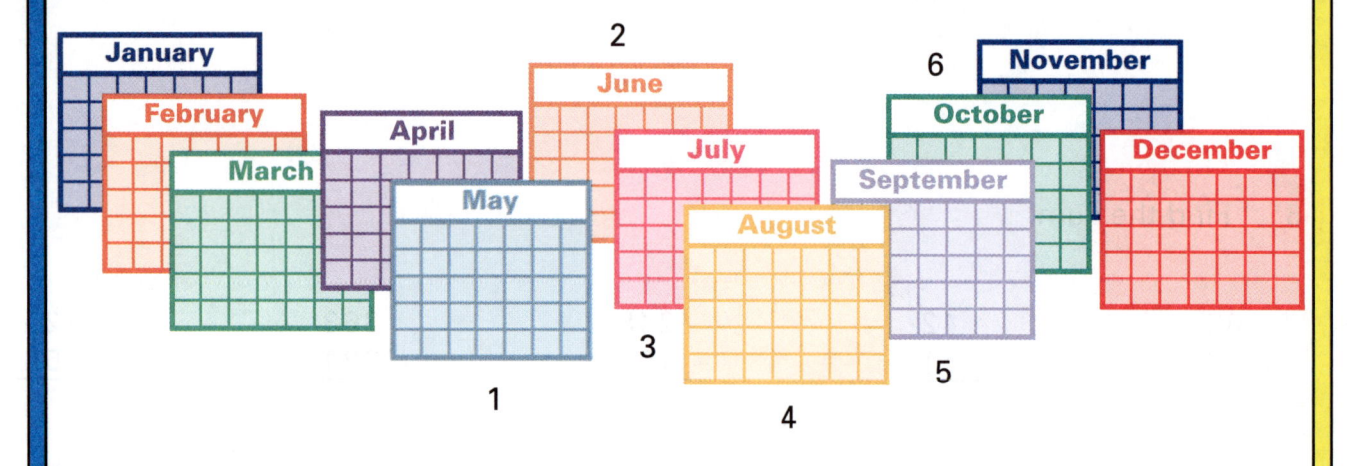

January, February, March, April, May, June, July, August, September, October, November, December

1. May
2. June
3. July
4. August
5. September
6. October

The birds leave in October because October is 6 months after April.

### CALENDAR UNITS

| 1 year | = 365 days |
| 1 leap year | = 366 days |
| 1 year | = 52 weeks |
| 1 year | = 12 months |

10 years = 1 decade
100 years = 1 century
1,000 years = 1 millennium
1 week = 7 days
1 month = 30 or 31 days (except February)

### November

| S | M | T | W | T | F | S |
|---|---|---|---|---|---|---|
|   |   |   |   |   | 1 | 2 |
| 3 | 4 | 5 | 6 | 7 | 8 | 9 |
| 10 | 11 | 12 | 13 | 14 | 15 | 16 |
| 17 | 18 | 19 | 20 | 21 | 22 | 23 |
| 24 | 25 | 26 | 27 | 28 | 29 | 30 |

208  Horizons Math 5, Student Workbook 1

**1.** Use the calendar and calendar units chart to answer these questions.

If Thanksgiving is the last Thursday in November, what date is that? _____

How many school days are there in November if school starts on the fourth of the month, and the students have the last week off for Thanksgiving? _____

Some school years have 182 days. How many full weeks is that? _____

How many weeks are there in a decade if we ignore leap year? _____

How many months are there in a century? _____

How many weeks are there in 49 days? _____

Which is more, 369 days or one leap year? _____

Which is more, 27 hours or 2 days? _____

**2.** Use the clock at the right to solve the questions.

If Sarah needs to be at work by 12:00, does she have time to take a 2 hour tour at the museum?

Kevin will go to lunch at 1:30. How much longer does he have to wait?

Lisa has been at school since 8:00. How long has she been in class?

If Tom just arrived at work and will stay there until 6:00, without leaving, how many hours will he work?

**3.** Complete the chart.

| Hours | Minutes | Seconds | Days (if applicable) |
|---|---|---|---|
| 3 |  | 10,800 |  |
| 1 |  | 3,600 |  |
| 24 | 1,440 |  |  |
|  | 2,880 |  | 2 |
| 2 |  | 7,200 |  |

**4** Average.

24, 56, 89, 90

56, 78, 43, 10, 13, 20

5, 8, 9, 4

**5** Find the product and solve the puzzle.

Across
1. 50 × 168 =
2. 12 × 516 =

Down
3. 451 × 31 =
4. 25 × 203 =

**6** Find the sum.

```
  699,560          498,124         56,091          1,634
+ 173,703        + 780,543       + 11,805        + 3,489
```

**7** Find the missing addend.

```
   1,99☐            6,318           5☐
 + 9,960          + ☐,☐33        + 1 2
  ──────          ───────         ─────
  11,954            8,251           6 8
```

210  Horizons Math 5, Student Workbook 1

# Lesson 67

## Time Zones

Cathy is traveling from Savannah, Georgia to San Francisco, California. Before leaving, she decides to set her watch to California time. If it is 8:00 A.M. in Georgia, what time is it in San Francisco?

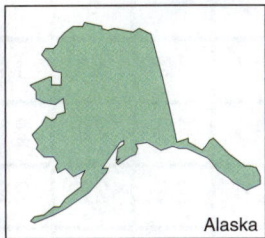

There are 24 different time zones in the world. The diagram below shows the different time zones that affect the United States. There are 6 of them. As you travel from east to west, subtract one hour for each time zone. This means that at 8:00 A.M. in Georgia, which is in the Eastern time zone, it is 5:00 A.M. in California. If you were traveling from west to east, then you would add an hour for each time zone

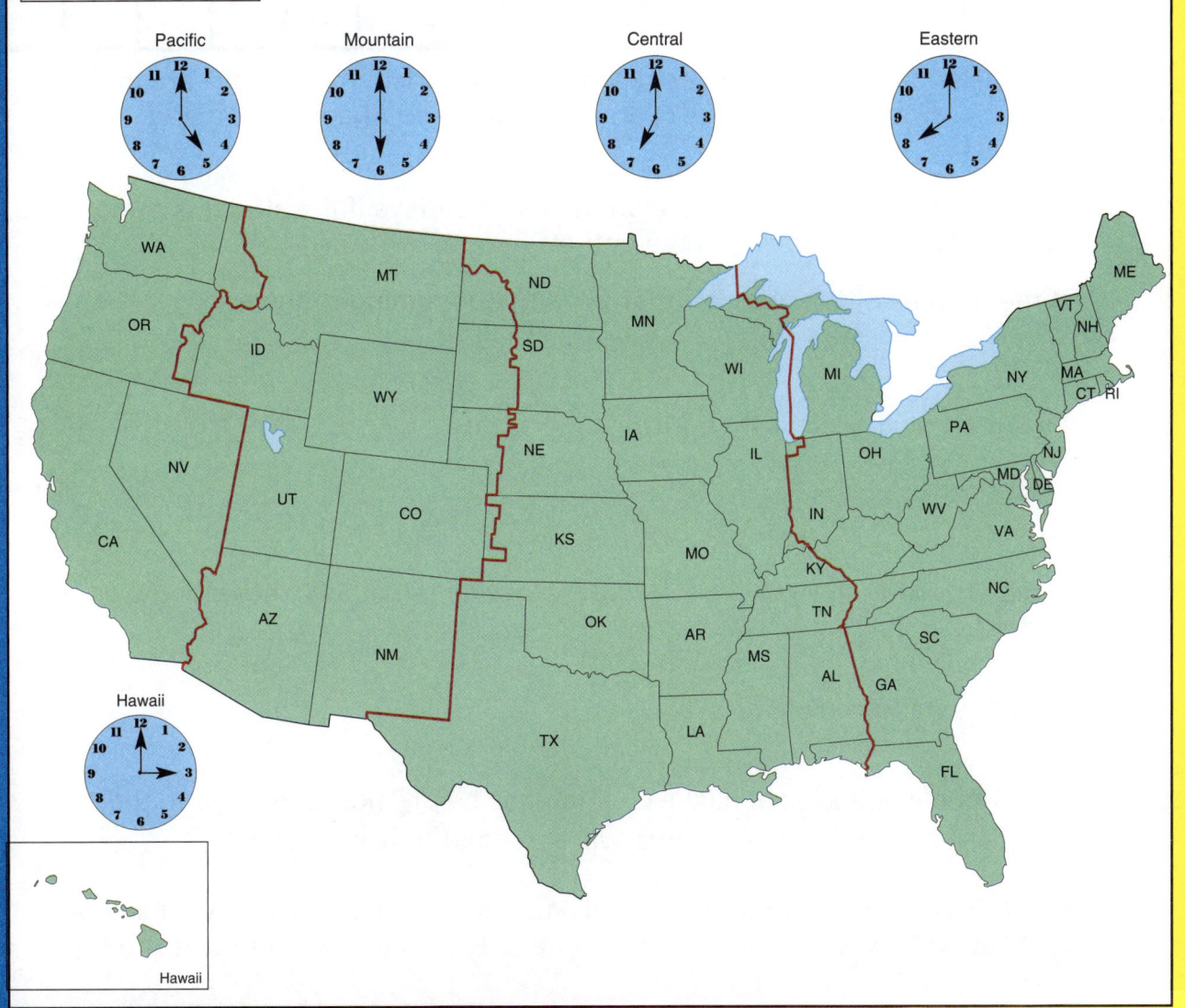

**1** Use the map to answer these questions.

In which time zone is Nevada?

In which time zone is Texas?

If is it 6:00 P.M. in Dallas, Texas, what time is it in Boston, Massachusetts?

If it is 11:00 A.M. in Atlanta, GA, what time is it in Phoenix, Arizona?

**2** Solve.

**November**

| S | M | T | W | T | F | S |
|---|---|---|---|---|---|---|
|   |   |   |   |   | 1 | 2 |
| 3 | 4 | 5 | 6 | 7 | 8 | 9 |
| 10 | 11 | 12 | 13 | 14 | 15 | 16 |
| 17 | 18 | 19 | 20 | 21 | 22 | 23 |
| 24 | 25 | 26 | 27 | 28 | 29 | 30 |

**December**

| S | M | T | W | T | F | S |
|---|---|---|---|---|---|---|
| 1 | 2 | 3 | 4 | 5 | 6 | 7 |
| 8 | 9 | 10 | 11 | 12 | 13 | 14 |
| 15 | 16 | 17 | 18 | 19 | 20 | 21 |
| 22 | 23 | 24 | 25 | 26 | 27 | 28 |
| 29 | 30 | 31 |   |   |   |   |

On the calendars above, the Thanksgiving and Christmas holidays are indicated in blue. How many whole weeks are there between Thanksgiving and Christmas?

How many school days are between the two holidays if the students are out the entire Thanksgiving week and the entire Christmas week?

List the months of the year in order from the beginning to the end.

Which months have less than 31 days?

**3** Solve.

Tabitha arrived at the movies at 12:30 P.M. If she left at 3:00, how long was the matinee?

How many minutes is this?

Kimberly's plane leaves at 6:00 P.M. If it takes her $1\frac{1}{2}$ hours to drive to the airport and park her car, what time will she need to leave home?

Christy drove from Orlando, Florida to Atlanta, Georgia in one day. If she left Florida at 10:30 A.M. and arrived in Atlanta at 6:30 P.M., how long was the trip?

**4** Find the quotient. Check your answers. The first one has been done for you.

Worked:          Checked:

$$60\overline{)251}^{\ 4\ R11}$$          $60 \times 4 = 240 + 11 = 251$          $40\overline{)167}$

$20\overline{)90}$          $70\overline{)273}$

$33\overline{)167}$

**5** Find the product.

717
x 502

109
x 120

271
x 512

721
x 851

404
x 164

**6** Solve.

The preschool director needs to calculate salaries for the coming year. If each teacher makes $8.50 an hour, how much is her salary for a four week month? (She works 4 days a week for 4 hours a day).

If each teacher's assistant makes $6.00 per hour, how much money will be made in a four week month?

How much more money per month does a teacher make than an assistant?

**Lesson 68**

# Counting Money

Timmy purchased a bicycle and a tire pump. The total cost was $125.78. He gave the cashier $130.00 and received $4.22 back from the sale. How many bills and coins did the cashier give him?

Four Dollars     and     twenty-two cents = $4.22

The dollar amount is always given before the change amount. Remember place value! Dollars are whole numbers and coins are fractional (decimal) parts of a dollar. The word "and" signals a decimal is present in the number.

**1** Give the value in bills and coins.

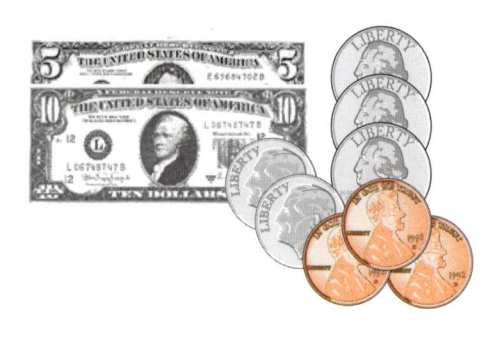

**2** Find the quotient.

22)826        40)720        32)920        50)2,800

**3** Solve.

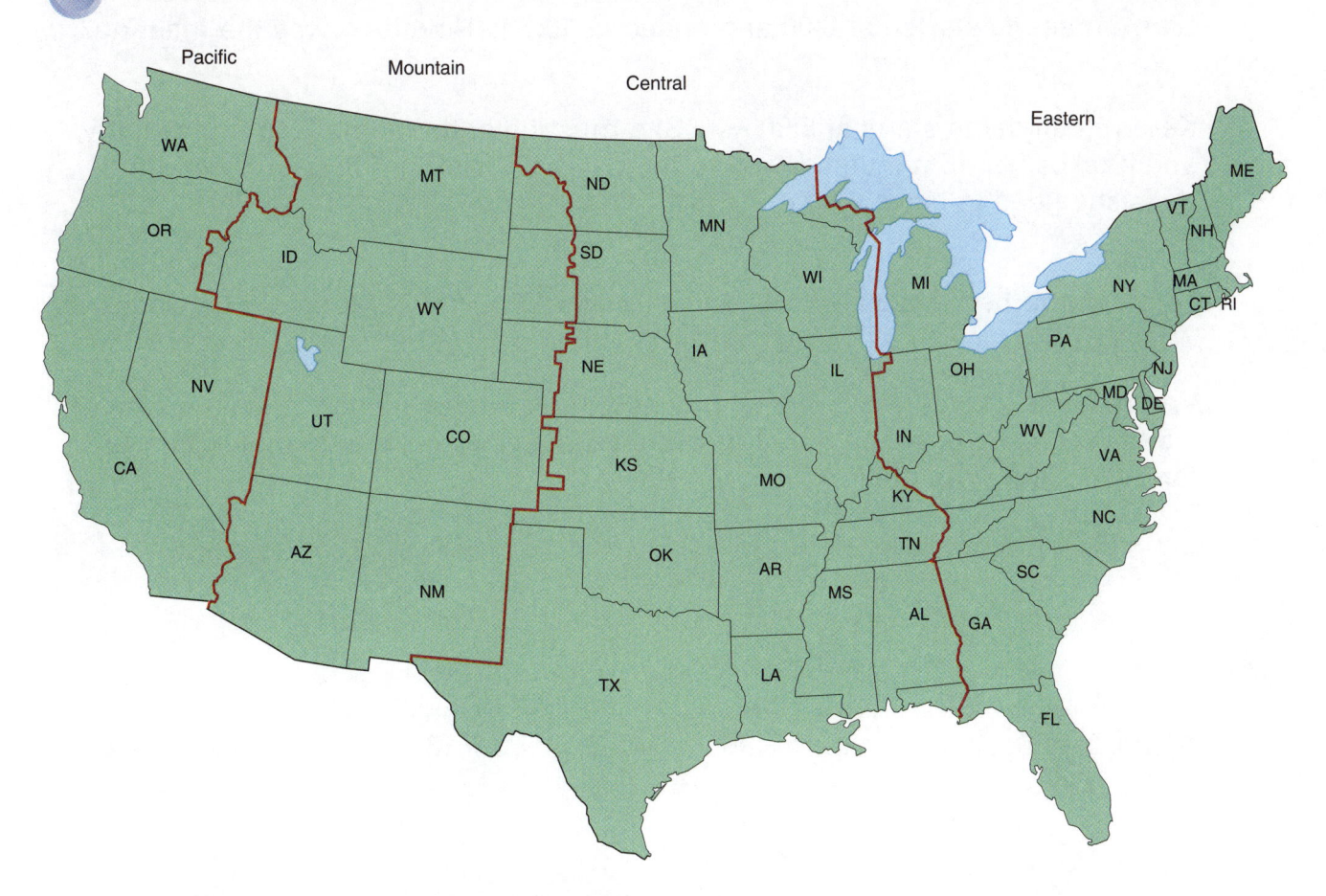

In what time zone is Seattle, Washington? _____

Suppose it is 3:00 Mountain time; what time is it in Central time? _____

What time is it in Salt Lake City when it is 4:00 in New York City? _____

When it is 2:00 P.M. in Houston, Texas, what time is it in Los Angeles? _____

**4** Answer.

How many weeks are in a year? _____

How many days are in a year? _____

How many months are in a year? _____

How many days are in a week? _____

Which months have 31 days? _____

_____

**5** Solve.

Sam's meeting started at 8:00 and ended at 10:30. How long was the meeting?

Karen's ball game starts at 5:30 P.M. She must be at the game 30 minutes early, and it takes her 15 minutes to get to the ball field from her house. What time does she need to leave?

Tom went to bed at 9:30 P.M. He woke up at 7:15 A.M. How long did he sleep?

When Jamie arrived at work and punched in on the time clock, it gave a time of 7:58. When she punched out at lunch, the time clock gave a time of 1:05. How long did Jamie work before lunch?

**6** Solve.

$n \times 5 = 30$

$n \times 4 = 36$

$n \times 6 = 18$

$12 \times 2 = n \times 8$

**7** Solve.

Science World had a winter attendance of 12,593 for January, 13,967 for February, and 11,274 for March. In the summer they had an attendance of 20,473 in June, 26,385 in July, and 28,583 in August. What was the difference between the total winter attendance and the total summer attendance?

Elmer went on a hiking and camping trip. He paid $55.00 for a pack, $38.00 for a cook stove, and $100.00 for a thermal sleeping bag. His food bill totaled $40.00, and he paid $5.00 per day to park his car at the secured parking area at the head of the hiking trail. If he was gone 7 days, how much did the entire trip cost him?

**Lesson 69**

# Giving Change

Christy bought a package of computer diskettes for $14.67. She paid for them with a $20.00 bill. What change should she get?

1. To count change, start with the cost of the item ($14.67).
2. Using coins with the smallest value, begin to count up to the amount given as payment for the item ($20.00).

$14.67        +        $.03         +        $.05       +       $.25         +       $5.00
($14.67)        ($14.68  $14.69  $14.70)        ($14.75)        ($15.00)              ($20.00)

Christy should receive $5.33 in change

```
  9 91
$20.00
-14.67
  5.33
```

Another way to find change is to subtract.

**1** Count the change. Use the fewest coins and bills possible. Write the total amount due.

| Price | Paid | Change Due |
|---|---|---|
| Ex: $1.55 | $2.00 | 2 dimes, 1 quarter = $.45 |
| $3.74 | $5.00 | |
| $8.29 | $10.00 | |
| $11.36 | $15.00 | |
| $32.15 | $40.00 | |
| $17.19 | $20.00 | |

Horizons Math 5, Student Workbook 1   217

**2** Match.

$2.71

$2.45

$2.81

**3** Label and color each time zone.

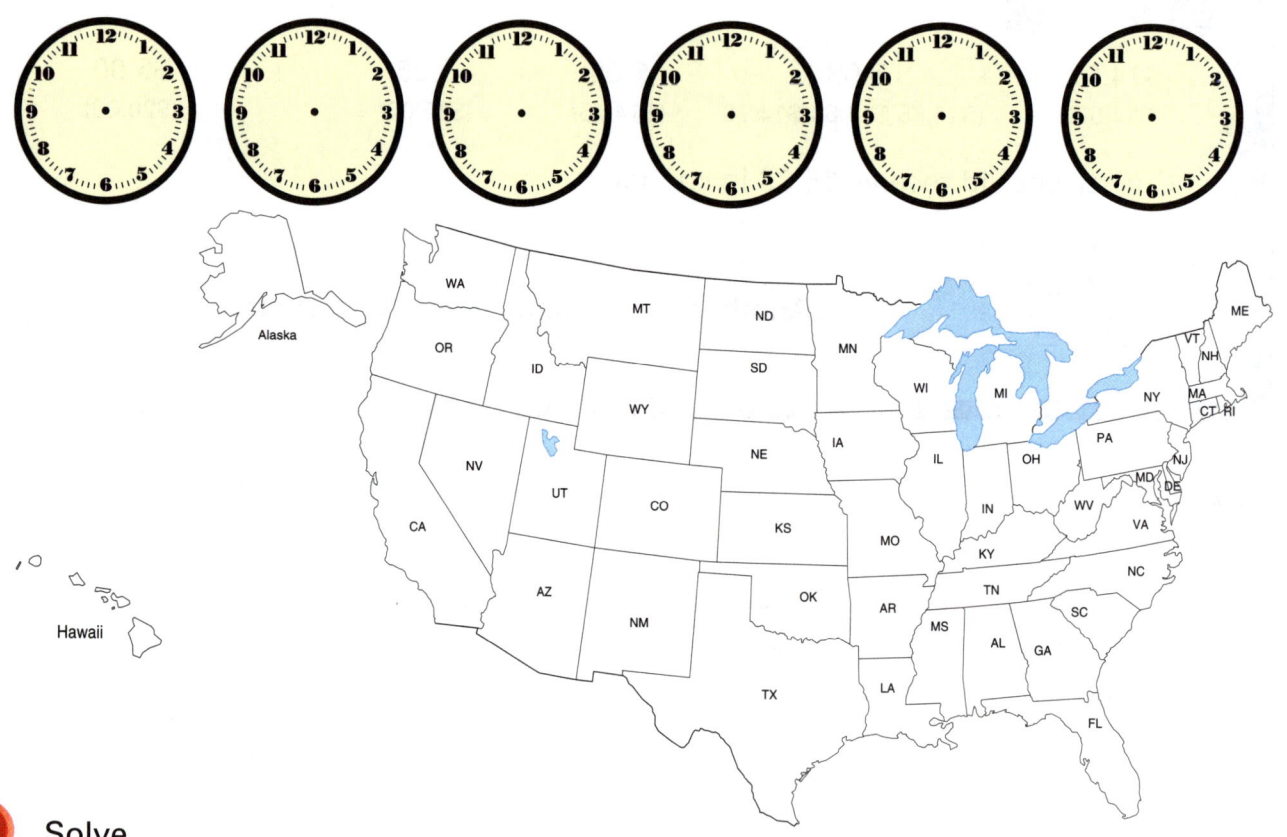

**4** Solve.

If a dog is 144 months old, how many years old is it?

A century is 100 years. How many weeks are there in a century, if leap year is ignored?

How many total days are there in the months of April, May, and June?

How many weeks are there in a decade ignoring leap years?

218 Horizons Math 5, Student Workbook 1

### 5. Complete the table.

| Factors | | Product | Exponent | Number of Zeros |
|---|---|---|---|---|
| | 10 x 10 | | 2 | 2 |
| $10^3$ | | 1,000 | 3 | 3 |
| | 10 x 10 x 10 x 10 | | | |
| $10^5$ | 10 x 10 x 10 x 10 x 10 | | | |
| $10^6$ | | | | |

### 6. Find the sum or difference.

$3.20
+ 1.35

$8.75
+ 2.39

$5.82
+ 1.65

$15.70
−   8.90

$13.30
−   6.99

### 7. Solve.

$n + 45 = 90$

$n + 87 = 190$

$n + 178 = 550$

$n + 21 = 400$

### 8. Find the quotient.

6)4,707

9)4,229

7)2,705

# Lesson 70

## Problem Solving

When in the working stage of problem solving, look at your work and answer to see if it is reasonable.

Chad wanted to purchase 4 baseball tickets for the Friday night game. If each ticket costs $15.00 how much will he spend?

Answer: about $100.00

Is this answer reasonable or not?

Think logically. $15.00 x 2 = $30.00 then $15.00 x 4 = $60.00.

$100.00 is not a reasonable answer.

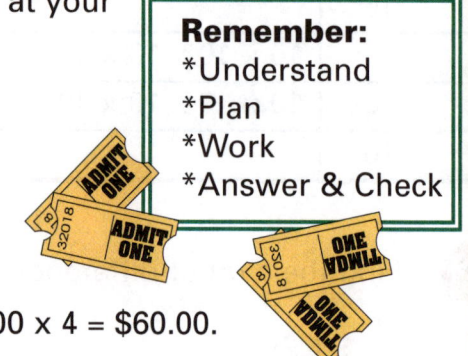

**Remember:**
*Understand
*Plan
*Work
*Answer & Check

**1** Write yes or no to tell if each answer is reasonable or not.
(Hint: Use estimation to help you decide)

The attendance at 3 baseball games was 120,352; 135,072; and 150,123. How many total fans attended all three games combined?

Answer: 1,305,555

Reasonable? _____

A set of 5 knives is on sale for $55.00. How much does each knife cost?

Answer: $10.00

Reasonable? _____

Leslie has $15.00. She wants to buy a CD for $18.95 and a book for $5.25. How much more money does she need to purchase both of these items?

Answer: $5.00

Reasonable? _____

John purchased 4 baseball cards for his collection. They cost $1.25 each. How much was the total cost of the baseball cards?

Answer: $5.00

Reasonable? _____

Tara priced two pair of earrings. One pair was $35.00. The other pair was $17.95. What is the difference in the price of the earrings?

Answer: $30.00

Reasonable? _____

**2** Write down the amount of change due and the coins and bills you would give for change.

A customer bought a coke for $ .85. How much change should he receive from a $1.00 bill?

_____

A set of highlighters cost $2.59. How much is the change from a $5.00?

_____

Kara bought a jacket for $62.95. How much change should she receive from $80.00?

_____

Mr. Hill purchased a plant for $12.95, a shovel for $15.75, and some fertilizer for $9.95. How much change did he receive from a $50.00 bill?

_____

**3** Solve.

Suppose it is 12:00 Eastern time:    Suppose it is 3:00 Mountain time:

   What is the Central time? _____    What is the Eastern time? _____

   What is the Pacific time? _____    What is the Alaska time? _____

   What is the Hawaii time? _____    What is the Central time? _____

**4** Color the numbers which are divisible by 2, 3, or 5.

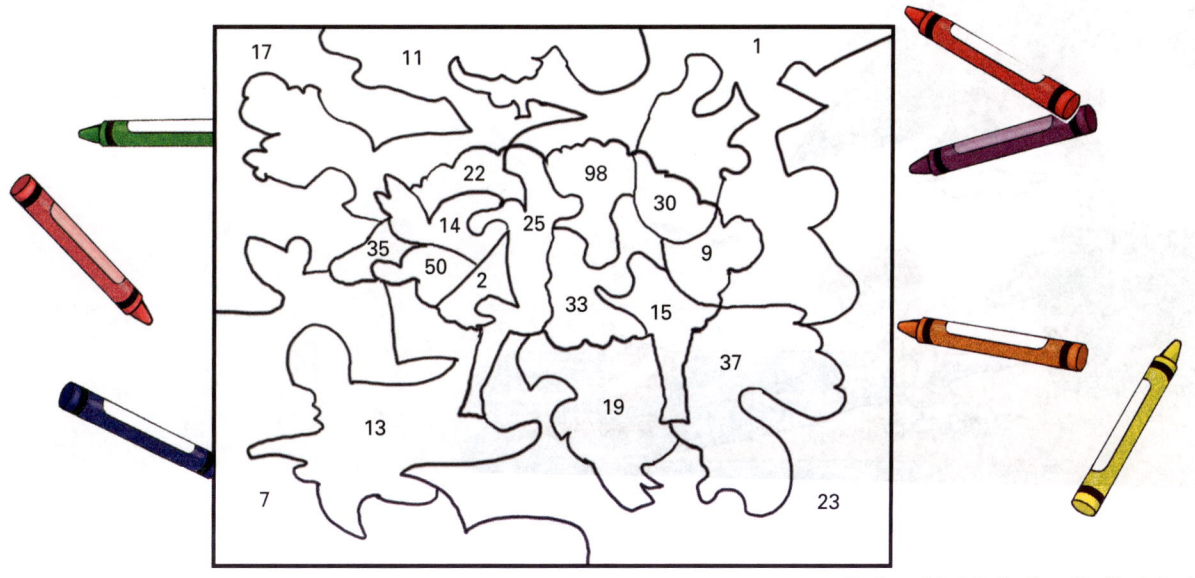

17, 11, 1, 22, 98, 30, 14, 25, 35, 9, 50, 2, 33, 15, 37, 13, 19, 7, 23

5. Complete the table. The first one is done for you.

| | Factors | Product | Exponent | Number of Zeros |
|---|---|---|---|---|
| $10^4$ | 10 x 10 x 10 x 10 | 10,000 | 4 | 4 |
| $10^5$ | | | | |
| $10^6$ | | | | |
| $10^7$ | | | | |
| $10^8$ | | | | |

6. Solve.

$n - 34 = 154$

$n - 78 = 213$

$n - 89 = 513$

$n - 512 = 120$

Test 7

**1** Find the quotients. 8 pts. total for this exercise.

29)5,249     16)6,528     13)2,613     35)6,755

82)8,856     13)$26.39    15)$45.00    27)$378.00

**2** Round the dividend and divisor to estimate each quotient. 4 pts. total for this exercise.

53)382     28)902     84)4,341     33)62,899

**3** Test each number to see if it is divisible by 2, 5, 10, or 3. Circle the correct responses. The first one has been done for you. 4 pts. total for this exercise.

| | | | | |
|---|---|---|---|---|
| 48 is divisible by | (2) | 5 | 10 | (3) |
| 820 is divisible by | 2 | 5 | 10 | 3 |
| 9,420 is divisible by | 2 | 5 | 10 | 3 |
| 8,000 is divisible by | 2 | 5 | 10 | 3 |
| 6,024 is divisible by | 2 | 5 | 10 | 3 |

**4** Answer each question using the words decade, century, millennium, A.D., or B.C.

The Mondas were married in 1987. In 1997 how long will they have been married? 4 pts. total for this exercise.

_____

Christ was born almost 2 _____ ago.

James graduated in 1990 _____ .

In 740 _____ Isaiah became a prophet.

Horizons Math 5, Student Workbook 1   223

**5** Some problems have information that is not needed. Underline the data that is not needed Solve the problems. 4 pts. total for this exercise.

1. John bought a pizza for $6.50 and a soft drink for $0.95. He purchased a watch for $12.95. How much did John's lunch cost?

2. Kim bought a calculator for $20.75, a package of pencils for $0.95, and a package of erasers for $0.95. How much did Kim spend in all?

3. Alice bought lunch for $4.65 on Tuesday, and she spent $6.95 on Wednesday. On Friday she spent $9.50. How much more did she spend on Friday than Tuesday?

4. Garrett spent $100.00 a month for eating lunch at various restaurants. If he ate out 20 times, about how much did it cost him each day?

**6** Write the time. Be sure to include A.M. or P.M. 4 pts. total for this exercise.

| Activity: | Eating an early lunch | Watching the morning news | Ending the school day | Eating a late breakfast |
|---|---|---|---|---|
| | | | 3:20 A.M./P.M. | 9:27 A.M./P.M. |
| Time: | _____ | _____ | _____ | _____ |

**7** Match. 8 pts.

_____ 1 hour          A.  300 seconds
_____ 90 seconds      B.  18th Century
_____ 24 hours        C.  60 minutes
_____ 72 hours        D.  14th Century
_____ 120 Minutes     E.  $1\frac{1}{2}$ minute
_____ 5 minutes       F.  1 day
_____ 1394            G.  3 days
_____ 1788            H.  2 hours

**8** Find the elapsed time. Write the new time on the blank. 5 pts. total for this exercise.

| Add 2 hours | Add 30 min. | Add 30 min. | Add $4\frac{1}{2}$ hours | Add 45 min. |
|---|---|---|---|---|
| _____ | _____ | _____ | _____ | _____ |

41 pts. Total

Lesson 71

# Points, Lines, Segments, Rays, and Planes

A **point** shows an exact location. It is named by a capital letter. (K)

A **line** goes on and on in both directions. ($\overleftrightarrow{DE}$)

A **line segment** is part of a line. It has two endpoints. ($\overline{LM}$)

A **ray** is part of a line. It has one endpoint and goes on and on in one direction. ($\overrightarrow{UV}$)

A **plane** is a set of points on a flat surface that extends without end in all directions.

| Geometry Terms | Geometry in Pictures | Geometry in Symbols | Geometry in Words |
|---|---|---|---|
| Point | • K | K | Point K |
| Line | D — E | $\overleftrightarrow{DE}$ | Line DE |
| Line Segment | S — T | $\overline{ST}$ | Line Segment ST |
| Ray | X — Y | $\overrightarrow{XY}$ | Ray XY - Always name the endpoint first. |
| Plane | R | Plane R | A plane is a flat surface that goes on and on in all directions. |

**1** Write the name of each figure using both symbols and words.

1. • V

2. A——B

3. C←——→D

4. E——→F

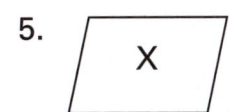

5. X (plane)

**2** Read the clues and find the mystery number in the data bank.

| 75 | 10 | 17 | 45 |
|---|---|---|---|
| 11 | 8 | 21 | 16 |

The number is divisible by 3.
The number is less than 50.
The sum of the digits is 3.
    The mystery number is _____ .

| 16 | 71 | 28 | 3 |
|---|---|---|---|
| 12 | 4 | 17 | 13 |

The number is prime.
The sum of the digits is 8.
The product of the digits is 7.
The number is greater than 50.
    The mystery number is _____ .

**3** Find the difference. Make sure the answer is in lowest terms.

$\frac{8}{10} - \frac{1}{10} =$      $\frac{6}{8} - \frac{2}{8} =$      $\frac{11}{13} - \frac{10}{13} =$      $\frac{6}{8} - \frac{1}{8} =$

$\frac{9}{11} - \frac{6}{11} =$      $\frac{5}{12} - \frac{1}{12} =$      $\frac{11}{12} - \frac{6}{12} =$      $\frac{18}{20} - \frac{8}{20} =$

**4** Use the table to help you make the following conversions.

1 gallon (gal) = 4 quarts
1 quart (qt) = 2 pints
1 pint (pt) = 2 cups (c)

12 qt = _____ gal      6 c = _____ pt

8 pt = _____ qt      24 c = _____ pt

16 qt = _____ gal      18 pt = _____ qt

**5** Use the definitions to help answer the questions.

| B.C. | = | Before Christ |
| A.D. | = | Anno Domini (after Christ's birth *in the year of our Lord*) |
| 10 years | = | a decade |
| 100 years | = | a century |
| 1,000 years | = | a millennium |

Moses was born c. 1520 _____ .

Elizabeth is $9\frac{1}{2}$. She will soon be a _____ old.

When Christ returns to Earth, He will reign for 1,000 years, or a _____ .

Great-Aunt Emily was born in 1896. She is over a _____ old.

You were born in (write the date) _____ (A.D. or B.C.) _____ .

**6** Find the quotient.

70)280           50)950           80)640


30)639           60)982           40)928

# Parallel, Perpendicular, and Intersecting Lines

Lesson 72

**Intersecting lines** cross each other, or intersect.

**Parallel lines** run next to each other the same distance apart.

**Perpendicular lines** form right angles where they intersect.

| Geometry Terms | Geometry in Pictures | Geometry in Symbols | Geometry in Words |
|---|---|---|---|
| Intersecting Lines | | $l$ intersects $m$ | Line $l$ intersects line $m$. |
| Parallel Lines | | $x \parallel y$ | Line $x$ is parallel to line $y$. |
| Perpendicular Lines | | $a \perp b$ | Line $a$ is perpendicular to line $b$. |

**1** Use $\parallel$, $\perp$ or **intersects** to write a statement about the pairs of lines.

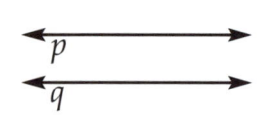

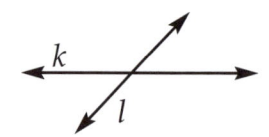

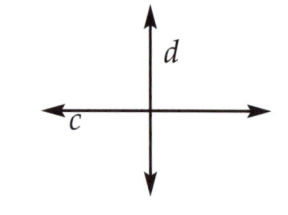

**2** Write the name for each figure.

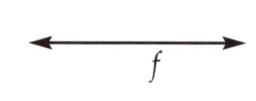

228 Horizons Math 5, Student Workbook 1

**3** Add. Rename in lowest terms. Find the answer to each fraction under the lines in the puzzle. Above the answer, place the letter next to each problem to discover the verse.

$\frac{8}{12} + \frac{1}{12} =$ _____ L   $\frac{1}{7} + \frac{3}{7} =$ _____ Y   $\frac{1}{6} + \frac{3}{6} =$ _____ D

$\frac{5}{12} + \frac{1}{12} =$ _____ O   $\frac{1}{12} + \frac{1}{12} =$ _____ T   $\frac{2}{20} + \frac{4}{20} =$ _____ A

$\frac{2}{17} + \frac{1}{17} =$ _____ U   $\frac{1}{9} + \frac{2}{9} =$ _____ R   $\frac{1}{8} + \frac{1}{8} =$ _____ H

$\frac{3}{5} + \frac{1}{5} =$ _____ E   $\frac{1}{17} + \frac{12}{17} =$ _____ W   $\frac{4}{9} + \frac{3}{9} =$ _____ F

$\frac{1}{11} + \frac{3}{11} =$ _____ G   $\frac{5}{19} + \frac{4}{19} =$ _____ I

___ ___ ___    ___ ___ ___
$\frac{4}{7}$ $\frac{1}{2}$ $\frac{3}{17}$    $\frac{3}{10}$ $\frac{1}{3}$ $\frac{4}{5}$

___ ___ ___    ___ ___ ___ ___ ___
$\frac{1}{6}$ $\frac{1}{4}$ $\frac{4}{5}$    $\frac{3}{4}$ $\frac{9}{19}$ $\frac{4}{11}$ $\frac{1}{4}$ $\frac{1}{6}$

___ ___    ___ ___ ___
$\frac{1}{2}$ $\frac{7}{9}$    $\frac{1}{6}$ $\frac{1}{4}$ $\frac{4}{5}$

___ ___ ___ ___ ___
$\frac{13}{17}$ $\frac{1}{2}$ $\frac{1}{3}$ $\frac{3}{4}$ $\frac{2}{3}$

**A city set on a hill cannot be hidden. Matthew 5:14**

**4** Write A.M. or P.M. in the lines below.

1. John ate his breakfast at 7:00 _____ .

2. Suzanne had soccer practice after school at 4:30 _____ .

3. Paul ate his lunch at 12:30 _____ in the afternoon.

4. Trevor was awakened at 12:30 _____ at night.

5. Steve and his dad got up at 4:00 _____ , before sunrise, to go fishing.

**5** Use the data bank to complete the sentences.

> 1 foot = 12 inches
> 1 yard = 3 feet = 36 inches
> 1 mile = 1,760 yards = 5,280 feet

72 inches = _____ yards

3 yards = _____ feet

12 feet = _____ yards

24 inches = _____ feet

1,760 yards = _____ mile

3 miles = _____ yards

To change inches to yards, divide by _____ .

To change yards to feet, multiply by _____ .

To change feet to yards, divide by _____ .

**6** Divide and check.

22)68          44)150          17)87          89)270


61)189                          58)375

Lesson 73

# Angles

An **angle** is two rays that share a common end point.

The rays $\vec{BA}$ and $\vec{BC}$ are called *sides*. They meet at vertex B to form an angle. The angle can be referred to as ∠ABC, ∠B, or ∠CBA.

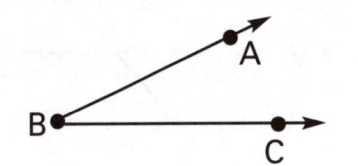

There are three kinds of angles:

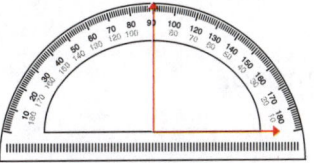

A **right angle**. It measures 90°.

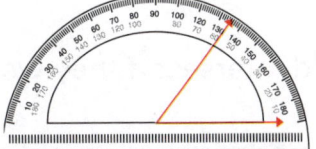

An **acute angle**. It measures less than 90°.

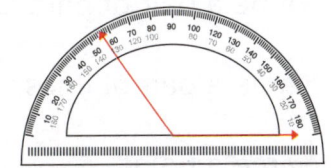

An **obtuse angle**. It measures greater than 90°.

**1** Write **obtuse**, **acute**, or **right** angle.

1. 30° _____
2. 100° _____
3. 90° _____
4. 78° _____

5. 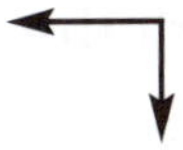 _____
6.  _____
7.  _____
8. _____

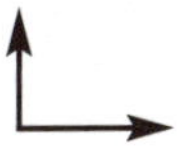

**2** Answer the questions regarding the figures below.

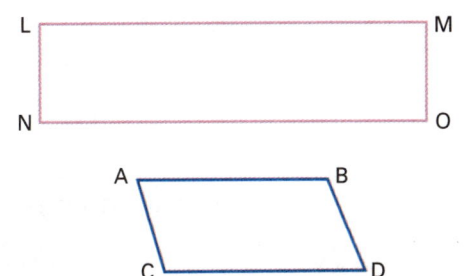

1. ∠CAB is _____ . (obtuse, acute, right)

2. ∠ABD is _____ . (obtuse, acute, right)

3. ∠MON is _____ . (obtuse, acute, right)

4. Line LM and line NO are _____ . (parallel, perpendicular, intersecting)

5. Line LN and line NO are _____ . (parallel, perpendicular, intersecting)

6. Line CD and line DB are _____ . (parallel, perpendicular, intersecting)

**3**

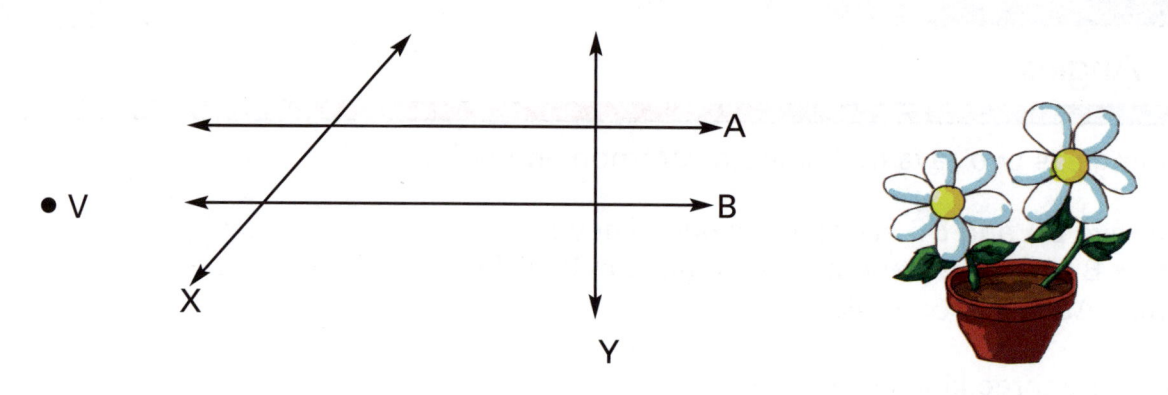

Name a pair of parallel lines.

Name a pair of lines that would intersect if they were extended.

Name a point.

Name a pair of perpendicular lines.

**4** Connect the term with the matching picture.

1. point

2. parallel

3. line

4. line segment

5. ray

6. intersecting lines

7. perpendicular lines

8. plane

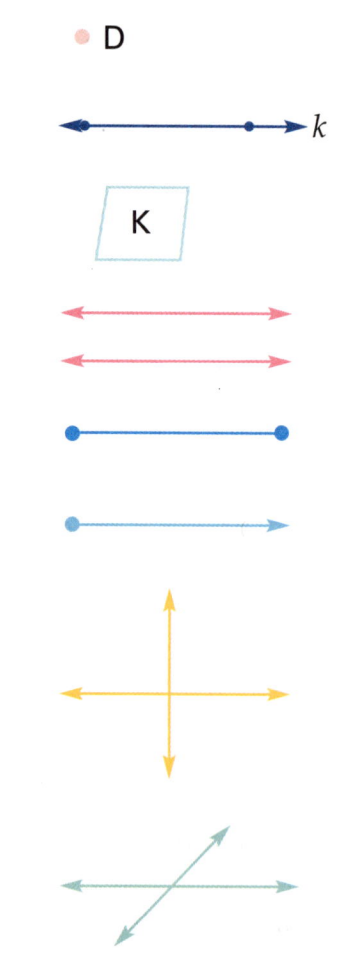

**5** Find the missing numerator.

$\frac{2}{3} = \frac{}{30}$  $\frac{7}{12} = \frac{}{36}$  $\frac{3}{15} = \frac{}{90}$

$\frac{5}{6} = \frac{}{18}$  $\frac{6}{7} = \frac{}{49}$  $\frac{1}{8} = \frac{}{16}$

**6** State the century.

1998 _____

1289 _____

1843 _____

1509 _____

894 _____

**7** Use the data bank to answer the questions.

> 1 minute = 60 seconds
> 1 hour = 60 minutes
> 1 day = 24 hours

3 minutes = _____ seconds

5 hours = _____ minutes

48 hours = _____ days

180 seconds = _____ minutes

600 minutes = _____ hours

5 days = _____ hours

# Protractors

Lesson 74

A *protractor* is an instrument used to measure angles. The angles are measured in degrees. The protractor is marked with 180 degree (180°) units. What is the measure of ∠LMN?

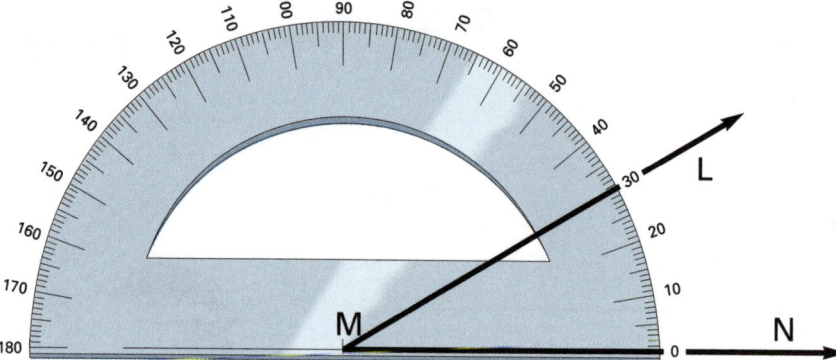

Follow these simple steps to measure an angle with a protractor
1. Place the arrow on the protractor on the vertex of the angle.
2. Place the zero edge on the side of the angle.
3. Read the measure of the angle.

∠LMN measures 30°

**1** Give the measure of each angle. You may need to extend the sides of the angle for easier reading.

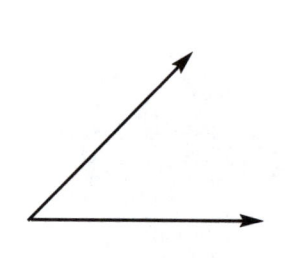

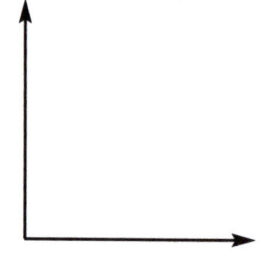

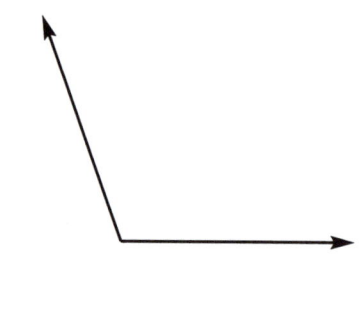

_____    _____    _____

**2** Draw the lines as indicated.

| Perpendicular | Parallel | Intersecting |
| --- | --- | --- |
|  |  |  |

234   Horizons Math 5, Student Workbook 1

3. Draw the geometric terms in pictures.

| Point | Line | Line Segment | Ray | Plane |
| Label K | Label AB | Label RS | Label LM | Label T |
|  |  |  |  |  |

4. Use the data bank to answer the questions.

1 minute = 60 seconds
1 hour = 60 minutes
1 day = 24 hours

5 minutes = _____ seconds

3 hours = _____ minutes

120 hours = _____ days

480 seconds = _____ minutes

6000 minutes = _____ hours

9 days = _____ hours

To change minutes to seconds, multiply by _____ .

To change hours to minutes, multiply by _____ .

To change days to hours, multiply by _____ .

To change hours to days, divide by _____ .

5. Find the missing addend.

```
   180          145          411          497
 + 56?        + 2?5        + ?68        + ?30
 -----        -----        -----        -----
   743          420          679        1,027
```

**6** Use a factor tree to find prime numbers. Write the missing numbers in the circles.

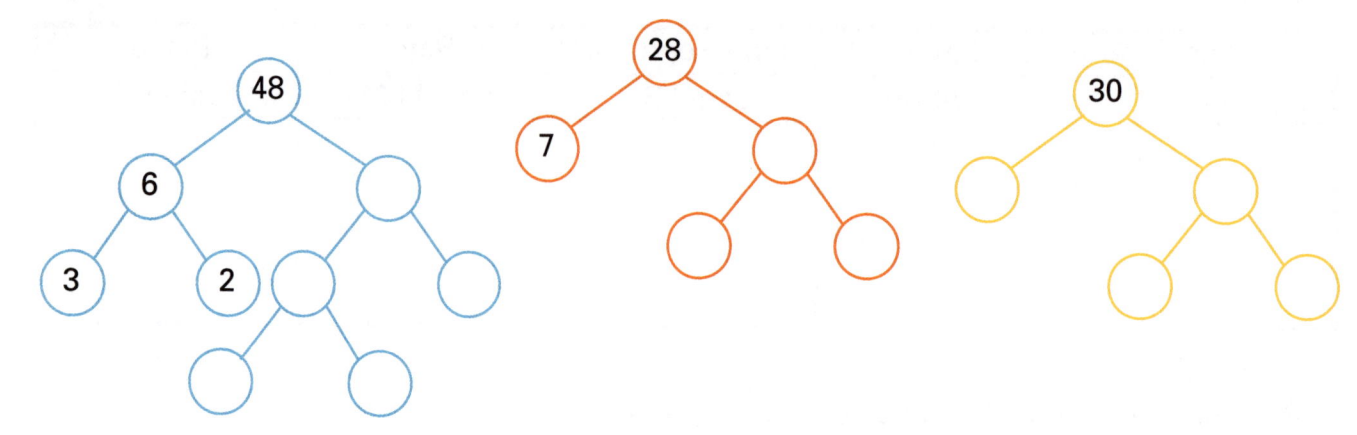

**7** Find each quotient. Look for the answer in the data bank. Write the letter above each number in the puzzle that corresponds with the problem numbers. Read the verse. The first one has been done for you.

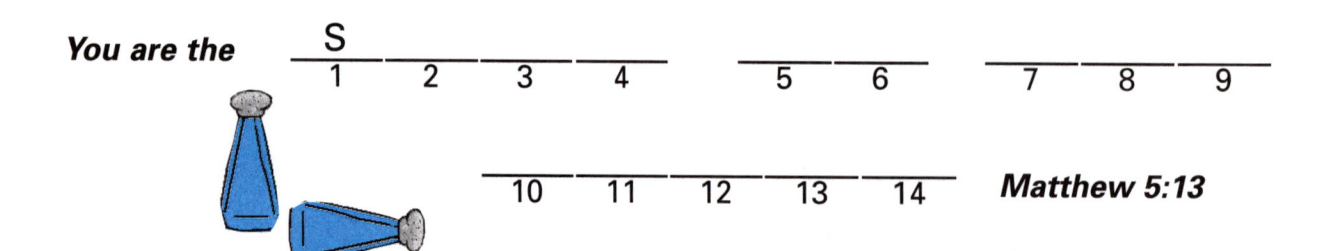

$\overset{25}{5\overline{)125}}$   $8\overline{)256}$   $7\overline{)154}$   $4\overline{)132}$   $6\overline{)186}$

$7\overline{)161}$   $9\overline{)297}$   $7\overline{)392}$   $8\overline{)624}$   $6\overline{)468}$

$5\overline{)160}$   $6\overline{)534}$   $3\overline{)99}$   $3\overline{)168}$

| A = 32 | E = 78 | F = 23 | H = 56 | L = 22 | O = 31 | R = 89 | S = 25 | T = 33 |

You are the  $\underset{1}{S}$  $\underset{2}{\_}$  $\underset{3}{\_}$  $\underset{4}{\_}$   $\underset{5}{\_}$  $\underset{6}{\_}$   $\underset{7}{\_}$  $\underset{8}{\_}$  $\underset{9}{\_}$

$\underset{10}{\_}$  $\underset{11}{\_}$  $\underset{12}{\_}$  $\underset{13}{\_}$  $\underset{14}{\_}$   **Matthew 5:13**

236   Horizons Math 5, Student Workbook 1

**Lesson 75**

# Triangles

**Naming Triangles**

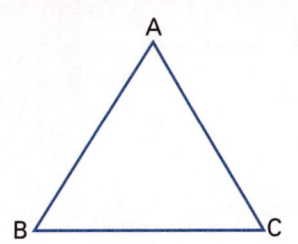

Triangles have three sides: $\overline{AB}$, $\overline{BC}$ and $\overline{AC}$. Triangles have three angles, ∠A, ∠B, and ∠C. We refer to a triangle in writing as △ABC.

## Three Types of Triangles

| Scalene | Equilateral | Isosceles |
| --- | --- | --- |
| No sides the same length.<br><br>No angles the same measure.  | All sides the same length.<br><br>All three angles the same measure. 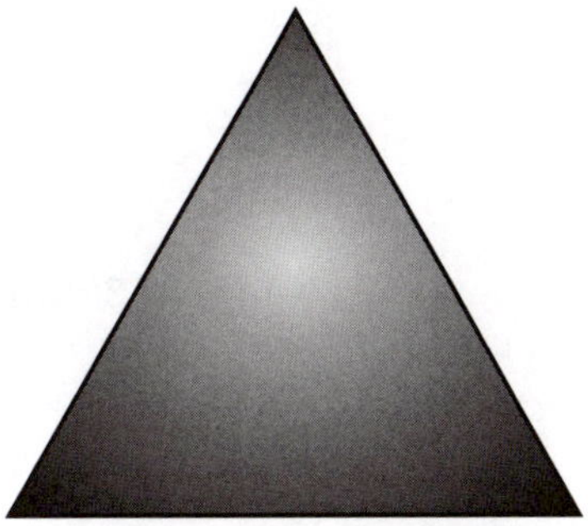 | At least 2 sides the same length.<br><br>At least 2 angles the same measure. 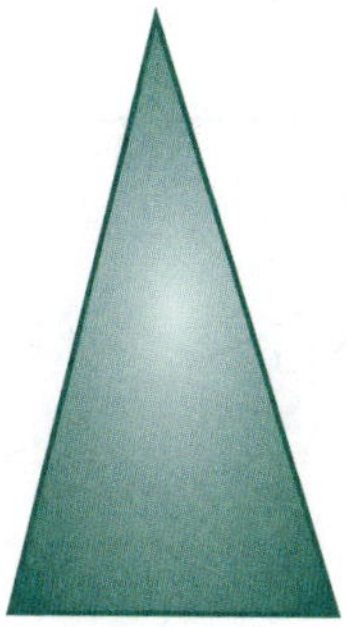 |

**Right Triangles**

A triangle with a right angle (90° angle) is called a right triangle. Both isosceles and scalene triangles can have a right angle.

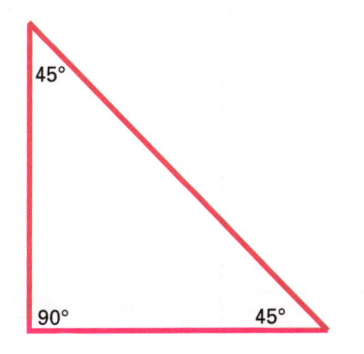

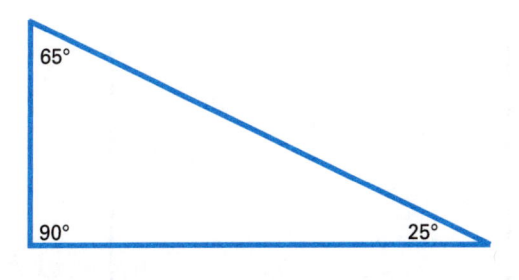

**1** Use the diagram to answer the questions.

Name the triangle. _____

Name the sides to the triangle. _____

Name the angles. _____

Name the type of triangle. _____

Is the triangle a right triangle? _____

**2** Identify each triangle as equilateral, isosceles or scalene. Circle the right triangle.

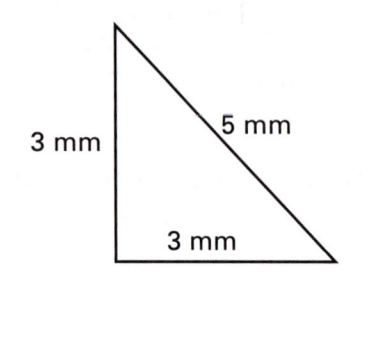

3 mm, 5 mm, 3 mm

_____

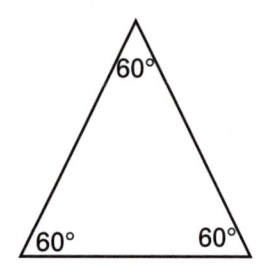

60°, 60°, 60°

_____

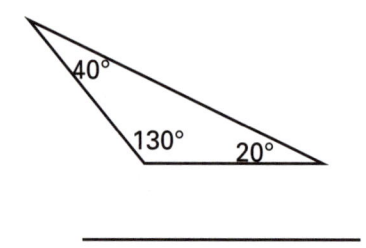

40°, 130°, 20°

_____

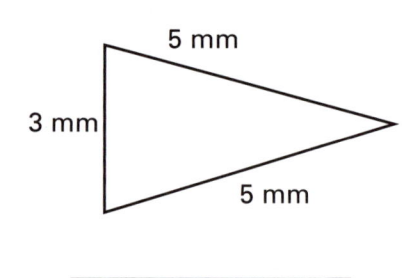

3 mm, 5 mm, 5 mm

_____

**3** Draw the angles indicated.

| Acute Angle | Obtuse Angle | Right Angle |
| --- | --- | --- |
|  |  |  |

238   Horizons Math 5, Student Workbook 1

**4** Measure each angle in the triangle with a protractor. Write the measurement on the lines provided.

∠R _____     ∠S _____     ∠T _____

Define the type of triangle. _____

Is the triangle a right triangle. _____

**5** Solve.

Jeannine leaves for gymnastics at 3:45. She gets home from school at 3:10. How much time does she have between the two activities?

Jeannine's Wednesday gymnastics class starts at 4:00 and ends at 5:30. How long does her class last?

Jeannine's Friday gymnastics class begins at 5:00 and ends at 6:00. How long does her class last?

How much time does Jeannine spend in gymnastics classes each week?

**6** Divide.

41)567        58)963        78)876        91)456

**Lesson 76**

## Quadrilaterals

A quadrilateral has four sides; $\overline{JK}$, $\overline{KM}$, $\overline{ML}$, and $\overline{JL}$.
A quadrilateral has four angles; $\angle J$, $\angle K$, $\angle M$, and $\angle L$.

| Square | Rectangle | Parallelogram | Trapezoid | Rhombus |
|---|---|---|---|---|
| All sides the same length. All angles right angles. | Two pairs of sides the same length. All right angles. | Two pairs of sides the same length. Two pairs of parallel sides. | One pair of parallel sides. | All sides the same length. |

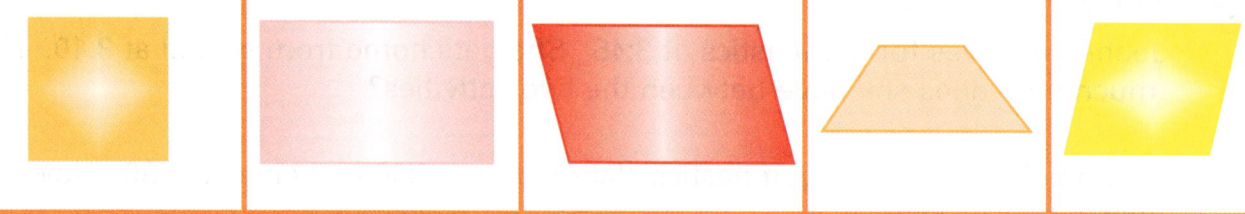

A square is a special type of a rectangle having all sides the same length. Also, a rhombus is a special type of a parallelogram having all sides the same length.

**1** Look at the figure below and answer the questions.

1. Name four angles. _____

2. Name two pairs of parallel segments. _____

3. Circle the definitions that apply to the above figure.

trapezoid,   parallelogram,   rhombus,   rectangle,   square

240    Horizons Math 5, Student Workbook 1

**2** Name each quadrilateral.

_____    _____    _____

_____    _____

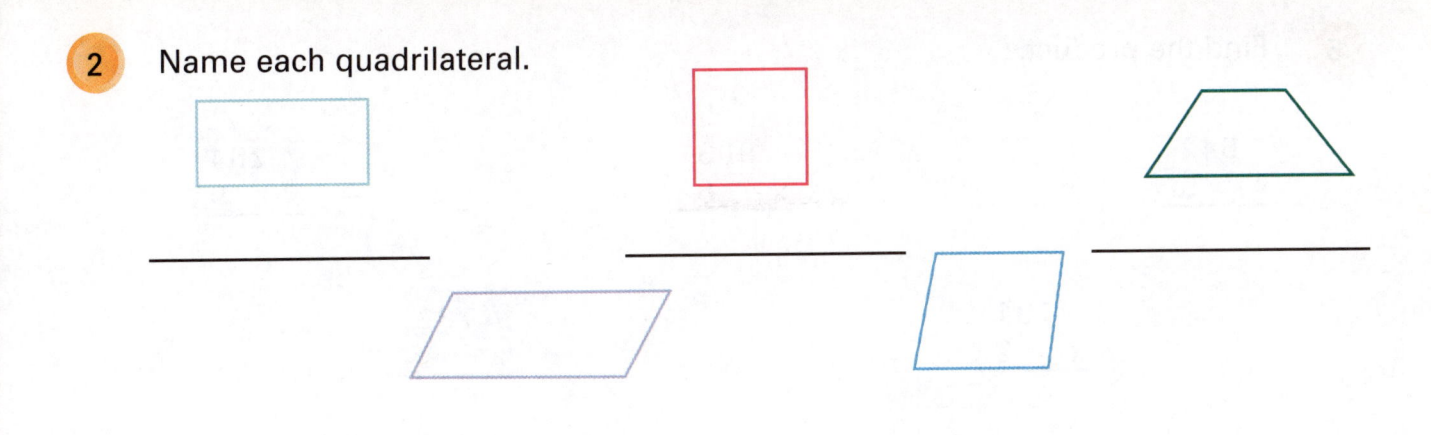

**3** Read the definitions and name the quadrilateral(s) described.

1. Two pairs of opposite sides are parallel. _____

2. These quadrilaterals are parallelograms with all sides the same length. _____

3. These quadrilaterals are parallelograms with all right angles. _____

4. One pair of opposite sides are parallel. _____

5. This figure is a special rectangle with all sides the same length. _____

6. This figure has all right angles, but not all sides the same length. _____

**4** Look at the pictures and answer the questions.

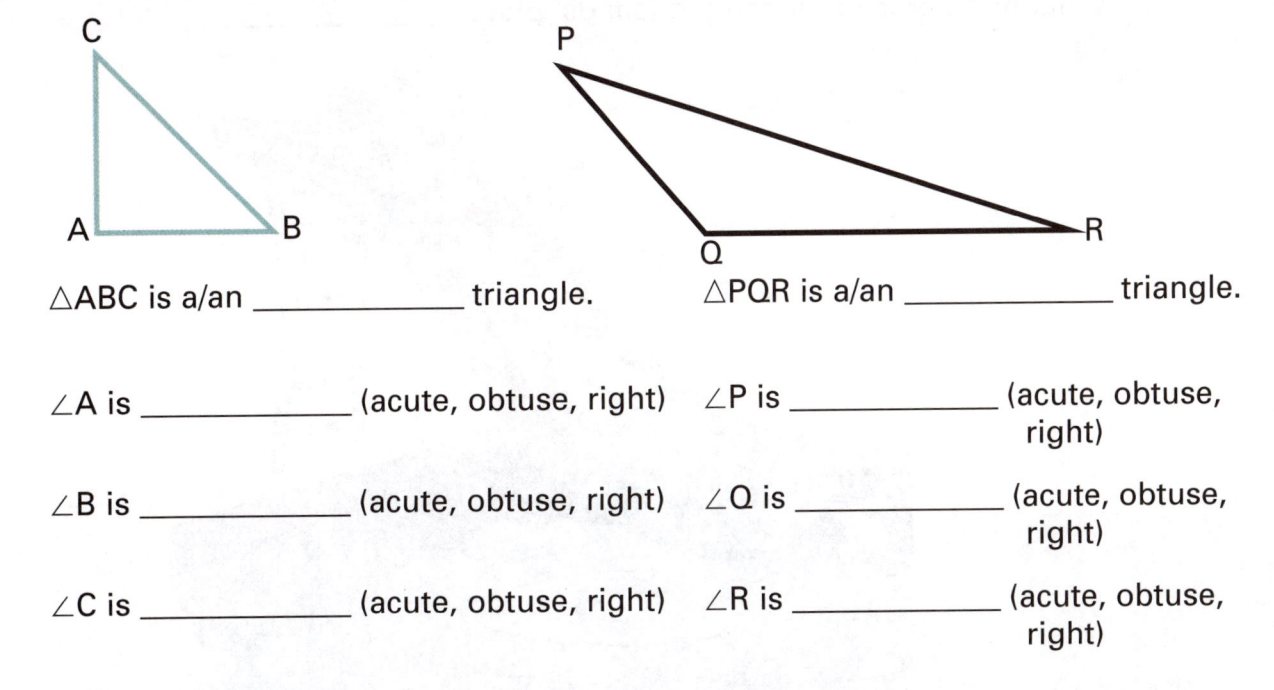

△ABC is a/an _____ triangle.     △PQR is a/an _____ triangle.

∠A is _____ (acute, obtuse, right)     ∠P is _____ (acute, obtuse, right)

∠B is _____ (acute, obtuse, right)     ∠Q is _____ (acute, obtuse, right)

∠C is _____ (acute, obtuse, right)     ∠R is _____ (acute, obtuse, right)

**5** Find the product.

```
  542        903        284
x   5      x   8      x   9
```

```
  731        732
x   2      x   3
```

**6** Answer the questions about the number below.

# 365,891,027,000

1. Write the number in words. _____
   _____

2. The seven is in the _____ place.

3. What number is in the ten billions' place? _____

4. What number is in the hundred millions' place? _____

5. What number is in the ten thousands' place? _____

**Lesson 77**

# Identifying Polygons

**Polygons** are closed plane figures with three or more straight sides.
A **vertex** is formed where two sides meet.
**Regular polygons** have all sides the same length and the same measure. The hexagon is a regular polygon.

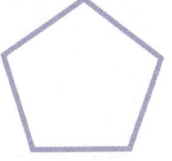

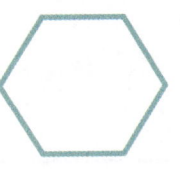

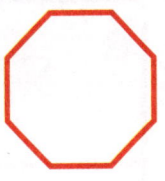

| triangle | quadrilateral | pentagon | hexagon | octagon | decagon |
|---|---|---|---|---|---|
| 3 sides | 4 sides | 5 sides | 6 sides | 8 sides | 10 sides |
| 3 vertices | 4 vertices | 5 vertices | 6 vertices | 8 vertices | 10 vertices |

**Drawing Diagonals.**
A diagonal of a polygon is a line segment that joins two vertices but is not a side. A quadrilateral has two diagonals. How many diagonals does a pentagon have?

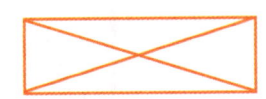

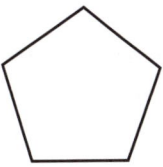

A quadrilateral has two diagonals      A pentagon has five diagonals.

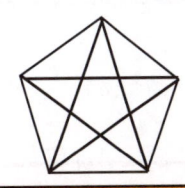

**1** Use the word bank to answer the questions. Some words may be used more than once.

1. I am a three-sided figure. _____

2. I have eight vertices. _____

3. I have four right angles. _____

4. I have ten sides and ten vertices. _____

5. I have six sides and nine diagonals. _____

6. I have five sides. _____

7. I am a four sided figure. _____

8. I have all sides the same length and all angles the same measure. _____

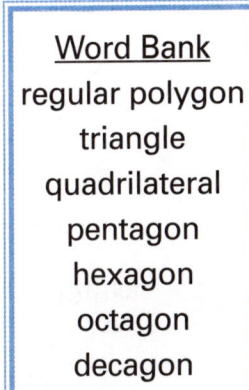

**Word Bank**
regular polygon
triangle
quadrilateral
pentagon
hexagon
octagon
decagon

**2** Draw a picture for each polygon. Draw all the diagonals and complete the table.

| Polygon | Draw the Polygon and Diagonals | # of Sides | # of Diagonals |
|---|---|---|---|
| triangle | | | |
| quadrilateral | | | |
| pentagon | | | |
| hexagon | | | |
| octagon | | | |
| decagon | | | |

**3** Label the triangles isosceles, scalene or equilateral.

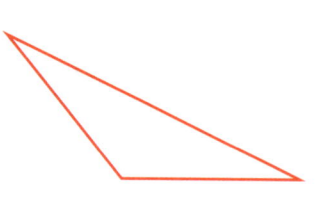

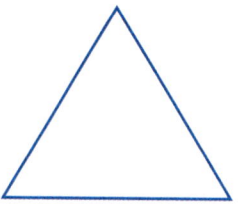

**4** Multiply.

$$\begin{array}{r}63\\\times\ 28\end{array} \qquad \begin{array}{r}99\\\times\ 23\end{array} \qquad \begin{array}{r}89\\\times\ 78\end{array} \qquad \begin{array}{r}209\\\times\ 92\end{array} \qquad \begin{array}{r}391\\\times\ 76\end{array}$$

**5** Use a protractor to measure the following angles and write each measurement on the lines provided. Circle the correct definition.

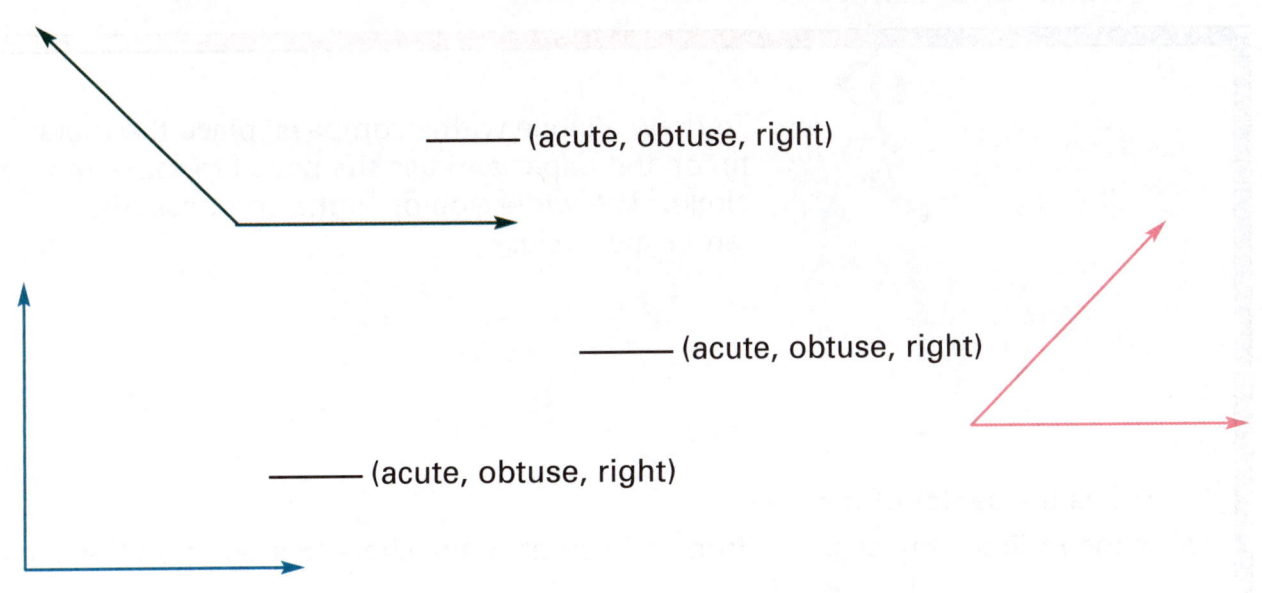

_____ (acute, obtuse, right)

_____ (acute, obtuse, right)

_____ (acute, obtuse, right)

**6** Refer to the time zone map when answering the questions.

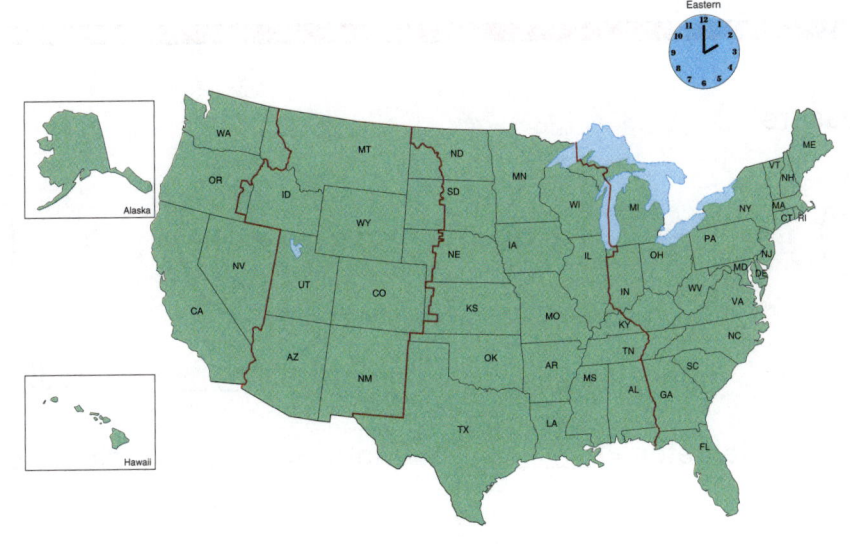

If it is 2:00 P.M. in the Eastern time zone, what time is it in the following time zones?

a. Central time   _____

b. Mountain time   _____

c. Pacific time   _____

d. Alaska time   _____

e. Hawaii time   _____

Horizons Math 5, Student Workbook 1   245

**Lesson 78**

## Circles and Compass

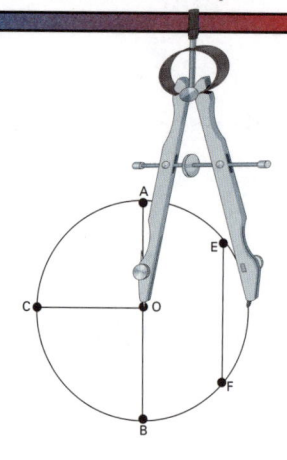

To draw a circle with a compass, place the metal tip on the paper and use the pencil to make the circle. The wider you open the compass, the larger the circle.

Point O is the **center** of the circle.

$\overline{OC}$ is the **radius**. Any segment from the center of the circle to a point on the circle is the radius.

$\overline{EF}$ is the **chord**. A chord is any line segment that begins and ends on the circle.

$\overline{AB}$ is the **diameter**. A diameter is a chord that passes through the center of the circle.

**1** Find the measure.

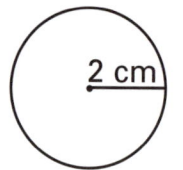

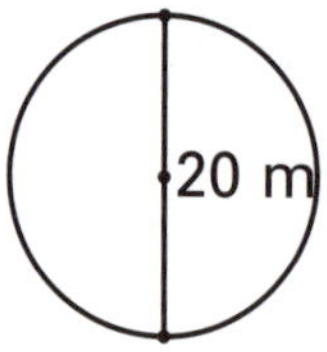

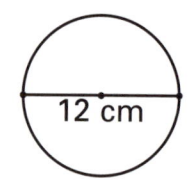

2 cm    20 m    16 cm    12 cm

radius = _____    radius = _____    radius = _____    radius = _____

diameter = _____    diameter = _____    diameter = _____    diameter = _____

**2** Use a calculator to average these grades. Round each answer to the nearest whole number.

78%, 99%, 82%, 66%, 93%

100%, 92%, 88%, 96%, 50%

88%, 78%, 86%, 80%, 76%

89%, 56%, 10%, 92%, 90%

**3** Match the picture with the best name for each polygon.

trapezoid

octagon

parallelogram

pentagon

hexagon

rectangle

rhombus

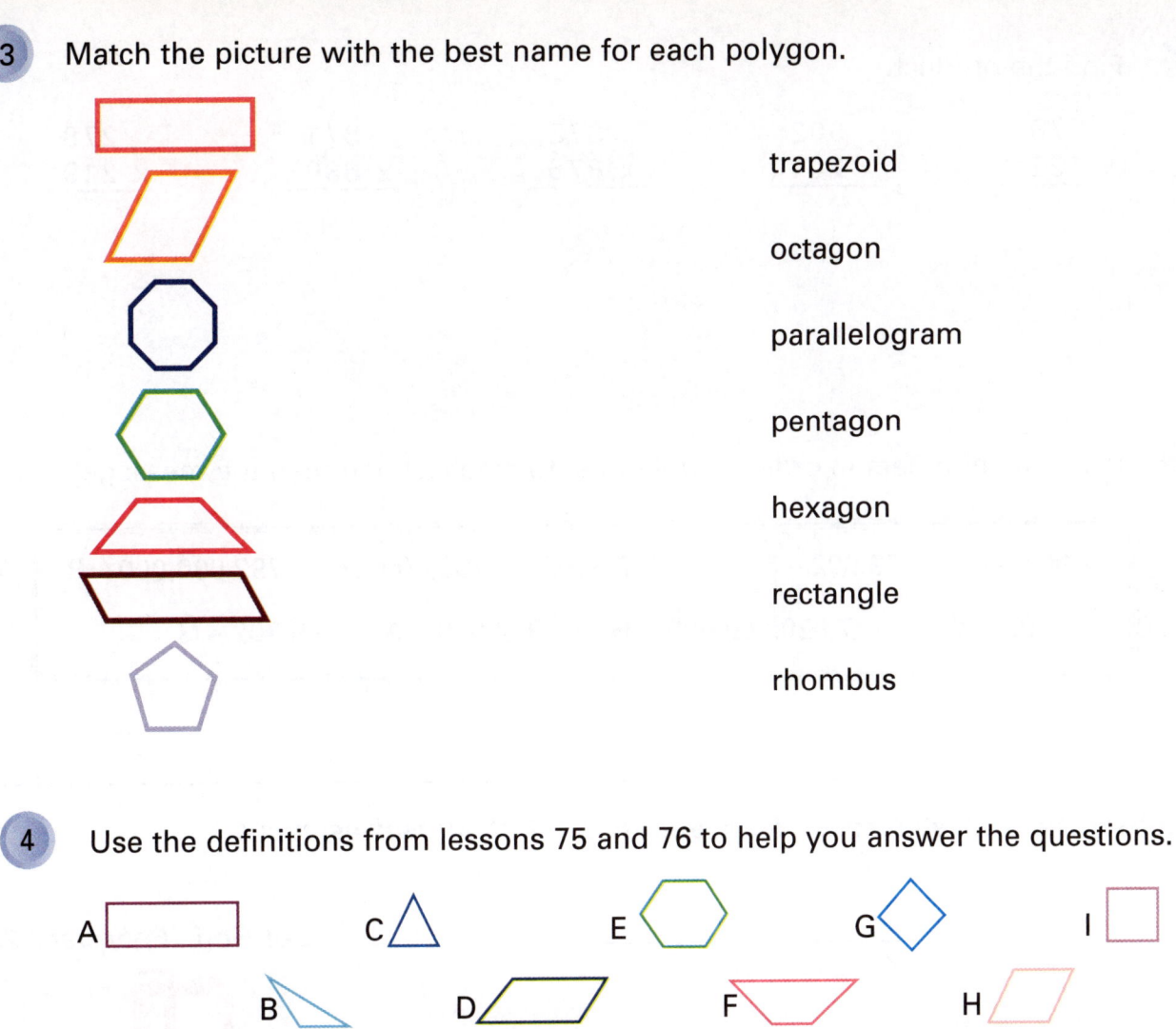

**4** Use the definitions from lessons 75 and 76 to help you answer the questions.

A   C   E   G   I
B   D   F   H

1. Which of the figures above are defined as quadrilaterals?

2. Which of the figures above are triangles?

3. Which of the figures are defined as rectangles?

4. Which of the figures are defined as parallelograms?

5. Which of the figures are defined as a square?

6. Which of the figures are defined as a rhombus?

7. Which triangle is scalene?

8. Which triangle is equilateral?

**5** Find the product.

| 576 | 902 | 378 | 871 | 278 |
|---|---|---|---|---|
| x 132 | x 204 | x 876 | x 630 | x 219 |

**6** Place the numbers in order from largest to smallest and read the message.

| 7,901 – I | 79,002 – E | 792 – F | 792,000 – C | 792,000,000 – R |
|---|---|---|---|---|
| 92 – T | 7,920,000,000 – G | 972,000 – A | 9,702 – G | |

For by _____ _____ _____ _____ _____

You have been saved through faith; and that not of yourselves, it is a

_____ _____ _____ _____ of God.  Ephesians 2:8

**7** Find the mystery number.

| 30 | 17 | 28 | 60 |
|---|---|---|---|
| 15 | 80 | 13 | 16 |

I am an even number.

I am a multiple of 10.

The sum of my digits is 6.

I am _____ .

**Lesson 79**

## Graphing

You can locate each point on the grid with an ordered pair of numbers.
Point A is at (3, 1). To locate it, start at 0 and move three units to the right. Move up one unit.
Point B is at (5, 4). To locate it, start at 0 and move five units to the right. Move up four units.
Can you name the ordered pair of numbers for Point C? (6, 2)

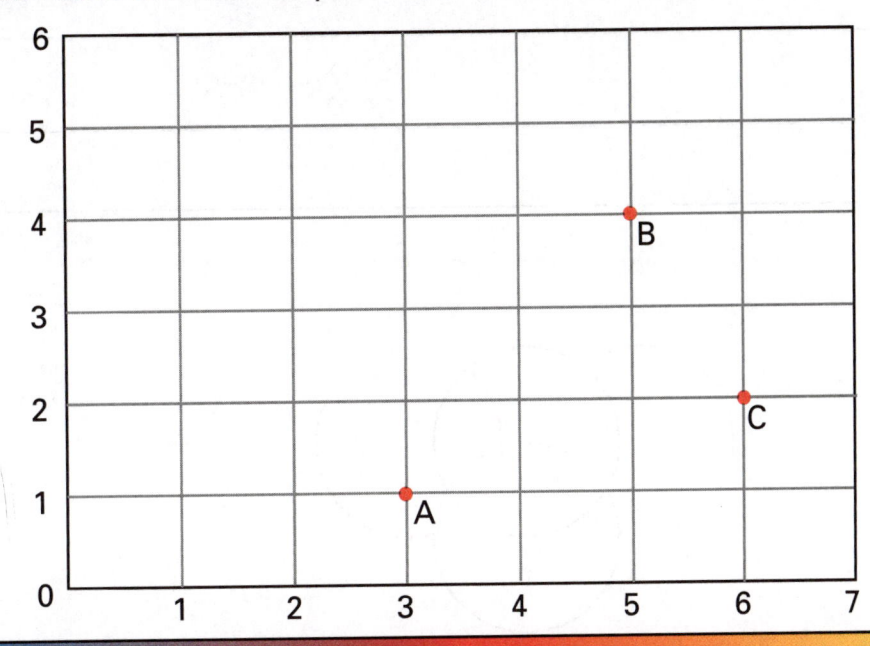

**1** Find the ordered pairs below to solve the riddle:
### Where do baby ears of corn sleep?

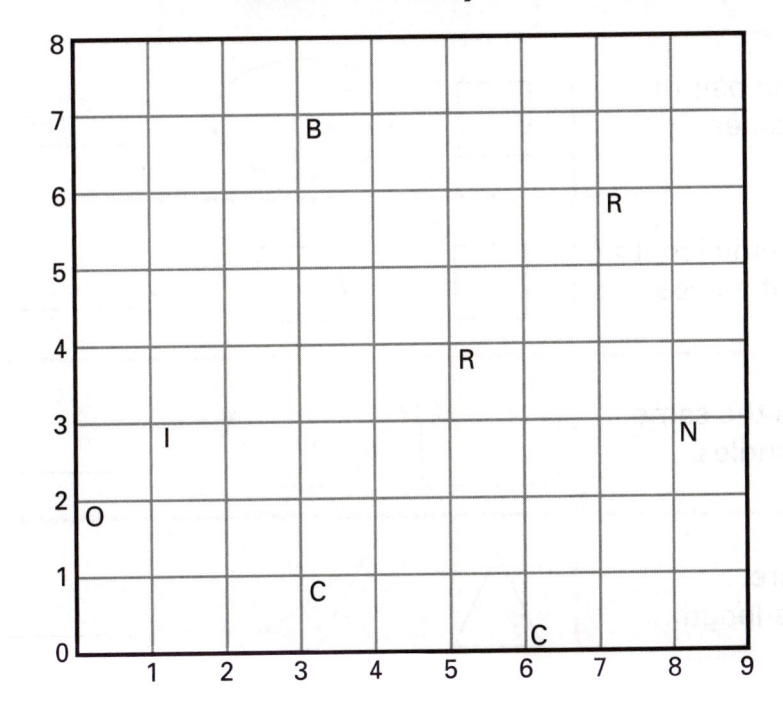

(3, 1) _____

(0, 2) _____

(5, 4) _____

(8, 3) _____

(6, 0) _____

(7, 6) _____

(1, 3) _____

(3, 7) _____

**2** Define the terms. Use your compass to draw this design on a separate sheet of paper.

1. radius – _____

   _____

2. diameter – _____

   _____

3. chord – _____

   _____

**3** Circle the polygon that fits the definition. Write the name of the figure. The first one has been done for you.

| Definition | Figures | Name |
|---|---|---|
| This figure has one pair of opposite parallel sides. | □  ⬡(circled) | trapezoid |
| All sides are the same length. All angles are right angles | □  ▱ | _____ |
| Two pairs of sides the same length. All right angles. | ▭  ▱ | _____ |
| A three-sided figure. All sides the same length. | △  △ | _____ |

**4** Solve the equations.

| $2 \times n = 18$ | $3 \times n = 27$ | $7 \times n = 49$ | $6 \times n = 36$ |

**5** Write each number and place in order from largest to smallest.

1. twenty-seven thousand, five
2. forty-five million, nine hundred sixteen
3. four million, two
4. seventeen thousand, eight hundred four
5. two thousand, seven hundred twenty-two

_____   _____   _____   _____   _____

**6** Find the sum.

| 9 | 7 | 8 | 3 | 2 |
| + 9 | + 7 | + 8 | + 9 | + 9 |

| 8 | 7 | 5 | 7 | 6 |
| + 9 | + 6 | + 9 | + 5 | + 8 |

# Problem Solving – Guess and Check

**Lesson 80**

A good plan for some problems is to guess the answer. Then test to see if it works.

*Understand → Plan → Work → Answer/Check*

Mrs. Blade is going to take 24 students on a field trip to the zoo. The total entrance fee per class is $72.00. Lunch will be $48.00 per class. How much money should each person bring for the field trip?

**Understand** – What is the question?
1. How much should each student bring for the field trip?

**Plan** – How do you solve the problem?
1. Add the entrance fee and lunch fee ($72.00 + $48.00 = $120.00).
2. Guess an amount for students to bring.
3. Multiply by the number of students and subtract that amount from step one.
4. Is it a close approximation? If not, guess again.

**Work** – First Guess
Total fee–$120.00
$4.00 per student
$4.00 x 24 = $96.00–not enough

Second Guess
Total fee–$120.00
$5.00 per student
$5.00 x 24 = $120.00–Exactly correct

**Answer/Check** – Have you answered the question? Does the answer make sense? Reread the problem. Each child will bring $5.00 to total $120.00. The answer is correct.

**1** Solve.

1. Amy and Pauline had 15 pieces of candy. Pauline had 5 more pieces than Amy. How many pieces did Amy have?

2. Candy bars cost $ .35 apiece. Pete had $3.00. After he bought the candy bars, he had $ .20 left over. How many candy bars did he buy?

3. Popcorn at the movies costs $1.25 per box. If the Nelson family gave the cashier $5.00 and received no change, how many boxes did they buy?

**2** Draw these circles on a separate sheet of paper. You will need a compass and a centimeter ruler.

1. Draw a circle with a radius of 3 cm.

2. Draw a circle with the diameter of 12 cm.

**3** Use the word bank to fill in the blanks.

| octagon | rectangle | rhombus | trapezoid |
| pentagon | hexagon | triangle | parallelogram |

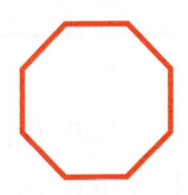

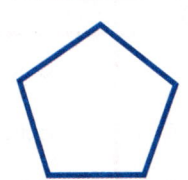

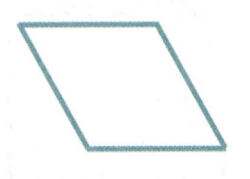

_____    _____    _____    _____

_____    _____    _____    _____

**4** Check the boxes that apply.

| Figure | Square | Parallelogram | Quadrilateral | Polygon |
|---|---|---|---|---|
| triangle | | | | |
| rectangle | | | | |
| trapezoid | | | | |
| circle | | | | |
| rhombus | | | | |
| pentagon | | | | |
| hexagon | | | | |

1. Are all rectangles squares?

2. Are all squares rectangles?

*Horizons Math 5, Student Workbook 1*

## 5. Write the value of each number.

$5^3$     $2^6$     $10^2$     $3^4$     $2^5$     $5^4$

## 6. Find the difference.

```
  17        43        89        40        56
- 13      - 39      - 38      - 37      - 47
```

```
  67        78        92        84        73
- 59      - 49      - 25      - 68      - 57
```

## 7. Circle the correct answer and write it on the lines below.

| Round each number to the nearest 10. | Choose A | Choose B | Round each number to the nearest 10 | Choose A | Choose B |
|---|---|---|---|---|---|
| 1. 56 | 50 (N) | 60 (M) | 10. 681 | 680 (I) | 690 (O) |
| 2. 35 | 30 (O) | 40 (Y) | 11. 895 | 890 (R) | 900 (V) |
| 3. 64 | 60 (P) | 70 (I) | 12. 1,247 | 1,240 (R) | 1,250 (E) |
| 4. 19 | 10 (O) | 20 (E) | 13. 6,672 | 6,670 (T) | 6,680 (S) |
| 5. 93 | 90 (A) | 100 (E) | 14. 8,808 | 8,800 (M) | 8,810 (O) |
| 6. 81 | 80 (C) | 90 (L) | 15. 9,999 | 9,990 (E) | 10,000 (Y) |
| 7. 13 | 10 (E) | 20 (S) | 16. 12,781 | 12,780 (O) | 12,790 (E) |
| 8. 127 | 120 (K) | 130 (I) | 17. 16,001 | 16,000 (U) | 16,010 (R) |
| 9. 399 | 390 (R) | 400 (G) | | | |

**Peace I leave with you;** __ __   __ __ __ __ __
                            1   2     3  4  5  6  7

__ __ __ __ __   __ __   __ __ __ ;
 8  9 10 11 12   13 14   15 16 17

not as the world gives do I give to you.  Let not your hearts be troubled, neither let them be afraid.      John 14:27

**Test 8**

**1** Use the calendar and your knowledge of calendars, to answer the questions. **5 pts.**

How many full weeks are there in this month? _____

In which whole week does Christmas fall? _____

How many weeks are there in a decade? _____

How many months are there in a century? _____

How many weeks are there in 49 days? _____

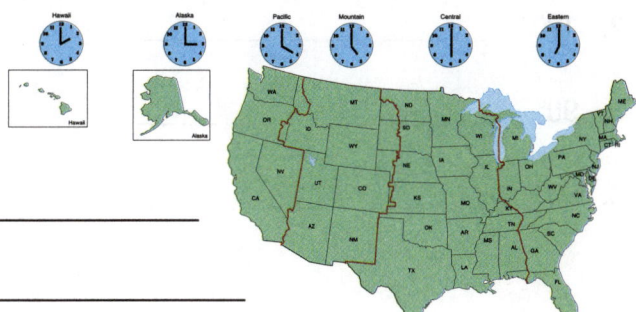

December

| S | M | T | W | T | F | S |
|---|---|---|---|---|---|---|
|   |   |   |   |   | 1 | 2 |
| 3 | 4 | 5 | 6 | 7 | 8 | 9 |
| 10| 11| 12| 13| 14| 15| 16|
| 17| 18| 19| 20| 21| 22| 23|
| 24| 25| 26| 27| 28| 29| 30|

**2** Use the map to answer the questions
4 pts. total for this exercise.

In which time zone is Seattle, Washington? _____

In which time zone is Kansas City, Kansas? _____

If it is 6:00 P.M. in Dallas, Texas, what time is it in Boston, Mass? _____

If it is 11:00 A.M. in Savannah, GA., what time is it in Denver, Colorado? _____

**3** Count the change. Use the fewest coins and bills possible. Write the total due.
5 pts. total for this exercise.

| Price | Paid | Change Due |
|-------|------|------------|
| Ex: $1.55 | $2.00 | 2 dimes, 1 quarter, = $.45 |
| $13.74 | $15.00 | |
| $18.25 | $20.00 | |
| $11.36 | $15.00 | |
| $39.15 | $50.00 | |
| $17.19 | $20.00 | |

**4** Write the name of each figure using symbols. Name it using words. **5 pts.**

1. • M

2. C————————B

3. A————————D (arrows both ends)

4. E————————F (arrow right)

5. [ X ]

Horizons Math 5, Student Workbook 1   255

## 5. Use ||, ⊥, or intersects to write a statement about the pairs of lines. 3 pts.

1. 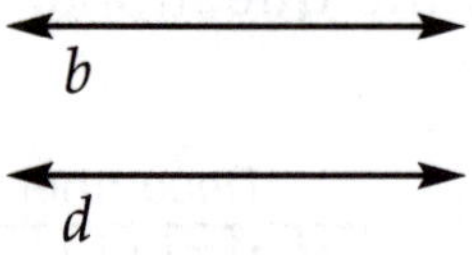  b  
    d  
    _____

2. 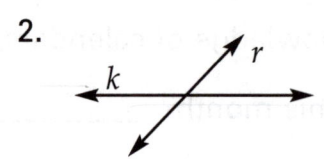  k, r  
    _____

3. 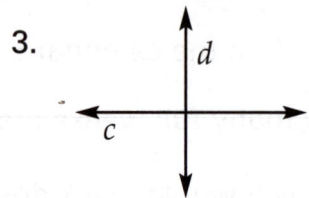  d, c  
    _____

## 6. Write obtuse, acute, or right angle. 8 pts.

1. 50° _____
2. 120° _____
3. 90° _____
4. 68° _____

5. 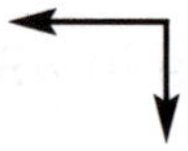 _____
6.  _____
7.  _____
8. _____

## 7. Give the measure of each angle. You may need to extend the sides of the angle for easier reading. 3 pts.

1. 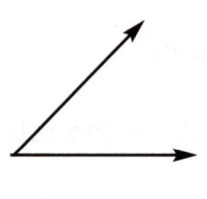 _____
2. 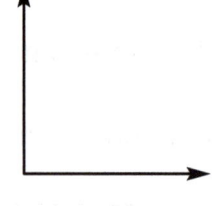 _____
3. _____

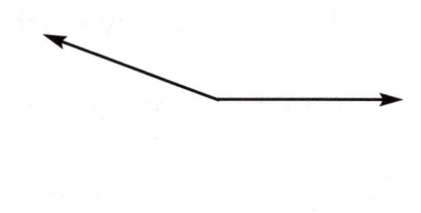

## 8. Use the diagram to answer the questions. 4 pts. total for this exercise.

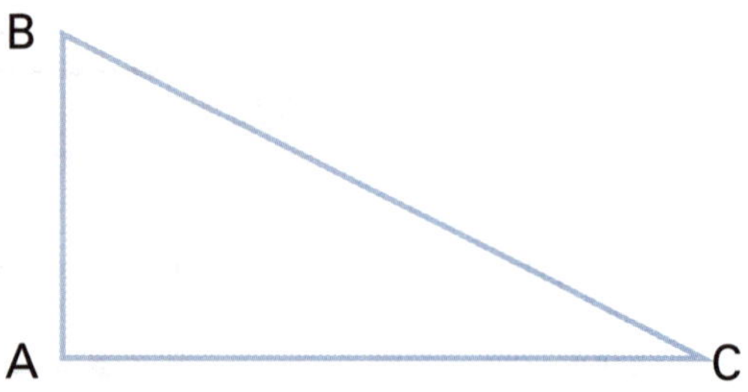

Name the triangle. _____

Name the sides to the triangle. _____

Name the type of triangle. _____

Is the triangle a right triangle? _____

256    Horizons Math 5, Student Workbook 1                    37 pts. Total